All-Stars for All Time

ALSO BY WILLIAM F. MCNEIL
AND FROM MCFARLAND

*Miracle in Chavez Ravine:
The Los Angeles Dodgers in 1988* (2008)

*Black Baseball Out of Season:
Pay for Play Outside of the Negro Leagues* (2007)

*Backstop: A History of the Catcher
and a Sabermetric Ranking of 50 All-Time Greats* (2006)

The Evolution of Pitching in Major League Baseball (2006)

*Gabby Hartnett: The Life and Times
of the Cubs' Greatest Catcher* (2004)

*The Single-Season Home Run Kings:
Ruth, Maris, McGwire, Sosa, and Bonds* (2d ed., 2003)

*The California Winter League: America's First
Integrated Professional Baseball League* (2002; paperback 2008)

*Cool Papas and Double Duties:
The All-Time Greats of the Negro Leagues* (2001; paperback 2005)

*Baseball's Other All-Stars: The Greatest Players
from the Negro Leagues, the Japanese Leagues, the Mexican League,
and the Pre–1960 Winter Leagues in Cuba,
Puerto Rico and the Dominican Republic* (2000)

*The King of Swat: An Analysis of Baseball's Home Run Hitters
from the Major, Minor, Negro and Japanese Leagues* (1997)

ALL-STARS FOR ALL TIME

A Sabermetric Ranking of the Major League Best, 1876–2007

WILLIAM F. MCNEIL

McFarland & Company, Inc., Publishers
Jefferson, North Carolina, and London

LIBRARY OF CONGRESS CATALOGUING-IN-PUBLICATION DATA

McNeil, William.
　All-stars for all time : a sabermetric ranking of the major league best, 1876–2007 / William F. McNeil.
　　　p.　　cm.
　Includes bibliographical references and index.

　ISBN 978-0-7864-3500-5
　softcover : 50# alkaline paper ∞

　1. Baseball — United States — History.　I. Title.
GV863.A1M427　2009
796.3570973 — dc22
　　　　　　　　　　　　　　　　　　2008039635

British Library cataloguing data are available

©2009 William F. McNeil. All rights reserved

No part of this book may be reproduced or transmitted in any form or by any means, electronic or mechanical, including photocopying or recording, or by any information storage and retrieval system, without permission in writing from the publisher.

On the cover: Shoeless Joe Jackson (author's collection)

Manufactured in the United States of America

McFarland & Company, Inc., Publishers
　Box 611, Jefferson, North Carolina 28640
　　www.mcfarlandpub.com

To the latest arrival in the McNeil clan,
Jamie Eileen Riley,
a beautiful Irish colleen with
lovely brown hair and bright blue eyes.
She weighed in at seven pounds, two ounces,
at 4:55 P.M., MDT, on August 3, 2007,
in Albuquerque, New Mexico.

Acknowledgments

I would like to acknowledge and thank the following people and organizations for their assistance.

Pete Palmer once again came to my rescue and has generously permitted me to use statistics from his book, *The Baseball Encyclopedia*.

James R. Madden, Jr., a friend, and a fine researcher and photographer, has authorized me to publish his photos of Barry Bonds, Randy Johnson, Alex Rodriguez, Ichiro Suzuki, and Ken Griffin, Jr.

Jay Sanford, another long-time friend, has authorized me to use several photos from his personal collection, including Lou Boudreau, Eddie Mathews, Ron Santo, and Brooks Robinson.

The Boston Red Sox gave me authorization to publish the photos of Pedro Martinez and Roger Clemens. They requested that credit for the Martinez photo be given to Julie Cordeiro.

Debbie Matson, publications manager of the Boston Red Sox, deserves a special thank you, not only for her help with the Martinez and Clemens photos, but for the above-and-beyond effort she has made over several years to assist me in the location and use of many photographs of Boston Red Sox players.

Authorization to use their photos was also given by John Thorn, the St. Louis Cardinals, the Texas Rangers and Jim Sundberg, the Ivan "Pudge" Rodriguez Foundation, and the New York Mets.

Contents

Acknowledgments viii
Preface 1

1. Baseball's All-Time All-Star Teams Through the Years 3
2. Methodology 13
3. The Nineteenth-Century All-Stars 36
4. Baseball's Greatest Catchers 62
5. Baseball's Greatest Pitchers 84
6. Baseball's Greatest First Basemen 113
7. Baseball's Greatest Second Basemen 133
8. Baseball's Greatest Shortstops 147
9. Baseball's Greatest Third Basemen 161
10. Baseball's Greatest Right Fielders and Left Fielders 175
11. Baseball's Greatest Center Fielders 199
12. Baseball's Legendary All-Stars 216

Appendix: The Steroid Problem 223
Bibliography 229
Index 231

Preface

The game of baseball is America's National Pastime. And selecting all-star teams has been a favorite hobby of its fans since the National League began operations in 1876. In addition to picking annual all-star teams, it has been common practice to select all-time all-star teams. Newspapers and magazines, Major League Baseball, active players, retired players, managers, coaches, and fans, have been polled at one time or another to identify baseball's greatest players.

In all cases, the process has been flawed. Most all-star teams that have been published were the result of polls conducted by the media, and were nothing more than popularity contests. The relative skills of the players were never taken into consideration except by one's memory, surely the most unreliable measurement of all. In those cases where baseball players, managers, and coaches were concerned, individual biases entered the equation. Players frequently selected men they played with, played against, or saw play in another league. The same was true of managers and coaches. Players they had close contact with, obviously, had an advantage.

In a few cases, all-time all-star teams were chosen based on a player's statistics, but in those cases, without exception, the players were measured only on their offensive contributions to the game. Defense was never taken into consideration. And the offensive statistics were the simple measurements of batting average and slugging average. The effect the physical dimensions of a ballpark had on a player's statistics were not taken into consideration. Neither were a player's other contributions to his team's offense, such as his stolen bases, sacrifice hits, and the number of times he hit into double plays.

This study was undertaken to overcome those shortcomings. Formulas were developed for measuring a player's overall contribution to his team's success, both offensively and defensively. And the necessary adjustments were made to put all the players on a level playing field, by accounting for differences in the various ballparks and for the era-to-era differences in the physical aspects of the game.

CHAPTER 1

Baseball's All-Time All-Star Teams Through the Years

The public's fascination with baseball's greatest players, and with selecting all-star teams, began back in the dawn of the game. In 1860, Jimmy Creighton, a handsome, 19-year-old pitcher for the Brooklyn Excelsiors, became an overnight celebrity when he pitched his team to the mythical national championship. The 5'7" fastball pitcher was unbeatable as the Excelsiors toured the Northeast, meeting and defeating the best teams in their respective towns. He defeated the Champion Club of Albany by a 24–6 score, knocked off the highly touted Niagaras of Buffalo, 50–19, and took the measure of the Athletics of Philadelphia, 15–4, before a raucous crowd of 3,000. Included in the gatherings were more than a few young ladies. Creighton, it seems, had become a matinee idol to the female set, and they flocked to the ballparks whenever the Excelsiors came to town. The attention also made the Brooklyn pitcher the first professional baseball player, as the Excelsiors secretly paid him in order to keep his loyalty.

Nine years after Jimmy Creighton rose to fame, Harry Wright traveled the East Coast looking for the best baseball players that money could buy. He was the manager of the Cincinnati Red Stockings, and he had been commissioned by the owners to assemble baseball's first professional team. It might also be called baseball's first all-star team since Harry Wright signed only the cream of the crop. The highest-paid player, and probably the greatest baseball player of his time, was Harry's younger brother, George, a slugging shortstop who would rip the ball at a .518 clip with 59 home runs in 52 games for Cincinnati in 1869.

The Redlegs put together an 80-game undefeated streak in 1869–70, the only blemish on their record being a 17–17 tie with the Haymakers of Troy,

New York. But, like all good things, the streak ended on June 14, 1870, when they fell to the Brooklyn Atlantics by the score of 8–7 in eleven innings. The Atlantics, like the Redlegs, were a solid team at every position.

A true all-star team for the period could have been made up of players from both teams.

Catcher:	Doug Allison — Cincinnati
	Bob Ferguson — Brooklyn
Pitcher:	Asa Brainard — Cincinnati
	George Zettlein — Brooklyn
First Base:	Charley Gould — Cincinnati
	Joe Start — Brooklyn
Second Base:	Charlie Sweasy — Cincinnati
	Lipman Pike — Brooklyn
Shortstop:	George Wright — Cincinnati
	Dickey Pearce — Brooklyn
Third Base:	Fred Waterman — Cincinnati
	Charles Smith — Brooklyn
Left Field:	Andy Leonard — Cincinnati
	John Chapman — Brooklyn
Center Field:	Harry Wright — Cincinnati
	George Hall — Brooklyn
Right Field:	Cal McVey — Cincinnati
	Dan McDonald — Brooklyn

The Reds disbanded after the 1870 season, but the game's first professional league the National Association of Professional Baseball Players, commonly known as the National Association (NA) was formed shortly thereafter. Some of the great players such as Harry Wright that brought the crowds to their feet in baseball parks up and down the East Coast were too old to play in the new professional league, but many of the younger players starred in the National Association and its successor, the National League, for ten or more years. The success of these players in the NA and the NL justified their selection to the all-star team.

- George Wright played in the NA for five years and the NL for seven years, batting a combined .301. His tactic of intentionally dropping a pop fly if there were two or more men on base and less than two out in order to get a double play led the introduction of the infield fly rule.
- Asa Brainard pitched in the NA for four years, compiling a 24–53 won-lost record, including a 5–22 record in his last year.

- George "The Charmer" Zettlein played in the NA for five years and in the NL for one year, retiring with a career record of 129 wins against 112 losses, including a record of 36–15 in 1873.
- Lip Pike played five years in the NA and five years in the NL, batting a combined .322.
- Cal McVey played for the Boston Beaneaters in the NA for five years, helping the powerful Boston team to four consecutive pennants. In 1876, he batted .347 for the Chicago White Stockings as they captured the first National League pennant. McVey batted .362 in the NA and .328 during his four-year NL career.
- George Hall, another five-year veteran of the NA, played two years in the NL, and won the first home run title in NL history by blasting five round-trippers in 268 at-bats. Hall batted .311 in the NA and hit .345 in two years in the NL before he was suspended for life in a gambling scandal.
- Bob "Death to Flying Things" Ferguson enjoyed a long professional career, playing in the NA for five years and in the NL for nine years. The switch-hitting third baseman batted .254 in the NA and .271 in the NL and played sensational defense at third base.
- Dickey Pearce, who was 35 years old when the National Association was formed, played five years in the NA and two years in the NL, batting a combined .251. The 5'4", 161-pound infielder defined the shortstop position. Prior to Pearce, the shortstop was more of an outfielder than an infielder. Pearce also developed the fair-foul bunt that drove third basemen crazy before the rules were changed to prevent such a maneuver.
- Charlie Gould played four years in the NA and two years in the NL, batting a combined .257.
- First baseman Joe "Old Reliable" Start played five years in the NA followed by an eleven-year career in the NL. He retired in 1886 at the age of 43 with a combined batting average of .299, including an even .300 average in the National League. He played on two NL pennant-winners with the Providence Grays, hitting .319 for the 1879 squad and .276 for the powerful 1884 club. In the first World Series, matching the NL champions against the American Association champions, the Grays swept the New York Mets three straight to claim the crown.

Allen & Ginter, one of the country's leading tobacco companies, advertised their "World's Champion" athletes in 1887, a group of fifty athletes that included western rifle marksmen Annie Oakley and Buffalo Bill Cody, heavyweight boxing champion John L. Sullivan, several pool players and strong men, and ten baseball players, representing the game's greatest players. The baseball "all-star team" consisted of:

- Michael J. "King" Kelly, star outfielder for the Boston Nationals, who led the National League in batting in 1886 with a hefty .388 average.
- Cap Anson, first baseman and leader of the Chicago Cubs, who had batted .371 in 1886.
- Bob Caruthers, the St. Louis Brown's ace pitcher, who had gone 30–14 in 1886.
- John Montgomery Ward, shortstop for the New York Giants, who led the National League in fielding in 1887 with a .919 fielding average.
- John Clarkson, pitcher for the Chicago Cubs, who won 36 games against 17 losses in 1886.
- Tim Keefe, ace of the New York Giant pitching staff, who led the National League with 42 victories against 20 losses in 1886.
- Jack Glasscock, shortstop for the St. Louis Maroons, who led the National League in fielding in 1886 with a .906 average while tattooing the ball at a .325 clip.
- Charles Comiskey, first baseman for the St. Louis Browns, who batted .325 in 1887.
- Charlie Bennett, catcher for the Detroit Wolverines, who led National League catchers in fielding in 1886 with a .955 average.
- Joe Mulvey, third baseman for the Philadelphia Athletics, who batted .287 with an .865 fielding average in 1887.

Various newspapers, magazines, and other media outlets continued to present their major league baseball all-time all-star teams to interested fans down through the years. Even the board game manufacturers got into the picture. Cadaco Ellis, manufacturer of the popular Ethan Allen's All-Star Baseball Game that was introduced in 1941 and provided thousands of boys with hundreds of thousands of hours of enjoyment over the next half-century, included in some editions of the game approximately 20 discs of what the company's staff felt were baseball's all-time all-stars in addition to playing discs of active players. Their selections were:

Catchers: Mickey Cochrane, Bill Dickey.
Pitchers: Walter Johnson, Grover Cleveland Alexander, Christy Mathewson, Cy Young.
First Base: Lou Gehrig, George Sisler.
Second Base: Rogers Hornsby, Eddie Collins.
Shortstop: Honus Wagner, Joe Cronin.
Third Base: Pie Traynor, Joe Dugan.
Outfield: Babe Ruth, Tris Speaker, Ty Cobb, Earle Combs, Paul Waner, Al Simmons.

1. Baseball's All-Time All-Star Teams Through the Years

The Cadaco Ellis squad was probably as good an all-time all-star baseball team as could be assembled for the period from 1900 to 1940.

Branch Rickey, a baseball legend and a veritable genius when it came to evaluating talent, selected his all-time all-star team in his book, *The American Diamond*, in 1965. It is presented here without comment.

Catcher:	Mickey Cochrane
	Roy Campanella
Pitcher:	Cy Young
	Kid Nichols
	Rube Waddell
	Addie Joss
	Christy Mathewson
	Walter Johnson
	Ed Walsh
	Grover Cleveland Alexander
	Carl Hubbell
	Dizzy Dean
	Bob Feller
	Warren Spahn
First Base:	George Sisler
	Lou Gehrig
Second Base:	Rogers Hornsby
	Eddie Collins
	Jackie Robinson
Shortstop:	Honus Wagner
Third Base:	Pie Traynor
	Frankie Frisch
Outfield:	Ty Cobb
	Babe Ruth
	Joe Jackson
	Tris Speaker
	Joe DiMaggio
	Ted Williams
	Stan Musial
	Willie Mays

Another all-star team was reported by Gerald Secor Couzens in his book, *A Baseball Album*. According to Couzens, Major League Baseball conducted a survey of baseball fans, writers, and sportscasters in 1969 to identify the greatest players of the first one hundred years. The team selected by the voters included:

Catchers— Mickey Cochrane, Bill Dickey, Roy Campanella

Pitchers (right-handed)— Walter Johnson, Cy Young, Christy Mathewson

Pitchers (left-handed) — Lefty Grove, Sandy Koufax, Carl Hubbell
First Basemen — Lou Gehrig, George Sisler, Stan Musial
Second Base — Rogers Hornsby, Charlie Gehringer, Eddie Collins
Shortstop — Honus Wagner, Joe Cronin, Ernie Banks
Third Base — Pie Traynor, Jackie Robinson, Brooks Robinson
Outfield — Joe DiMaggio, Babe Ruth, Ty Cobb, Ted Williams, Tris Speaker, Willie Mays.

In 1990, *Street & Smith's Baseball* magazine presented its Dream Team, the greatest players of the previous 50 years. The magazine polled active and retired players, managers, coaches, general managers, and media to identify the best of the best.

The team, as selected by the panel, was interesting, with the usual number of popularity choices, such as Johnny Bench, Ozzie Smith, and Don Mattingly, but on the whole it was a valid representation of the greatest major league players between 1941 and 1990.

	National League	*American League*
Best Player	Willie Mays	Joe DiMaggio
Best Hitter	Stan Musial	Ted Williams
Left-handed Pitcher	Sandy Koufax	Whitey Ford
Right-handed Pitcher	Bob Gibson	Bob Feller
Relief Pitcher	Bruce Sutter	Rollie Fingers
Catcher	Johnny Bench	Yogi Berra
First Base	Willie McCovey	Don Mattingly
Second Base	Joe Morgan	Bobby Doerr
Shortstop	Ozzie Smith	Luis Aparicio
Third Base	Mike Schmidt	Brooks Robinson
Outfield	Willie Mays	Joe DiMaggio
Outfield	Hank Aaron	Ted Williams
Outfield	Roberto Clemente	Mickey Mantle
Pinch Hitter (LH)	Stan Musial	Carl Yastrzemski
Pinch Hitter (RH)	Ernie Banks	Frank Robinson
Utility	Pete Rose	Harmon Killebrew
Pinch Runner	Lou Brock	Rickey Henderson

In 1999, Mike Kallay wrote an article for *Street & Smith's Baseball* in which he conducted a survey to identify the 50 greatest players of the twentieth century. A panel of writers and editors as well as the staff of Stats, Inc., were recruited to review the eligible players and to select the 50 greatest players from the pack. The team called "the Team of the Century" had five unan-

Barry Bonds broke Hank Aaron's career home run record in 2007 (courtesy James R. Madden, Jr.).

imous choices — Babe Ruth, Lou Gehrig, Mike Schmidt, Walter Johnson, and Sandy Koufax.

There were a few problems associated with the selection process, however. To begin with, active players who had not yet experienced the downside of their careers were included in the voting, and several of them made the team — Ken Griffey, Jr., Roger Clemens, Mike Piazza, Tony Gwynn, Mark McGwire, Cal Ripken, Jr., and Greg Maddux. A case might be made for the inclusion of Clemens, Maddux, Ripken, McGwire, and Gwynn, whose careers were nearing an end, but the fallacy of including active players on the eligibility list became clear when Griffey and Piazza suffered setbacks in their careers after 1999. Griffey, who had been on track to hit 800 career homers, spent four years battling injuries while his career stagnated, and Piazza, suffering the effects of the physical abuse of many years behind the plate, saw his batting average deteriorate after 2000 and his power follow suit after 2002.

Another problem with the "Team of the Century" poll was the apparent need to include token Negro league players Satchel Paige and Josh Gibson. It was obvious that many, if not most, of the panel were not familiar with the legends of Negro league baseball; nevertheless, having to include them in the voting, they selected the two most visible names while ignoring such giants as Smokey Joe Williams, Oscar Charleston, and Martin Dihigo.

Noticeable by his absence was Barry Bonds, who in 1999 was considered to be a very good major league player, but not one of the top 50 players of the century. But in 2000, the big left fielder's statistics exploded. Over a four-year stretch, from 2001 through 2004, between the ages of 37 and 40, a time when most players have retired, he batted a robust .349, 60 points above his previous career average, and crushed 209 home runs in 1,642 at-bats, an average of 70 home runs for every 550 at-bats. Some respected baseball experts even went so far as to call him the greatest baseball player of all-time. As I noted in *The Evolution of Pitching in Major League Baseball*, "It is well known that wine gets better with age. But ballplayers, obviously with the exception of Barry Bonds, do not. Coincidentally, Bonds' rise to a power icon began after his move to San Francisco. The big slugger has claimed that the above batting and slugging statistics are the result of his weight-lifting program. But people don't bulk up by forty pounds and get puffy faces from lifting weights."

The men selected for *Street & Smith*'s "Team of the Century" were:

	"A" Team	"B" Team
Catcher	Johnny Bench	Yogi Berra
Pitchers	Walter Johnson	Cy Young
	Sandy Koufax	Steve Carlton
	Christy Mathewson	Nolan Ryan
	Warren Spahn	Bob Feller
	Grover Cleveland Alexander	Juan Marichal
Relief	Bob Gibson	Jim Palmer
	Lefty Grove	Whitey Ford
	Roger Clemens	Greg Maddux
	Satchel Paige	Dennis Eckersley
	Tom Seaver	Hoyt Wilhelm
First Base	Lou Gehrig	Mark McGwire
Second Base	Rogers Hornsby	Jackie Robinson
Shortstop	Honus Wagner	Ernie Banks
Third Base	Mike Schmidt	Eddie Mathews
Outfield	Babe Ruth	Hank Aaron
	Ty Cobb	Roberto Clemente
	Ted Williams	Tris Speaker
Utility	Willie Mays	Tony Gwynn
	Stan Musial	Jimmie Foxx
	Joe DiMaggio	Mike Piazza
	Mickey Mantle	Cal Ripken, Jr.
	Josh Gibson	Joe Morgan
	Pete Rose	Brooks Robinson
	Ken Griffey, Jr.	Ozzie Smith

1. Baseball's All-Time All-Star Teams Through the Years

Major League Baseball conducted its own All-Century Team poll in 1999, involving fans from around the country. The objective of the poll was to stimulate fan interest in our National Pastime and, as such, it was immensely successful. More than one million fans cast votes for their favorite players. It was, of course, nothing more than a popularity contest, with no measurement of skill involved. And, as most of the voters were on the sunny side of forty, hardly any of them saw any player who played prior 1970. They were familiar with the exploits of such recent players as Bob Gibson, Willie McCovey, and Brooks Robinson, and they had heard about some of the players of yesteryear, the "ancients" like Ted Williams, Yogi Berra, and Mickey Mantle, but names like Honus Wagner, Nap Lajoie, and Christy Mathewson were unfamiliar to them. As might be expected, the results were so outlandish that MLB had to quickly convene a special panel of baseball executives, media, and historians to try to salvage the project. The panel added five players to the team, legends like Honus Wagner, Christy Mathewson, Stan Musial, Warren Spahn, and Lefty Grove. The original team, as selected by the fans, is shown below, with the top voters listed first, and so on down the line.

Catchers	Johnny Bench, Yogi Berra, Carlton Fisk
Pitchers	Nolan Ryan, Sandy Koufax, Cy Young, Roger Clemens, Bob Gibson, Walter Johnson, Greg Maddux, Steve Carlton, Satchel Paige
First Basemen	Lou Gehrig, Mark McGwire, Jimmie Foxx
Second Basemen	Jackie Robinson, Rogers Hornsby, Joe Morgan
Shortstops	Cal Ripken, Jr., Ernie Banks, Ozzie Smith
Third Basemen	Mike Schmidt, Brooks Robinson, George Brett
Outfielders	Babe Ruth, Hank Aaron, Ted Williams, Willie Mays, Joe DiMaggio, Mickey Mantle, Ty Cobb, Ken Griffey, Jr., Pete Rose, Roberto Clemente.

Ozzie Smith finished just ahead of Honus Wagner in the voting. Major League Baseball, obviously realizing that to present that end result to the fans of America would be a travesty, quietly voted Wagner into the number three spot. Similar adjustments had to be made to rescue Musial (number 11), Mathewson (number 14), Grove (number 18), and Spahn (number 10), from the garbage heap.

The selection of all-time all-star teams via a voting process, whether by fans, writers, managers, or coaches, has never resulted in a true depiction of the greatest players in the game. Memory is a bad measure of a player's skills. There also are the normal biases that enter into the voting, such as players that are liked or disliked by the voter, and the total disregard of obvious baseball legends because of the lack of the historical knowledge of the voters.

Unfortunately, there are no perfect measuring devices for evaluating the skills of individual baseball players. The only thing baseball historians and statisticians can do is provide the most equitable formulas that are available to compare one player with another, offensively and defensively, in order to identify the greatest players at each position.

Chapter 2

Methodology

Baseball's All-Time All-Star team was determined by a comparison of each player's offensive and defensive contributions as measured by his most important statistics. Each position had to be evaluated separately since each position had unique responsibilities that required its own measurements. For instance, catchers had to be evaluated for their ability to throw out potential base stealers, while pitchers were evaluated for their success in the art of pitching. Other position players were measured primarily for their success at producing runs on offense and for preventing runs on defense. Each player's statistics had to be adjusted to eliminate the differences in the game from one era to another, and to eliminate any contributing factors resulting from the geometry of a player's home park.

There have been several statistical studies conducted over the years by the country's foremost baseball historians and statisticians. In my opinion, the studies all have weak spots that make them unacceptable for identifying baseball's greatest players. Bill James' Win Shares is a theoretical evaluation system based on a team concept and each player's contribution to the team's success. It does not evaluate players independently using their individual statistics; player ratings are related to the supposed contributions the player makes to his team. When James was asked for the calculations for Joe DiMaggio's 1937 Win Shares, he said it would take him at least eight hours to calculate that number because he would have to do the entire team first in order to arrive at DiMaggio's contribution. Win Shares does not use individual park factors, but rather one generalized park factor for each stadium. For instance, there is only one park factor for Yankee Stadium even though the distances to the left-field area are much greater than the distances to the right-field area. Under that scenario, left-handed batters like Yogi Berra and Bill Dickey, who had individual park factors of 1.34 and 2.01, respectively, would be rewarded while right-handed batters like Joe DiMaggio and Elston Howard, with individual park factors of 0.71 and 0.48, would be penalized. Win Shares also makes the assumption that players are getting better every year so today's players receive more points, based on their birthday, than players of thirty years ago, and players of thirty years ago receive more points than players of sixty years ago, and so on. Finally, James' rating system includes a subjective factor that allows the statistician to add points to a particular player's total if he believes it is warranted for some reason. James, as reported in *Backstop*, noted a quirk in his rating system that gave Mickey Mantle a higher overall rating than Ty Cobb. He admitted, "I gave Cobb a higher subjective factor than I gave Mantle, and allowed him to edge back ahead. My heart is not in it, but as I see it, the world believes that Cobb was a better player than Mantle, and I would be unable to sustain a logical argument to the contrary under rigorous attack. I have to give Cobb the edge." A more detailed review of Bill James' Wins Shares system can be found in *Backstop*.

Pete Palmer, one of the early editors of *Total Baseball* and one of the editors of *The Baseball Encyclopedia*, has developed the best overall rating system available at the present time. His Player Overall Wins Rating system (POWR) adds a player's batting wins, fielding wins, base running wins, and pitching wins to rate his overall value compared to an average player. But it is a value system as opposed to a skill system, which explains why a player like Bert Blyleven, who pitched in the major leagues for 22 years, is rated above Sandy Koufax, who pitched for only 12 years. Blyleven has a POWR of 31.1 compared to a rating of 22.3 for Koufax. Palmer's data is adjusted for the era in which a player was active, but it does include a generalized park factor similar to the one used by James. As a result, depending on the park, a significant advantage could be given to a right-handed batter or a left-handed batter. In other words, all players are not competing on a level playing field. Pete Palmer has also noted that his system is not yet satisfactory for rating catchers because a caught-stealing factor is not included in his equations.

The statistics used in this study will be outlined position by position, and the reason for using each statistic will be fully explained. First, each player was measured for both his offensive and defensive contributions, but the weight assigned to each player's offense compared to his defense varied depending on his position. The shortstop position was considered to be the most critical defensive position on the team for several reasons. Since most batters hit right-handed, more balls are hit to the left side of the infield, between third base and second base. The shortstop is responsible for covering about two-thirds of the territory between second base and third base, and since many of the balls he runs down are in the hole between his position and the third base position, he must have a strong throwing arm in order to throw out the base runner before the batter reaches first base. He must also have quick reactions to batted balls and above-average speed in order to charge balls that are hit slowly to his position, and he must be able to range far and wide for pop flies that are hit anywhere from the left field foul line to straight-away center field. Many teams carry a shortstop who is a defensive wizard but who has a weak bat, in appreciation of his defensive contributions to his team's success. For this study, a shortstop's defensive contributions were rated equal to his offensive contributions.

Another player who is often carried on a team for his defensive contributions to the team is the catcher. A catcher's primary responsibility is to run the game from his position behind the plate. He is considered to be the field general of the team. He has the whole field in front of him, and he sometimes positions the fielders depending on the particular batter, the game situation, or the strategy that is being used. He calls the pitches a pitcher throws, both the type of pitch and the location of the pitch. It is his responsibility to know the strengths and weaknesses of every batter in the league and to keep them off-balance by mixing up the pitches thrown by his pitcher. He must also be the team psychologist, who knows the temperament of every pitcher on his staff. He must know how to get the most out of each pitcher, when to stroke him, when to cajole him, and when to get tough with him.

A catcher is also responsible for keeping base runners honest by not letting them take too long a lead off base and by not letting them steal bases. If a runner takes too long a lead off base, even second base, the great catchers will invariably pick him off. And if he attempts to steal a base, the great catchers will throw him out a high percentage of the time, usually about half the time. Some baseball experts believe that catchers on good teams will generally throw out more prospective base stealers than catchers on poor teams, but that theory is flawed. A study of the great catchers through the years has shown that good catchers throw out a high percentage of base runners whether they play for a good team or a poor team. Ivan "Pudge" Rodriguez is a good example. He has thrown out a high percentage of base runners whether he was playing for a pennant-contender or for a basement-dweller. So, too, did Gabby Hartnett. And Wes Westrum. And Ray Mueller. And Jim Sundberg. Conversely, Mike Piazza had a poor caught-stealing record wherever he played. He usually played for a strong, pennant-contending club, yet his caught-stealing percentage was never above 30 percent and was often in the low teens. Other catchers who had poor caught-stealing records, even with strong teams, included Mickey Cochrane, Carlton Fisk, Bill Freehan, and Chris Hoiles. Pudge Rodriguez may be the most underrated catcher in the game today. He is a .300 hitter with decent power and the most dominant defensive catcher still active. His career caught-stealing percentage of 49 percent is one of the highest ever recorded. And, in 2006, at 34 years old, an advanced age for a catcher, he gunned down 51 percent of all would-be base stealers, an amazing accomplishment.

A catcher also needs to have quick reflexes in order to respond to the batted ball, whether it is a pop-up, a bunt, or a ball that is topped in front of the plate, and he should have good speed in order to reach those balls in time to retire the batter. He is also responsible for backing up first base on ground balls hit to the infield. Roy Campanella, a high school track star, and Gabby Hartnett, who was taught the position by his father, were two of the best at backing up first base. In addition to those characteristics, a catcher has to be physically tough because he is responsible for blocking the plate to prevent base runners from scoring on close plays and the abuse he is subjected to from base runners determined to make him drop the ball can be brutal. Unfortunately, some of a catcher's greatest skills are intangible and cannot be measured, such as calling the game and handling the pitchers. But a review of the great catchers in baseball history reveals that essentially all of them are strong in intangibles, so the fact that those strengths cannot be measured should not affect the final ratings. For this study, the catcher's defensive statistics, like those of the shortstop, were rated equal to his offensive statistics.

Third base is known as the hot corner for good reason. The third baseman is in a direct line of fire for balls screaming off the bats of right-handed sluggers, and it is his responsibility to prevent those balls from reaching the outfield. Admittedly, the third baseman is required to cover much less ground than the shortstop because his position is near the foul line and, in general, his range requirement is about half that of the shortstop. Nevertheless, he still must protect the area between the shortstop and the third base foul line, and he must have a cannon for a throwing arm since his throws have to make their way across the diamond to first base, occasionally from foul territory behind the base. He does not need to possess the speed of a shortstop, but he must have quick reflexes, because balls hit down the line or in the hole are often hit hard, making it imperative that he react quickly in order to catch the ball or stop it before it goes into the outfield that, in many cases, turns the hit into a two-base hit. And he needs to react quickly to bunts or topped balls down the third base line. From an offensive standpoint, the third baseman in today's environment is usually one of the power hitters on the team and one of its top run-producers. Since the third baseman's offensive contribution is a significant part of his overall value to the team, his offense-to-defense ratio was set at two-to-one for this study.

Second base is another key infield position that requires superior defense. The second baseman has as much ground to cover as the shortstop, but he does not need to have as strong a throwing arm since his throws usually cover a much shorter distance. He does have one critical attribute that puts him in the upper echelons of team defense. He has to be an expert in starting or turning the double play. He has to have good foot speed to get to a ball to start a double play or to get to the bag to force the base runner if the ball is hit to another fielder, and he must have the necessary acrobatic skills to pivot, avoid the slide of the base runner, and make a strong, accurate throw to first base in time to retire the batter. A world-class second baseman must also have good foot speed in order to reach pop flies hit down the right-field foul line, pop flies hit into no-man's land between the infield and the outfield, and slow-hit infield grounders in his direction. A top second baseman is also required to contribute to the offense much more than the shortstop but perhaps less than the third baseman. He is frequently a contact hitter with a good batting average and an above-average on-base percentage. Many of the top base stealers in baseball history were second basemen, such as Joe Morgan, Davey Lopes, Jackie Robinson, Eddie Collins, and Steve Sax. The offense-to-defense ratio for second basemen was set at two-to-one for this study.

The first baseman is usually selected for his offensive contributions to the team as opposed to his defensive contributions. If he is a strong defensive player, that's a bonus. Often, when a team has one or more strong offensive players on the team, it is challenging to find a position for all of them to play; hence, the designated first baseman. That position is usually a last resort. If the player can play the outfield without embarrassing himself, he will be assigned to either right field or left field. If he does not have the requisite skills for playing the outfield, he may find a home at first base. And in today's American League culture, if he and a fielder's glove are mortal enemies, he can serve the team as its designated hitter. For a first baseman, his offense was considered to be four times as important as his defense in this study.

The center fielder is another of those critical defensive players whose skills with the glove are paramount to a team's success. It is an old but accurate truism that, for a team to contend for the title, it must be strong up the middle. That means a team must have outstanding pitching plus strong defense at catcher, second base, shortstop, and center field. Since the right and left fielders are often selected for their bats rather than their gloves, the center fielder is the key defensive player in the outfield. One humorist wrote that on a team with slow-moving pachyderms in the corner outfield spots, the center fielder has to cover the acreage from foul line to foul line. In many cases, that is not far from the truth. Suffice it to say, center field is one of the team's most important defensive positions. And because the center fielder has to cover large expanses of ground, he must have outstanding speed, and that characteristic often means he is an offensive threat, particularly after he gets on base. He is often one of the team's leading base stealers. He frequently bats leadoff, is capable of drawing a significant number of bases on balls, is a good bunter, and a good base runner. The center fielder's offensive-to-defensive ratios in this study were set at three-to-one.

The left fielder and right fielder, as noted previously, are primarily in the lineup for their offensive contributions, not their skill with the glove. They, like the first baseman, were weighted at four-to-one in this study.

The offensive and defensive statistics that were used to determine baseball's all-time all-star team, position by position, follow.

Catcher

The offensive statistics used to determine the offensive skills of the catcher included on-base percentage (OBP), slugging average (SLG), stolen bases (SB), sacrifice hits (SH), and double plays grounded into (GIDP). These same statistics were used for each of the position players. Every statistic had to be adjusted for the era in which the player was active, and the SLG also had to be adjusted for the individual park factor. Base hits had to be eliminated from the XSLG calculation since they are part of OBP and to include them in XSLG would be double-dipping. Only the extra bases in extra-base hits were counted, not the initial base. The era adjustment was determined by selecting a base point year, and by subtracting that value from the league average for the years played by the individual. The base point year selected was 1960, which is near the midpoint for the league's yearly averages for OBP and SLG. Coincidentally, it is also near the midpoint of the first year of the lively ball era and the present year, and it is also the last year in which the major leagues were represented by 16 teams. In 1961 the American League expanded to ten teams, with the addition of the Minnesota Twins and the Los Angeles Angels and, the following year, the National League followed suit, with the addition of the Houston Colt .45s and the New York Mets. Actually, the Washington Senators were one of the new teams admitted to the American League in 1961, with the existing Washington team relocating to Minnesota under its new name, "Twins." Two of the most obvious offensive statistics, runs scored and runs batted in (RBIs), were not used in this study, for good reason. There is a strong correlation between runs scored and OBP, meaning that players with a high OBP are the same players who have a high runs scored total. There is also a strong correlation between SLG and runs batted in, meaning that players who have a high SLG are the same players who have a high RBI total. To include the runs scored and RBI statistics along with OBP and SLG would be another case of double-dipping.

Finally, each statistic was normalized in order to determine not only which player was better or worse than another player in a particular category, but to what extent he was better or worse. Roy Campanella's statistics will be used to demonstrate the method for calculating a player's offensive and defensive point totals. All statistics were not rated equally. For the offensive ratings, normalized statistics NOBPA and NXSLGA were rated at a maximum of 20 points, while NSB, NSH, and NGIDP were rated at one point maximum, for a total of 43 points maximum.

On-Base Percentage (OBP)

Hits plus walks plus hit by pitch, divided by hits plus walks plus hit by pitch, plus official at-bats.

ADJUSTED ON-BASE PERCENTAGE (OBPA)

$$\text{Campanella's OBPA} = A - (B - C)$$
$$\text{OBPA} = .362 - (.332 - .322) = .352$$

Where:

OBPA = Official OBP adjusted for the era in which Campanella played.
A = Campanella's official OBP, .362.
B = League average OBP during Campanella's career, .332.
C = Base point OBP (National League 1960), .322.

NORMALIZED ON-BASE PERCENTAGE (NOBPA)

$$\text{Campanella's NOBPA} = (A/B) \times 20$$
$$\text{NOBPA} = (.352/.401) \times 20 = 17.506$$

Where:

NOBPA = Normalized OBPA
A = Campanella's OBPA, .352.
B = Highest OBPA of the candidates, in this case, Mickey Cochrane's .401 OBPA.
20 = Maximum weight assigned to the statistic.

Slugging Average (SLG)

The number of total bases a batter accumulates — one base for a single, two bases for a double, and so on — divided by his official at-bats.

ADJUSTED SLUGGING AVERAGE (XSLG)

This calculation adjusted the player's slugging average (SLG) for his individual park factor. For players from 1958 to the present, a calculation had to be made for both a player's home statistics and his away statistics. First, a player's average statistics, both home and away, per 550 at-bats, had to be determined for runs, singles, doubles, triples, and home runs. For players prior to 1961, with eight teams in the league, each home statistic (S, D, T, HR) was multiplied by one, then added to the player's away statistic that was multiplied by seven, and the resulting sum was divided by eight to arrive at the player's adjusted total of singles, doubles, triples, and home runs. The adjusted base hits were then subtracted from 550 to give the player's adjusted at-bats for extra-base hits only. The adjusted slugging average (XSLG) was determined by adding the player's doubles per 550 at-bats (D × 1), triples (T × 2), and home runs (HR × 3), and dividing the sum by the player's adjusted at-bats (550 − base hits).

For players who played prior to 1957, for the most part, the splits of home stats and away stats were not available, so some assumptions had to be made. Home run factors (HRF) are available for every major league player, so they were used to determine the player's home and away home runs. A player's home and away at-bats and his home and away doubles could be estimated fairly accurately based on information obtained from a study of the home and away splits for players after 1957. That study indicated that, in general, a player has 5 percent more at-bats on the road than he does at home. That is easily explained by the fact that players often do not bat in the bottom half of the ninth inning at home, meaning they would be expected to have fewer at-bats at home than away. The study also showed that the difference in a player's home and away home runs is normally accompanied by an equal and opposite difference in his doubles; therefore, for players whose statistics included only a home run factor, an assumption was made that the player's doubles changed by an equal and opposite amount to his home runs. Triples are essentially the same, home and away. In Campanella's case, he averaged 32 home runs for every 550 at-bats, and his park factor for home runs was 1.37, meaning he hit 37 percent more home runs at home than on the road. His at-home home run total was 32 × 1.185 (one-half of the spread) = 38, and his away home run total was 32 divided by 1.185 = 26. He averaged 23 doubles a year, so his adjusted doubles were 17 doubles at home and 29 doubles on the road. If there were eight teams in the league (prior to 1960), his adjusted doubles and home run totals would be:

Adjusted home runs = (7 × 26 + 1 × 38) = 220 divided by 8 = 28 home runs.
Adjusted doubles = (7 × 29 + 1 × 17) = 220 divided by 8 = 28 doubles.

As more teams entered the major leagues, a player's away statistics became more and more important in determining the player's adjusted extra-base hits. For instance, if there were 16 teams in the league, the player's home statistics would still be multiplied by one, but his away statistics would now be multiplied by 15, with the sum of those stats divided by 16. It is obvious from these examples that a player's away statistics are much more important for measuring his skills than his home statistics are. One of the more eye-popping examples of the difference between a player's home stats and his away stats can be found in the statistics of Todd Helton of the Colorado Rockies. Helton, playing in the rarified air of Denver, Colorado, compiled a home batting average of .374 from 1998 through 2005 compared to an away batting average of .297. He also averaged 40 home runs a year at home compared to 25 homers on the road.

$$\text{Campanella's XSLG} = (A + B + C)/D$$
$$\text{XSLG} = (28 + 4 + 84)/398 = .291$$

Where:

XSLG = Campanella's slugging average adjusted
for his home park factor (PF).
A = adjusted doubles per 550 at-bats × 1
B = adjusted triples per 550 at-bats × 2
C = adjusted home runs, per 550 at-bats × 3
D = 550 at-bats − 152 base hits = 398

FINAL ADJUSTED SLUGGING AVERAGE (XSLGA)

The final adjusted slugging average (XSLGA) was an era adjustment to the XSLG to account for the difference between the league slugging average for the period the player was active and the base point slugging average.

$$\text{Campanella's XSLGA} = A - (B - C)$$
$$\text{XSLGA} = .291 - (.396 - .388) = .283$$

Where:

XSLGA = Campanella's XSLG adjusted for
the era in which the player was active.
A = Campanella's XSLG, .291.
B = League average SLG during Campanella's career, .396.
C = Base point SLG (National League 1960), .388.

NORMALIZED FINAL ADJUSTED SLUGGING
AVERAGE (NXSLGA)

The player's final adjusted slugging average (XSLGA) was normalized to account for the difference between players and the amount of the difference.

$$\text{Campanella's Normalized Adjusted Slugging}$$
$$\text{Average (NXSLGA)} = (A/B) \times 20$$
$$\text{NXSLGA} = .283/.302 \times 20 = 18.742$$

Where:

A = Campanella's XSLGA.
B = Highest XSLGA of the candidates, in this case, Johnny Bench's .302.
20 = Maximum weight assigned to the statistic.

Roy Campanella had the deadliest throwing arm in the history of the game.

Stolen Bases (SB)

The average number of stolen bases by the player per 550 at-bats during his career.

NORMALIZED STOLEN BASES (NSB)

$$\text{Campanella's NSB} = (A/B) \times 1$$
$$\text{NSB} = 3/8 \times 1 = .375$$

Where:

A = Campanella's SB, 3.
B = Highest SB of the candidates, in this case Carlton Fisk with 8.
1 = Maximum weight assigned to the statistic.

Sacrifice Hits (SH)

The average number of sacrifice hits made by the player per 550 at-bats during his career.

NORMALIZED SACRIFICE HITS (NSH)

Campanella's NSH = (A/B) × 1
NSH = 4/16 × 1 = .250

Where:

A = Campanella's SH, 4.
B = Highest SH of the candidates, in this case Mickey Cochrane with 16.
1 = Maximum weight assigned to the statistic.

Number of Double Plays Grounded Into (GIDP)

Number of double plays grounded into by the player for every 550 at-bats during his career.

NORMALIZED DOUBLE PLAYS GROUNDED INTO (NGIDP)

Campanella's NGIDP = A/B × 1
NGIDP = (10/19 × .25) × 1 = .132

Where:

A = Fewest number of DPs grounded into by a candidate, in this case Cochrane, Porter, and Tenace, with 10 each.
B = Number of DPs grounded into by Campanella, 19.
.25 = GIDP factor assigned to the statistic.
1 = Maximum weight assigned to the statistic.

The defensive statistics used to evaluate catchers included fielding average (FA), caught stealing percentage (CS), passed balls (PB), wild pitches prevented (WP), range factor (RF), and other assists (ASSA). These factors were not all rated equally. FA, CS, and RF were rated at 20 points maximum, ASSA was rated at 10 points, PB was rated at 6 points, and WP was rated at 1.5 points, for a total of 77.5 points maximum.

The defensive statistics used to evaluate all other positions, with the exception of first base, were fielding average (FA) and range factor (RF). For first basemen, fielding runs (FR) was substituted for range factor as will be explained in the chapter on first basemen. Range factor, in most cases, is an imperfect method of measuring a player's defensive skills because of the differences in the geometrical configurations of the baseball stadiums in the major leagues. The amount of foul territory behind the plate, and around the infield from first base to third base, is markedly different from park to park. And the outfield dimensions are also vastly different. The right-field wall in Ebbets Field, for instance, had a significant effect on the range factor of players like Carl Furillo, who was penalized by the lack of territory to cover. And the famous Green Monster in Boston had a negative effect on the range factors of Red Sox left fielders like Ted Williams and Carl Yastrzemski.

Fielding Average (FA)

Putouts plus assists divided by putouts plus assists plus errors.

FIELDING AVERAGE DIFFERENTIAL (FAD)

Campanella's FAD = .988 − .984 = + 4

Where:

.988 = Campanella's career fielding average.
.984 = League fielding average for catchers during Campanella's career.

NORMALIZED FIELDING AVERAGE DIFFERENTIAL (NFAD)

Campanella's NFAD = (4 + 2)/10 × 20 = 12.000

Where:

4 = Campanella's FAD.
2 = Adjustment to bring the most negative FAD to zero (some players had a negative FAD).
10 = Total range of candidate's FADs.
20 = Maximum weight assigned to the statistic.

Caught Stealing Percentage (CS)

The number of times a catcher throws out a base runner attempting to steal a base, divided by the total number of attempts, multiplied by 100.

CAUGHT STEALING PERCENTAGE DIFFERENTIAL (CSD)

Campanella CSD = 58 − 40 = 18

Where:

58 = Campanella's career caught stealing percentage.
40 = National League average CS percent during Campanella's career.

NORMALIZED CAUGHT STEALING PERCENTAGE
DIFFERENTIAL (NCSD)

$$\text{Campanella's NCSD} = A/B \times 20$$
$$NCSD = 18/18 \times 20 = 20.000$$

Where:

A = Campanella's CSD.
B = The widest CS differential of the candidates, in this case Campanella's own 18-point differential.
20 = Maximum weight assigned to the statistic.

Passed Balls (PB)

The average number of passed balls per 154-game season during a player's career.

NORMALIZED PASSED BALL (NPB)

$$\text{Campanella's NPB} = A/B \times 6$$
$$NPB = 5/7 \times 6 = 4.286$$

Where:

A = Fewest passed balls by any candidate, in this case Mueller and Hoiles, 5.
B = Campanella's average number of passed balls per 154 games, 7.
6 = Maximum weight assigned to the statistic.

Wild Pitches (WP) Prevented

Average number of wild pitches allowed by the team's pitching staff per 154-game season, during the player's career.

WILD PITCH DIFFERENTIAL (WPD)

The difference between the number of wild pitches made by the candidate's team per 154-game season and the league average number of wild pitches per team per 154 games.

$$\text{Campanella's WPD} = A - C$$
$$WPD = 29 - 30 = -1$$

Where:

A = Number of wild pitches thrown by Campanella's team per 154 games.
B = League average number of wild pitches per team per 154 games.

NORMALIZED WILD PITCH DIFFERENTIAL (NWPD)
$$\text{Campanella NWPD} = A/B \times 1.5$$
$$NWP = -1/-16 \times 1.5 + 0.094$$

Where:

A = Campanella's WPD, -1.
B = Widest differential of any catcher in the study, in this case Carlton Fisk with -16.
1.5 = Maximum weight assigned to the statistic.

Range Factor (RF)
The total number of putouts and assists per game for the player during his career.

RANGE FACTOR DIFFERENTIAL (RFD)
$$\text{Campanella's RFD} = A - B$$
$$RFD = 5.98 - 4.66 = +1.32$$

Where:

A = Campanella's range factor (average number of putouts and assists per game).
B = League average range factor.

NORMALIZED RANGE FACTOR DIFFERENTIAL (NRFD)
$$\text{Campanella's NRFD} = (A + B)/C$$
$$NRFD = ((1.32 + .35)/1.67) \times 20 = 20.000$$

Where:

A = Campanella's Range Factor = 1.32.
B = Adjustment to bring the most negative range factor back to zero (some catchers had negative range factor).
C = Total range of range factors.
20 = Maximum weight assigned to the statistic.

Other Assists (ASSA)
The total number of a catcher's assists, less his caught stealing (CS) assists, per 154-game season.

OTHER ASSISTS DIFFERENTIAL (ASSAD)
$$\text{Campanella's ASSAD} = A - B$$
$$ASSAD = 40 - 45 = -5$$

Where:

$\qquad$ A = Campanella's ASSA = 40.
$\qquad$ B = League average ASSA = 45.

NORMALIZED OTHER ASSISTS DIFFERENTIAL (NASSAD)

$\qquad$ Campanella NASSAD = (A + B)/C × 10

Where:

$\qquad$ A = Campanella ASSAD = ((-5 + 9)/10) × 10 = 4.000.
$\qquad$ B = Adjustment to bring the most negative ASSAD to zero = 9.
$\qquad$ C = Total range of ASSAD's = 10.
$\qquad$ 10 = Maximum weight assigned to the statistic.

To review, the weights that were assigned to each of the calculations were:

OFFENSE

NOBPA — 20 points max.
NXSLGA — 20 points max.
NSB — 1 point max.
NSH — 1 point max.
NGIDP — 1 point max.
Total — 43 points max.

DEFENSE

NFAD — 20 points max.
NCSD — 20 points max.
NPB — 6 points max.
NWPD — 1.5 points max.
NRFD — 20 points max.
NASSAD — 10 points max.
Total — 77.5 points max.

OFFENSIVE POINT TOTALS — EXAMPLE

Name	NOBPA	NXSLGA	NSB	NSH	NGIDP	Total Points	Final Offensive Rating
Campanella	17.506	18.742	.375	.250	.132	37.005	4
Hartnett	17.257	17.417	.625	.938	.167	36.404	6

Defensive Point Totals — Example

Name	NFAD	NCSD	NPB	NWPD	NRFD	NASSAD	Total Points	Final Defensive Rating
Campanella	12.000	20.000	4.286	0.094	20.000	4.000	60.380	1
Hartnett	16.000	14.545	2.727	0.094	13.054	10.000	56.420	2

To determine the catcher's final all-around rating, based on a one-to-one offense-to-defense ratio, the total offensive points were divided by 43 and the total defensive points were divided by 77.5. The results were added together and the player with the highest point total was rated number one, the player with the second highest total was rated number two, and so on down the line.

Final All-Around Rating — Example

Name	Offense Divided by 43	Defense Divided by 77.5	Total Points	Final All-Around Rating
Campanella	0.861	0.779	1.640	1
Hartnett	0.847	0.728	1.575	2

Pitcher

The pitcher is a unique case in the determination of baseball's greatest players in that he is not judged primarily on either his skill with the bat or his skill with the glove. Rather, the pitcher's primary responsibility is to keep the opposing batters off base, by either striking them out or by causing them to hit balls that can be caught or fielded by the pitcher or his teammates. Still, a pitcher is required to bat (in the National League) and to field ground balls hit in his direction, as well as to catch an occasional pop fly or to catch a ball at first base.

In determining baseball's greatest pitchers, they had to be evaluated for all three skills — pitching, batting, and fielding — which obviously puts modern American League pitchers at a disadvantage. That disparity between the two leagues is unfortunate, but it had to be taken into consideration. Remember, the National League has been in operation since 1876, and the pitcher has always batted.

The American League introduced the designated hitter to major league baseball fans on April 6, 1973, when Ron Blomberg of the New York Yankees drew a bases-loaded walk off Luis Tiant of the Boston Red Sox en route to a one-for-three day in the Yankees' 15–5 loss to the Sox. The designated hitter, with no defensive position, relieved the pitcher of his batting responsibility. Fortunately, the National League has kept the game pure, with a lineup of nine players, all of whom play both offense and defense.

The history of baseball is filled with pitchers who were armed and dangerous with a bat in their hands. In fact, during the first fifty years of the twentieth century, there was a plethora of good hitting pitchers, including Walter Johnson, Wes Ferrell, and Don Newcombe.

Walter Johnson was one of baseball's best hitting pitchers, recording a career batting average of .235 with 22 doubles, 10 triples, and six home runs for every 550 at-bats. And two-thirds of his career was in the dead ball era. He batted .268 in the lively ball era.

Wes Ferrell, who was probably the greatest hitting pitcher who ever wore a major league uniform, compiled a career batting average of .280 during a fifteen-year career. He averaged 27 doubles, six triples, 18 home runs, and 97 RBIs for every 550 at-bats. In 1931, the 6'2", 192-pound right-handed hitter slugged the ball at a .319 clip with nine home runs in 116 at-bats, an average of 43 home runs for every 550 at-bats! Five years later, he batted a sizzling .347 with seven homers in 150 at-bats. Wes Ferrell's 38 career home runs is still the record for a pitcher.

Don Newcombe batted .271 over a ten-year career, with 15 home runs in 858 at-bats. He had a career season in 1955 when he batted .359 with nine doubles, seven homers, and 23 RBIs, in 117 at-bats. He also went 20–5 on the mound with 17 complete games.

Pitchers were evaluated for their pitching skills, their batting skills, and their fielding skills in this study. Their pitching performance represented 90 percent of their Final All-Around Rating (FAR), while their batting performance represented 6 percent of their FAR and their fielding performance represented 4 percent of their FAR.

Offensive Ratings

The pitcher's batting performance was evaluated for NOBP and NXSLG.

Name	NOBPA × 3	NXSLGA × 3	Total Points	Final Offensive Rating
W. Johnson	1.989	2.658	4.647	2
C. Mathewson	2.109	2.067	4.176	3
W. Ferrell	3.000	3.000	6.000	1

Defensive Ratings

The pitcher's defense was evaluated for NFAD and NRFD.

Name	NFAD × 2	NRFD × 2	Total Points	Final Defensive Rating
W. Johnson	1.839	0.451	2.290	13
C. Mathewson	1.977	1.461	3.438	3
W. Ferrell	1.793	1.490	3.283	4

Pitching Ratings

It was very difficult to arrive at a fair method for evaluating the pitching skills of the individual pitchers from one era to another and select those pitching statistics that would provide a level playing field for all pitchers due to the many changes that have been made in the position over the years. Some of the statistics that were considered were the number of complete games pitched per year, the number of innings per game a pitcher averaged, and a pitcher's winning percentage. Obviously winning percentage per se could not be used because pitchers who pitched for winning teams invariably had higher winning percentages than pitchers who toiled for losing teams. The mentality of the game has changed over the decades as well, particularly with regard to pitchers. Relief pitchers have gradually grown in importance since their introduction in 1892 by evolving into genuine closers whose responsibility it was to shut down the opposition for just one inning. Middle relievers and setup men were part of the same evolutionary process, putting less emphasis on the starting pitcher going the distance or even pitching seven or eight innings. These changes made the evaluation of complete games and innings pitched per game moot points.

After a careful study of all the factors that are available to measure a pitcher's skills, it was decided that the most equitable statistics that could be used to evaluate pitchers would be their normalized won-lost percentage and the normalized ERA. The individual won-lost percentage was compared to the team's won-lost percentage, with the difference between the two numbers identified as the differential winning percentage (WLPD). This number was then normalized (NWLPD), with an assigned maximum point total of 45. The adjusted ERA (AERA) was a value arrived at by dividing the league average ERA by individual pitcher ERA, with the result multiplied by the pitcher's park factor, as described in *The Baseball Encyclopedia*. A pitcher's park factor, like a position player's park factor, is the effect that a player's home park has on his statistics, but unlike a batter's park factor, it is a generalized term that is the same for all pitchers that pitch in that park. The

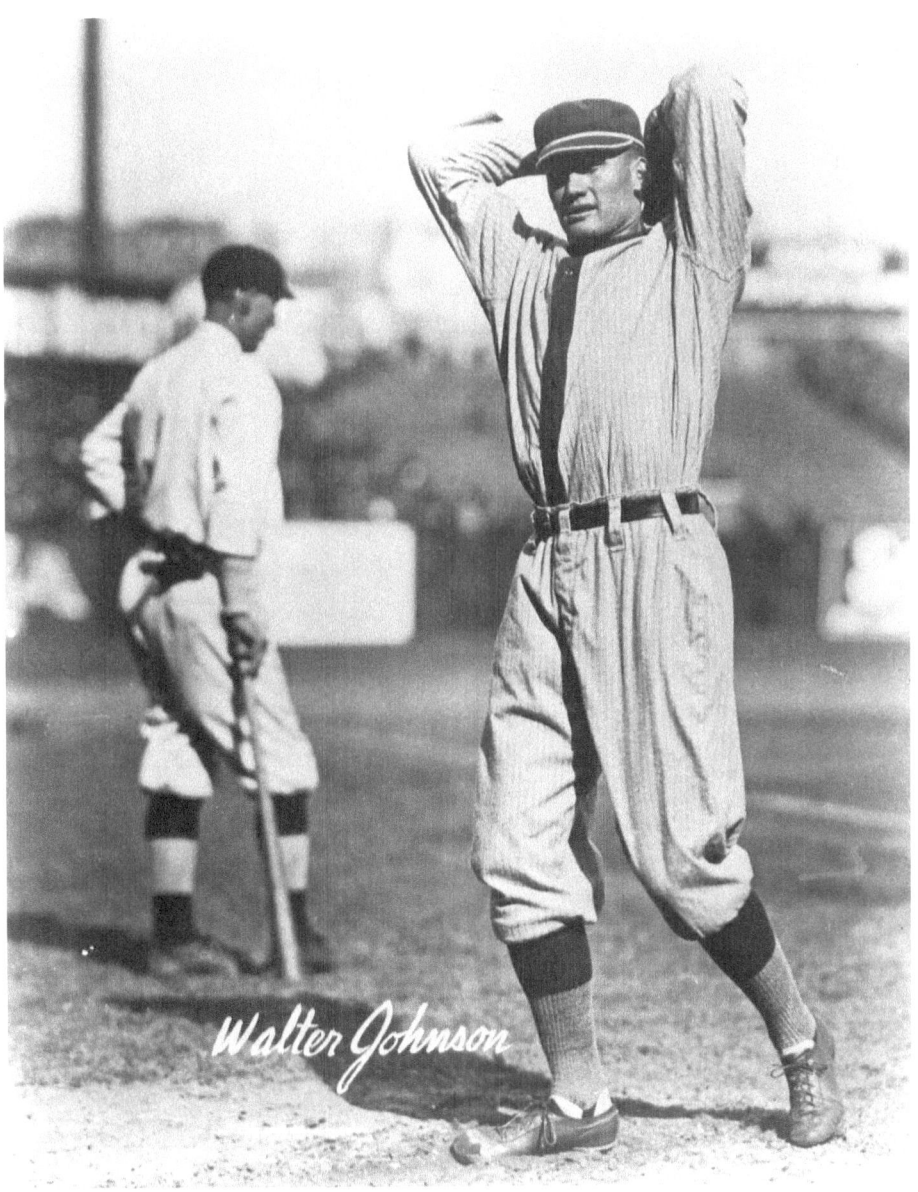

Walter Johnson won 417 games during his 21-year career, primarily with a second-division club.

pitcher's park factor is not individualized like a batter's park factor since the pitcher is facing both right-handed batters and left-handed batters. The adjusted ERA was normalized (NAERA) with an assigned maximum point total of 45.

Walter Johnson's won-lost percentage differential (WLPD) was:

$$\text{WLPD} = A - B$$
$$\text{WLPD} = .599 \text{ minus } .492 = +.107.$$

Where:

A = Walter Johnson's career won-lost percentage, .599.
B = Walter Johnson's team's won-lost percentage during his career, .492.

NORMALIZED WON-LOST PERCENTAGE DIFFERENTIAL

$$\text{NWLPD} = A/B \times 45$$
$$\text{NWLPD} = .107/.108 \times 45 = 44.583$$

Where:

A = Walter Johnson's WLPD, +.107.
B = Highest WLPD of the candidates, in this case Grover Cleveland Alexander's +.108.
45 = Maximum weight assigned to the statistic.

Walter Johnson's adjusted ERA, as determined by Pete Palmer, was 145. The highest AERA belonged to Lefty Grove at 148. Therefore, Walter Johnson's normalized ERA was:

$$\text{NAERA} = 145 \text{ divided by } 148 \times 45 = 44.088.$$

Where:

45 = Maximum weight assigned to the statistic.

Walter Johnson's total pitching rating (TPR) was the sum of his normalized won-lost differential percentage and his normalized adjusted ERA.

Name	NWLPD	NAERA	Total Points	Total Pitching Ratings (TPR)
W. Johnson	44.583	44.088	88.671	1
C. Mathewson	36.667	41.351	78.018	7
W. Ferrell	30.000	35.574	65.574	16

Final All-Around Rating

Name	Pitching @ 90%	Offensive @ 6%	Defensive @ 4%	Total Points	Final All-Around Rating
W. Johnson	88.671	4.647	2.290	95.608	1
C. Mathewson	78.018	4.176	3.438	85.632	6
W. Ferrell	65.574	6.000	3.283	74.857	13

First Base

The offensive statistics used for first basemen were the same statistics that were used for catchers: OBP, SLG, SB, SH, GIDP. There were a total of 43 offensive points, as noted previously, 20 points each for OBP and SLG, one point each for SB, SH, and GIDP. Since first basemen have been considered to be one of the primary offensive weapons on a team, they were normally selected for their batting prowess as opposed to their defensive skills; therefore, in this study their offensive point total was weighted at four times their defensive point total. If a team is fortunate enough to find a first baseman with both offensive and defensive skills, it is considered to be a bonus.

The defensive statistics used for first basemen were fielding average (FA) and fielding runs (FR). Other position players in the infield and outfield were rated for FA and range factor (RF), but RF is not of much value for first basemen since they have very few assists and most of their putouts are the result of throws made to them while they are standing stationary on first base. A more valuable statistic is Pete Palmer's fielding runs (FR), which is defined by the following formula.

$$FR = PFR/(PO - SO \text{ for team}) - LFR/(PO - SO \text{ for league}) \times \text{player innings}$$

Where:

PFR = Player fielding rate for first base = $.2 \times (2 \times A - E)$.
LFR = League fielding rate.

As with Palmer's other formulas, however, FR is a value formula, so it has to be modified slightly to make it a skill formula. Since the FR varies with the number of games played by the first baseman, the result had to be made equitable for all players by adjusting the result to fixed number of games played. The number of games played in this case was arbitrarily set at 2,000. Therefore, since Lou Gehrig played in 2,137 games during his career, his adjusted FR formula (AFR) would be:

$$AFR = FR \times A/B = -59 \times 2000/2137 = -55$$

Where:

FR = Lou Gehrig's career fielding runs, −59.
AFR = Lou Gehrig's career fielding runs adjusted to 2,000 games.
A = The 2,000 game base point.
B = Lou Gehrig's games played, 2,137.

An example of the defensive ratings for first basemen, with a maximum of 40 defensive points, is:

Name	FA	LFA	DIFF.	NFAD × 20	FR	AFR	NAFR × 20	Total Points	Rating
Gehrig	.991	.990	+1	7.500	−59	−55	5.300	12.800	17
V. Power	.994	.991	+3	17.500	116	178	20.000	37.500	1
Mattingly	.996	.992	+4	20.000	−19	−21	7.444	27.444	5
K. Hernandez	.994	.992	+2	15.000	133	132	17.098	32.098	2

Some examples of the Final All-Around Ratings for first basemen, based on a four-to-one offense-to-defense ratio are:

Name	Offense Divided by 43 × 4	Defense Divided by 40	Total Points	Final All-Around Rating
Gehrig	3.865	0.445	4.310	1
Foxx	3.620	0.659	4.279	2
V. Power	2.275	0.938	3.213	18

Second Base, Shortstop, Third Base

The offensive statistics for the second baseman, the shortstop, and third baseman were the same as those used by catchers and first basemen: OBP, SLG, SB, SH, and GIDP. The defensive statistics used for second basemen, shortstops, and third basemen were fielding average (FA) and range factor (RF).

Second basemen and third basemen were rated at two-to-one for their offense versus their defense, while the shortstop was rated at one-to-one.

Outfielders

All outfielders were rated for OBP, SLG, SB, SH, and GIDP on offense and FA and RF on defense. The only difference between the three outfield positions was that the left fielder and the right fielder were rated on an offense-to-defense ratio of four-to-one, while the center fielder was rated at three-to-one.

Fielding averages are deceptive, particularly for outfielders. Some outfielders can catch anything that comes their way, but not all have very good range and can fail to reach balls they should catch that eventually fall in for base hits. Pete Rose and Al Simmons, for instance, fall into that category. Other outfielders, like Tris Speaker, Kirby Puckett, and Willie Mays, had excellent fielding averages as well as outstanding range. Most of the outfielders with good range usually find themselves in center field. Unfortunately, some outfielders are penalized because of their outstanding speed. For instance, if a ball is hit beyond a fielder's reach, it is scored a base hit. If, on the other hand, a speedy outfielder reaches a ball after a long run and then cannot hold the ball, he is occasionally charged with an error.

This study does not include ratings for Barry Bonds, Mark McGwire, Sammy Sosa, or Rafael Palmeiro due to the suspicion that steroids may have contributed to their offensive statistics. If, at a future date, the steroid scandal is resolved favorably and Bonds, McGwire, Sosa, and Palmeiro are exonerated, their ratings will be included in the next edition of this book. At the present time it appears as if the four players will have a difficult time being elected to the National Baseball Hall of Fame in Cooperstown, New York, even though their statistics are worthy of the players' induction. Mark McGwire, the first of the group to be eligible for election, garnered only 23.5 percent of the vote in 2007, with 75 percent required for election. Rafael Palmeiro retired after the 2005 season and will be eligible for Hall of Fame consideration in 2010. Barry Bonds and Sammy Sosa were still active in 2007.

The steroid issue is discussed in greater detail in the Appendix.

CHAPTER 3

The Nineteenth Century All-Stars

Major league baseball in the nineteenth century, from its first official contest in 1845 through 1899, was a game in transition. The game slowly evolved from a Saturday afternoon social event to a spirited contest between two dedicated teams, and the rules were adjusted over the years to find the most equitable balance between batter and pitcher, without favoring one over the other. Identifying the game's greatest players during this period was difficult because of all the changes in the rules, such as allowing overhand pitching, extending the pitcher's mound from fifty feet from home plate to 60' 6", recording stolen bases, and awarding the batter first base after four balls had been thrown. Still, the feeling was that the greatest players of their time should be recognized, just as their twentieth century counterparts would be recognized.

The relative weights given to the offense and defense for the nineteenth century all-stars were the same as the weights assigned to the twentieth century team:

Catchers and shortstops were rated equally for their offense and their defense, so their offensive skills were measured against the same maximum point totals as their defensive skills.

Pitchers were rated at 90 percent for their pitching, 6 percent for their batting, and 4 percent for their fielding.

First basemen, left fielders, and right fielders were assumed to be essentially offensive members of the team. Their offense received four times the weighted point totals as did their defense.

Second basemen and third basemen were rated two-to-one, offense-to-defense.

Center fielders, who were considered to be the defensive anchors in the outfield, were rated at three-to-one, offense-to-defense.

Catchers

Five catchers were rated for their offensive and defensive skills.

- Buck Ewing was the quiet leader of the New York Gothams, later the Giants. He was one of the National League's best hitters during the 1880s and 1890s, rapping the ball at a .304 clip. He also excelled on defense and was reported to have had the strongest throwing arm in the league.
- Michael "King" Kelly was a flamboyant character who was as colorful off the field as on it. His charisma perhaps embellished his career achievements, but he was still one of the best players of the nineteenth century, compiling a .308 career batting average. And he was as fast on his feet as he was mentally quick. He was a daring base runner who stole 312 bases over one five-year period, and who once scored 155 runs in 118 games.

Buck Ewing was the field leader of the New York Giants during the 1880s.

- Charles "Chief" Zimmer, whose career covered nineteen years between 1884 and 1903, was considered to be the top defensive catcher of his era. He was the first catcher to play directly behind the batter on every pitch, a strategy previously frowned upon because of the danger of injury from foul tips. He was not, however, much of an offensive threat, posting a career batting average of .269.
- James "Deacon" McGuire caught in the major leagues for 26 years, a prodigious accomplishment under nineteenth-century conditions. When he retired, he held many catching records, two of which — most years

caught (26) and most career assists (1,859) — are still intact. The 6'1", 185-pound right-handed batter was primarily a defensive backstop, but he could also contribute at the plate, compiling a .278 career batting average.
- Jack Clements was a unique catcher in baseball history, a left-handed receiver who nonetheless enjoyed a 17-year major league career, primarily with the Philadelphia Phillies. The stubby Pennsylvanian, who packed 204 pounds on his 5'8" frame, was the first of the slugging catchers, averaging 10 home runs for every 550 at-bats during a time when many teams hit about 35 homers a year.

Offensive Ratings

Player evaluations for the nineteenth century all-star team were necessarily simple compared to the evaluations for the twentieth century team due to a paucity of statistics in the early game as well as many rule changes that affected the game, such as the four-ball rule, changes in the pitcher's mound height and distance to home plate, and the failure to record stolen bases. The offensive measurements consisted of on-base percentage differential (OBPD), and slugging average differential (SLGD). Each statistic was normalized as discussed earlier, and was rated at a maximum of 1.000 point, giving a total of two points maximum for offense. The individual statistics were not adjusted for the individual park factor, but that was probably not significant since most of the 19th century parks were large open fields with a wide expanse of outfield grass. There were, of course, a few exceptions, most notably Lakefront Park in Chicago with its 180-foot left-field fence and its 196-foot right-field fence. Home runs flew out of Lakefront Park with abandon. The White Stockings hit a total of 142 home runs in 1884, most of them at home, while the other seven National League teams hit a total of 179 homers combined. The following year the rules were changed to recognize balls hit over the left- and right-field fences as doubles.

As might be expected, Buck Ewing and King Kelly dominated the offensive statistics. Kelly's OBP was 53 points higher than the league average while Ewing's OBP was 22 points higher than the league average. Conversely, Chief Zimmer's OBP was 10 points below the league average. The offensive breakdown is shown below. The point totals for each category were arrived at by determining the ratio of each player's differential to the maximum differential. If some differentials were below the league average, an adjustment was made to bring the most negative differential back to zero, and that amount was added to each player's total before calculating the ratio. For example, the range for a catcher's OBP was 63 points, so ten points had to be added to each player's total in order to bring Zimmer's differential to zero. King Kelly, with a + 53 OBP, was awarded 1.000 point. Buck Ewing's normalized point total was arrived at by adding 10 points to his total and then calculating the ratio thusly.

Ewing's NOBPD = (22 + 10)/(53 + 10) = 0.508.

	OBPD	NOBPD × 1	SLGD	NSLGD × 1	Total Points	Final Offensive Ratings
Buck Ewing	+22	0.508	+85	1.000	1.508	2
King Kelly	+53	1.000	+77	0.913	1.913	1
Chief Zimmer	−10	0.000	−7	0.000	0.000	5
Deacon McGuire	+1	0.175	+2	0.098	0.273	4
Jack Clements	+9	0.302	+52	0.641	0.943	3

Defensive Ratings

The defensive ratings were similar in determination to the offensive ratings, with fielding average differential normalized (NFAD), and range factor differential normalized (NRFD). The results, shown below, awarded Buck Ewing with the title of the game's best defensive catcher, edging out the favorite, Chief Zimmer.

	FAD	NFAD × 1	RFD	NRFD × 1	Total Points	Final Defensive Ratings
Buck Ewing	+26	1.000	+68	1.000	2.000	1
King Kelly	−20	0.000	−75	0.000	0.000	5
Chief Zimmer	+16	0.783	+1	0.531	1.314	2
Deacon McGuire	−4	0.348	+18	0.650	0.998	4
Jack Clements	+13	0.717	+5	0.559	1.276	3

Final All-Around Ratings

The final all-around ratings were determined by adding the offensive point totals and the defensive point totals together, since both offense and defense were considered to be of equal weight. The results were somewhat surprising in that the game's foremost left-handed catcher finished in second place behind Buck Ewing on the strength of his fine overall skills. He finished in third place in both the offensive and defensive categories to give him the edge over King Kelly, who finished first in offense but dead last in defense. Buck Ewing, who was generally considered to be the nineteenth century's finest all-around catcher, justified that belief by finishing second in offense behind Kelly, finishing first in defense, and first overall.

	Offense × 1	Defense × 1	Total Points	Final All-Around Ratings
Buck Ewing	1.508	2.000	3.508	1
King Kelly	1.913	0.000	1.913	3
Chief Zimmer	0.000	1.314	1.314	4
Deacon McGuire	0.273	0.998	1.271	5
Jack Clements	0.943	1.276	2.219	2

Pitchers

Pitcher was the most difficult position to evaluate for nineteenth century players for the reasons noted earlier. They, like their twentieth century counterparts, were compared, not only for their pitching skills, but also for their batting skills and their fielding skills. After careful consideration, a pitcher's pitching skills were set at 90 percent of the point total, batting at 6 percent, and fielding at 4 percent. Pitching skills were determined by comparing a pitcher's won-lost percentage differential (WLPD) and his adjusted ERA (AERA). The batting and fielding categories were the same as that used for catchers.

A total of nine pitchers were in the running for the title of baseball's greatest all-around pitcher of the nineteenth century.

- Tim Keefe was the ace of the New York Giant pitching staff during the 1880s. From 1883 through 1888, his victory totals were 41, 37, 32, 42, 35, and 35. The side-arming right-hander, who was devastating while pitching from 50 feet, went 41–27 with 68 complete games in 68 starts in 619 innings in 1883. Over the course of his career, he won 342 games (number eight all-time) against 225 losses, while completing 93 percent of his starts.
- Michael Francis "Smiling Mickey" Welch, a pitching partner of Keefe, was a curveball specialist who also threw a changeup and a screwball. His greatest year was 1885 when he won 44 games against 11 losses for a league-leading .800 winning percentage. That year he completed all 55 of his starts. Smiling Mickey pitched in the major leagues for 13 years, winning 307 games against 210 losses while completing 96 percent of his starts.
- Charles "Kid" Nichols was the ace of the Boston Beaneaters' staff from 1890 through 1901. His seven consecutive 30+ victory seasons, from 1891

to 1898, has never been equaled. Nichols, who threw with an effortless overhand delivery, had a blazing fastball and pinpoint control. His 361 career victories rank sixth all-time, his 532 complete games are fourth, and his 5,067 innings pitched eleventh.

- Jack Stivetts, known as "Happy Jack," was a two-way player in the 1890s, pitching 388 games and playing other positions in 213 games. He pitched for eleven years, winning more than 20 games six times, with a high of 35 in 1892. His career won-lost record was 203–132, with 278 complete games. But Stivetts was also a deadly slugger who compiled a career batting average of .298 with 10 home runs and 99 RBIs for every 550 at-bats.
- Charles "Old Hoss" Radbourne had outstanding speed as well as a bewildering assortment of breaking pitches thrown from different arm angles. He produced baseball's greatest pitching performance in 1884, going 60–12 on the mound for the Providence Grays, with 73 complete games in 73 starts, eleven shutouts, a 1.38 ERA, and 441 strikeouts in 679 innings. Radbourne's career record was 309 victories against 194 losses.
- Amos Rusie, "The Hoosier Thunderbolt," was the major league's primary power pitcher in the 1890s, combining a blazing fastball with a sharp-breaking curveball to freeze batters in their tracks. The 6'1", 200-pound right-hander led the league in strikeouts five times and shutouts four times before tearing muscles in his shoulder, essentially ending his career with a record of 246 wins against 174 losses.
- John Clarkson, a slender right-handed underhand pitcher, combined speed, pinpoint control, and confusing curves to out-think opposing batters. In 1885, he led the league in victories (53), games started (70), complete games (68), shutouts (10), innings pitched (623), and strikeouts (308). Clarkson's twelve-year career produced 328 victories against 178 losses for a fine .648 winning percentage.
- Clark Griffith, "The Old Fox," small of stature at 5'6", 155 pounds, used a curveball and a slow ball, combined with such illegal pitches as a scuff ball and a spitball, to carve out a successful 20-year major league career. He won more than 20 games seven times while leading the National League in winning percentage, complete games, and ERA once each. His career record showed 237 wins against 146 losses.
- Robert "Parisian Bob" Caruthers, a diminutive right-hander, was a thinking-man's pitcher who pitched to the batter's weakness by using a live fastball and perfect control. His career won-lost percentage of .688, based on 218 victories against 99 losses, is the third-highest winning percentage in baseball history, behind Dave Foutz and Whitey Ford. He was also a .282 career hitter who played the outfield when not pitching.

Pitching Ratings

The most equitable won-lost percentage rating was determined to be the difference between the individual's won-lost percentage and the won-lost percentage of his team. Since most of the pitchers in the study had impressive won-lost records, and since most of them played for championship teams that also had impressive won-lost records, it would have been unfair to evaluate them based on their individual won-lost records alone. The won-lost percentage differential was intended to identify the pitchers who stood out, even on teams that compiled outstanding won-lost records. Surprisingly, at least to me, Bob Caruthers, who had the highest individual won-lost percentage, also produced the highest won-lost percentage differential (WLPD). His .688 winning percentage was 83 points higher than his team's .605 winning percentage. He was followed by Clark Griffith at +.70, Amos Rusie at +.62, and Old Hoss Radbourne at +.55.

The adjusted ERA (AERA), as presented by Pete Palmer and Gary Gillette in *The Baseball Encyclopedia*, was arrived at by dividing the league ERA by the individual pitcher's ERA and multiplying the result by the pitcher's park factor. The adjusted ERA compensated for the difference between the pre–1893 era, which was a pitcher's era with the pitcher's mound residing between 45 and 55 feet from home plate, and the post 1893 era, which was more of a hitter's era. The uncorrected ERAs confirmed that the early pitchers, Radbourne, Keefe, Welch, and Clarkson, topped the ratings, but when AERA was used, the results were completely different. Chet Nichols, who had the sixth-lowest ERA, finished first in AERA with a mark of 139. John Clarkson was close behind at 134, followed by Amos Rusie at 130 and Tim Keefe at 125.

The WLPD and AERA were then normalized, with each result multiplied by 45, giving a total of 90 points, or 90 percent of the final overall pitcher ratings. Amos Rusie, who finished third in both NWLPD and NAERA, deservedly walked off with top pitching prize. Kid Nichols, who finished first in NAERA but tied for seventh in NWLPD, was second, and Bob Caruthers, who set the pace in NWLPD and finished fifth in NAERA, came in third.

Name	NWLPD × 45	NAERA × 45	Total Pitching Points	Final Pitching Ratings
Amos Rusie	36.085	29.423	65.508	1
Kid Nichols	17.830	45.000	62.830	2
Bob Caruthers	45.000	17.308	62.308	3
John Clarkson	24.623	36.346	60.969	4
Clark Griffith	39.481	13.846	53.327	5

Name	NWLPD × 45	NAERA × 45	Total Pitching Points	Final Pitching Ratings
Old Hoss Radbourne	33.113	12.115	45.228	6
Tim Keefe	17.830	20.769	38.599	7
Mickey Welch	22.075	00.000	22.075	8
Jack Stivetts	00.000	12.115	12.115	9

Offensive Ratings

A pitcher's batting skills were evaluated for on-base percentage differential (OBPD), and slugging percentage differential (SLGD). The results were normalized, and the result was multiplied by three to produce a final offensive rating that was 6 percent of the total pitcher's rating. Jack Stivetts and Bob Caruthers, both of whom were outstanding hitters that often played the outfield when not pitching, dominated the batting category. Parisian Bob had a huge advantage in OBPD with a +66 points compared to a −21 points for the next man, Old Hoss Radbourne, and he also led in SLGD with a +52 point differential to a +44 differential for Jack Stivetts. When the total normalized batting points were computed for NOBPD and NSLGD, Bob Caruthers ran away from the other contenders.

	NOBPD × 2	NSLGD × 2	Total Points	Final Offensive Ratings
Bob Caruthers	2.000	2.000	4.000	1
Jack Stivetts	0.842	1.884	1.726	2
Old Hoss Radbourne	0.855	0.159	1.014	3
Mickey Welch	0.487	0.464	0.951	4
Amos Rusie	0.000	0.464	0.464	8
Clark Griffith	0.645	0.101	0.746	5
John Clarkson	0.013	0.478	0.491	6
Tim Keefe	0.408	0.072	0.480	7
Kid Nichols	0.066	0.000	0.066	9

Defensive Ratings

A pitcher's defensive ratings were based on the pitcher's fielding average differential (FAD) and his range factor differential (RFD). The results were normalized and multiplied by two to give a total of four points, or 4 percent of the overall pitcher's ratings. In general, pitchers were better-than-average fielders, with Nichols and Caruthers both exceeding the league fielding average for pitchers by 35 points. Caruthers also did well in range factor, finishing second to John Clarkson, but Nichols slipped to sixth place, dropping him to number two overall.

	NFAD × 2	NRFD × 2	Total Points	Final Defensive Ratings
Bob Caruthers	2.000	1.495	3.495	1
Kid Nichols	2.000	0.947	2.947	2
John Clarkson	0.571	2.000	2.571	3
Clark Griffith	1.524	0.947	2.471	4
Old Hoss Radbourne	1.238	1.200	2.438	5
Jack Stivetts	1.333	0.674	2.007	6
Tim Keefe	0.825	1.074	1.899	7
Amos Russie	0.444	1.432	1.876	8
Mickey Welch	0.000	0.000	0.000	9

Final All-Around Ratings

A pitcher's efforts on the mound accounted for 90 percent of his final rating, yet in this case, it was the pitcher's batting and fielding performance that determined the greatest all-around pitcher of the nineteenth century. Amos Rusie, who edged Bob Caruthers and Kid Nichols in the pitching competition, could not hold off Caruther's charge in the areas of batting and fielding. Parisian Bob outdistanced the group in batting by a wide margin, and also finished first in fielding. Rusie could do no better than fifth in batting and eighth in fielding. Nichols, with a .226 career batting average, finished dead last in batting, but came in second in fielding to finish third overall.

	Pitching	Offensive	Defensive	Total Points	Final All-Around Ratings
Bob Caruthers	62.308	6.000	3.495	71.803	1
Kid Nichols	62.830	0.099	2.947	68–876	2
Amos Rusie	65.508	0.696	1.876	68.080	3
John Clarkson	60.969	0.737	2.571	64.277	4
Clark Griffith	53.327	1.119	2.471	56.917	5
Old Hoss Radbourne	45.228	1.521	2.438	49.187	6
Tim Keefe	38.599	0.720	1.899	41.218	7
Mickey Welch	22.075	1.427	0.000	23.502	8
Jack Stivetts	12.115	2.589	2.007	16.711	9

First Base

Five players vied for the title of the nineteenth century's greatest all-around first baseman.

- Cap Anson was the first player in the game to accumulate more than 3,000 base hits and the first to hit more than 500 career doubles. His career batting average of .331 ranks 26th all-time. Cap, as he was called, was not only a terrific hitter, he was also an outstanding defensive player who led the league in fielding average four times.
- Jake Beckley was a talented all-around first baseman who had a .308 career batting average while also gaining a reputation as an excellent defensive player. The 5'10", 200-pound left-handed hitter batted .300 or better thirteen times in his 20-year career, with a high of .345 in 1895. On defense, he ranks number one in both games played (2,377) and putouts (23,709), and eighth in assists (1,315).
- Dan Brouthers compiled the highest slugging average of the nineteenth century (.519), while hitting against the dead ball from a distance of 50 to 55 feet from the pitcher. The 6'2", 207-pounder, the most feared batter of his time, averaged 38 doubles, 17 triples, and nine home runs for every 550 at-bats while hitting a robust .342. On the other side of the coin, he was considered a liability in the field and on the bases.
- Roger Connor, who stood 6'3" tall and weighed a husky 220 pounds, compiled a career batting average of .308 with 31 doubles, 16 triples, and 10 home runs a year. His 136 career home runs and 811 extra-base hits both rank number one for nineteenth-century batters, and his 233 career triples are fifth all-time. He was also an excellent defensive first baseman as well as an exceptional base runner.
- Dave Orr packed 250 pounds on his 5'11" frame, and he used it to

Dave Orr was the National League's foremost slugger until a stroke ended his career at the age of 30 (courtesy John Thorn).

pound out 57 extra-base hits for every 550 at-bats, the fifth highest extra-base hit totals in the nineteenth century. Sadly, Orr, who was also a fine defensive first baseman, suffered a paralyzing stroke in 1890, ending his career after just eight years. He left a .342 career batting average, a .366 on-base percentage, and a .502 slugging average, the fourth-highest slugging average in the nineteenth century.

Offensive Ratings

First base has always been considered to be an offensive position, one where big, burly sluggers are positioned when there is no other position they can play satisfactorily. First basemen who were outstanding defensive players were not in the majority, and teams who had an excellent all-around first baseman were fortunate. Since the position was primarily an offensive position, a first baseman's offense was weighted at four-to-one over his defense. Dan Brouthers led the way in both published on-base percentage and slugging average, but when the era adjustments were made, it was a different story. Big Dan had the highest on-base percentage differential (OBPD), with his .423 OBP topping the league average by 95 points. Orr, who walked only 16 times for every 550 at-bats, came in fourth. The slugging average differential was another two-man competition, with Dave Orr edging Dan Brouthers +156 to +150. Overall, Brouthers claimed the title of the game's best offensive first baseman, accumulating 1.931 points to 1.400 for Orr, thanks to his big lead in OBP.

Name	OBPD × 1	NOBPD	SLGD × 1	NSLGD	Total Points	Final Offensive Ratings
Dan Brouthers	+95	1.000	+150	0.931	1.931	1
Dave Orr	+50	0.400	+156	1.000	1.400	2
Roger Connor	+72	0.693	+118	0.563	1.256	3
Cap Anson	+67	0.627	+76	0.080	0.707	4
Jake Beckley	+20	0.000	+69	0.000	0.000	5

Defensive Ratings

First basemen were evaluated for fielding average differential (FAD) and fielding runs differential (FRD). All the first basemen in the study had positive fielding average differentials with the exception of Dan Brouthers, whose average was at the league average. Roger Connor set the pace in a close competition, finishing five points above the league average compared to four points for Orr, three points for Beckley, and two points for Anson. The fielding runs race was another close call with Anson topping the list. Roger Connor, thanks to a first-place finish in FA and a second-place finish in FR, claimed the title as the best defensive first baseman in the competition. Not surprisingly, Dan Brouthers finished last in the field of five.

Name	FAD	NFAD × 1	RFD	NRFD × 1	Total Points	Final Defensive Ratings
Jake Beckley	+3	0.600	+28	1.000	1.600	1
Roger Connor	+5	1.000	+18	0.412	1.412	2
Dave Orr	+4	0.800	+21	0.588	1.388	3
Cap Anson	+2	0.400	+22	0.647	1.047	4
Dan Brouthers	0	0.000	+11	0.000	0.000	5

Final All-Around Ratings

Obviously, the leader in the offensive ratings for first basemen had a distinct advantage over his rivals in the race based on the fact that offense was calculated at four times the defense. Big Dan Brouthers was the offensive leader, but his sad performance in the defensive competition almost wiped out his huge advantage over Dave Orr and Roger Connor. Still, he claimed the crown as the era's best all-around first baseman, followed by Connor, Orr, Anson, and Beckley, in that order.

Name	Offense × 4	Defense × 1	Total Points	Final All-Around Ratings
Dan Brouthers	7.724	0.000	7.724	1
Roger Connor	5.024	1.770	6.794	2
Dave Orr	5.600	1.084	6.684	3
Cap Anson	2.828	1.400	3.828	4
Jake Beckley	0.000	1.084	1.084	5

Second Base

Five players competed for the title of the nineteenth century's greatest all-around second baseman.

- John "Bid" McPhee was a threat both offensively and defensively during his 18-year career. The 5'8", 150-pound right-handed hitter compiled a .272 batting average while averaging 13 triples, 65 bases on balls, 50 stolen bases, 112 runs scored, and 71 RBIs per year. McPhee's forté, however, was defense, leading the league in fielding average eight times and double plays eleven times.

- Fred "Sure Shot" Dunlap earned his nickname for his hard, accurate throws to first base. A 12-year major league veteran, he batted .292 with 105 runs scored and 44 extra-base hits for every 550 at-bats. Dunlap, like McPhee, was considered to be a sensational defensive second baseman, once called "the greatest second baseman that ever lived" by Al Spink, the founder of the *Sporting News*.
- Hardy Richardson was the best hitter of the second-base candidates, with a .299 career average, 49 extra-base hits a year, 109 runs scored, 80 RBIs, and a .435 slugging average. He batted over .300 seven times in his 14-year career, with a high of .351 in 1886. He led the league with 189 base hits and 11 home runs that year, scored 125 runs, and contributed 27 doubles and 11 triples to the Detroit Tigers' offense.
- Fred Pfeffer was a .256 career hitter with little power, but he must have been an outstanding clutch hitter as he led all second-base candidates with 86 runs batted in for every 550 at-bats. In the field, he led the league in putouts eight times, assists four times, double plays six times, and total chances per game seven times. Pfeffer still ranks first in total chances per game (6.95), tenth in career putouts (4,714), and second in putouts per game (3.07).
- Thomas "Tido" Daly was recognized as a clutch hitter who was most dangerous when there were runners in scoring position. Daly, a former catcher, was converted to a second baseman in Brooklyn in 1893 to compensate for his weak throwing arm. He was an average defensive player and earned his keep with his bat, hitting .278 over 16 years, with 40 extra-base hits, 99 runs scored, 66 bases on balls, 78 RBIs, and 37 stolen bases.

Offensive Ratings

Fred Dunlap's career coincided with the most turbulent era in baseball history when the ancient game of base ball was gradually transformed into the modern game of baseball. From 1880 to 1891, when Dunlap played, overhand pitching became legal, four balls and three strikes were standardized, the distance from the pitching mound was lengthened from 45 feet to 55 feet, fielder's gloves, catcher's masks, and catcher's chest protectors became standard equipment, and stolen bases were defined and recorded. And within two years, relief pitchers were allowed to enter the game at any time and the pitcher's mound was established at its present distance of 60'6". Dunlap was a standout during this hectic period and, as it turned out, he was the game's best hitting second baseman, out-hitting the average National Leaguer by 38 points, the best performance by any second baseman. His OBP differential (OBPD) was 45 points above the league average, again setting the standard for second basemen. He was no slouch in the slugging department either, exceeding the National League average by 63 points, good enough for second place, behind Hardy Richardson.

Name	OBPD	NOBPD × 1	SLGD	NSLGD × 1	Total Points	Final Offensive Ratings
Fred Dunlap	+45	1.000	+63	0.862	1.862	1
Hardy Richardson	+30	0.769	+75	1.000	1.769	2
Tido Daly	+16	0.554	+11	0.221	0.775	3
Bid McPhee	+17	0.569	+5	0.125	0.694	4
Fred Pfeffer	−20	0.000	−5	0.000	0.000	5

Defensive Ratings

Bid McPhee and Fred Dunlap had a spirited competition for recognition as the greatest fielding second baseman of the nineteenth century, with McPhee nosing out his adversary by 0.300 points. There were not many differences between the two men, but Dunlap's range, although far above the league average, was no better than fourth in this group, and it cost him the title. Hardy Richardson and Fred Pfeffer also showed to good advantage in the competition, but Tido Daly was not in the same class with other members of the group.

Name	FAD	NFAD × 1	RFD	NRFD × 1	Total Points	Final Defensive Ratings
Bid McPhee	+25	1.000	+61	0.956	1.956	1
Fred Dunlap	+22	0.906	+47	0.750	1.656	2
Hardy Richardson	+10	0.531	+55	0.868	1.399	3
Fred Pfeffer	+3	0.313	+64	1.000	1.313	4
Tido Daly	−7	0.000	−4	0.000	0.000	5

Final All-Around Ratings

Since second basemen were considered to be among the strongest defensive players on the team, their offense was only given a two-to-one weight factor over their defense. Under those conditions, and with strong showings on both offense and defense, Fred Dunlap and Hardy Richardson finished one-two in the competition for baseball's all-time nineteenth century second baseman, with Dunlap edging Richardson, 7.380 points to 6.829 points. "Sure Shot" Fred held a slight advantage both offensively and defensively over his adversary. In the final analysis, Dunlap was the top offensive second baseman of the nineteenth century and the greatest all-around second baseman of his era. Bid McPhee was identified as the greatest defensive second baseman of the nineteenth century.

	Offense × 2	Defense × 1	Total Points	Final All-Around Ratings
Fred Dunlap	3.724	1.656	5.380	1
Hardy Richardson	3.535	1.399	4.934	2
Bid McPhee	1.388	1.956	3.344	3
Tido Daly	1.615	0.000	1.615	4
Fred Pfeffer	0.000	1.333	1.333	5

Shortstop

Seven players competed for the title of the greatest shortstop of the nineteenth century.

- William "Bad Bill" Dahlen, a twenty-year veteran of the National League in the nineteenth century, was a defensive specialist who is sixth all-time in career games played (2,132), third in chances per game (6.26), and second in both putouts (4,850) and assists (7,500). He could also hit. A .272 career batter with 40 extra-base hits and 75 RBIs a year, he hit .359 in 1894 and .352 two years later.
- Hughie "Ee-Yah" Jennings starred both offensively and defensively in the major leagues for 18 years, compiling a .312 career batting average with 111 runs scored and 94 RBIs a season. Jennings would do anything to get on base, even "taking one for the team," an art he perfected with the Baltimore Orioles between 1894 and 1898 when he absorbed 202 hits to his body. He also led the league in fielding average four times.
- John Montgomery Ward began his career as a pitcher, going 164–103 over six full years, then moved to shortstop when his pitching arm gave out. Ward was a decent hitter, a good defensive player, and an exciting base runner who stole 111 bases in 1887 and 88 in 1892. Over his career, he batted .275 with 2,107 base hits, 1,410 runs scored, and 540 stolen bases (after stolen bases were documented, between 1886 and 1894).

- Jack Glasscock was one of the top shortstops of his era, but he never seemed to get the recognition he deserved. "Pebbly Jack," as he was called for his grounds-keeping habit, was a dangerous hitter as well as a dazzling fielder. The .290 career hitter led the league in batting in 1890, and set the pace in base hits twice. In the field, he was magnificent, leading the league in fielding average six times in his first eleven years.
- Herman "Germany" Long was the shortstop on the great Boston Beaneaters teams of the 1890s. As *The Ballplayers* reported, "With a powerful arm, a quick release, and outstanding range, speed, and agility, Long played shortstop, according to the *Boston Globe*, 'like a man on a flying trapeze.'" The diminutive left-handed batter could also hit, topping the .300 mark four times, and scored more than 100 runs seven times.
- George "Germany" Smith, a 6', 175-pound infielder, was noted for his range and his dependable glove. Smith led the league in fielding average twice, assists four times, and double plays once during his 15-year career. He anchored the infield for the 1889 and 1890 league champions Brooklyn Bridegrooms. Unfortunately, his bat was not as deadly as his glove. His career average of .243 trailed all the other shortstops in the study.
- George Davis was a husky switch-hitter who starred at shortstop for the New York Giants from 1893 to 1901. He put together nine consecutive .300 seasons with the Giants, and he led the National League in RBIs in 1897 with 135. Davis was not only a good hitter, however. He was also one of the top defensive shortstops of his day. He led the league in fielding average four times, in assists five times, and in double plays five times.

Offensive Ratings

George Davis, in a spirited dogfight with Hughie Jennings, finished in first place in the shortstop's offensive category. He finished with a total of 1.876 points against 1.765 points for Jennings, based on his +46 point league-average differential in slugging compared to a +26 point differential for Jennings. Jack Glasscock, who finished third in both OBP and SLGD, was third at 1.502.

	OBPD	NOBPD	SLGD	NSLGD	Total Points	Offensive Rating
George Davis	+26	0.876	+46	1.000	1.876	1
Hughie Jennings	+37	1.000	+26	0.765	1.765	2
Jack Glasscock	+22	0.831	+18	0.671	1.502	3
Bill Dahlen	+16	0.764	+18	0.671	1.435	4

	OBPD	NOBPD	SLGD	NSLGD	Total Points	Offensive Rating
Herman Long	−11	0.348	−21	0.435	0.783	5
J.M. Ward	−5	0.528	−20	0.224	0.752	6
Germany Smith	−31	0.000	−52	0.000	0.000	7

Defensive Ratings

George Davis fell out of contention as a result of his poor showing in the defensive categories, but Jack Glasscock continued his war with Hughie Jennings, finishing first in NFAD and second in NRFD. Jennings, however, built a big lead in NRFD, which provided him with enough of a point spread to crown him the game's greatest nineteenth century defensive shortstop.

	FAD	NFAD	RFD	NRFD	Total Points	Final Defensive Ratings
Hughie Jennings	+21	0.720	+68	1.000	1.720	1
Jack Glasscock	+28	1.000	+36	0.347	1.347	2
George Davis	+17	0.560	+35	0.327	0.887	3
Bill Dahlen	+11	0.320	+36	0.327	0.647	5
Germany Smith	+15	0.480	+24	0.102	0.582	6
Herman Long	+3	0.000	+32	0.265	0.265	7

Final All-Around Ratings

A shortstop's defensive play was regarded as the most critical component in a team's defensive strategy. Therefore, many teams carried a shortstop with a dependable glove but a weak bat. The reverse has never been true. This study, recognizing that school of thought, measured a shortstop's offense and defense with equal weight. Hughie Jennings, however, demonstrated such a well-balanced game that he would have been declared the nineteenth century's greatest all-around shortstop whether the offense was rated at one-to-one, two-to-one, or four-to-one over defense. He led all shortstops in on-base percentage and slugging average, and he also showed the way in range factor while finishing second in fielding average.

	Offense × 1	Defense × 1	Total Points	Final All-Around Ratings
Hughie Jennings	1.765	1.720	3.485	1
Jack Glasscock	1.502	1.347	2.849	2

	Offense × 1	Defense × 1	Total Points	Final All-Around Ratings
George Davis	1.876	0.887	2.763	3
Bill Dahlen	1.435	0.647	2.082	4
Herman Long	0.783	0.265	1.048	5
J. M. Ward	0.752	0.080	0.832	6
Germany Smith	0.000	0.582	0.582	7

Third Base

Six third basemen competed for the title of the nineteenth century's foremost all-around protector of the hot corner.

- John McGraw was a feisty offensive sparkplug for the great Baltimore Oriole ballclubs of the 1890s. He was a career .334 hitter who batted over .300 nine consecutive years. The 5'7", 155-pound New Yorker, known as "Mugsy," was always ready to fight when the situation warranted it — and sometimes when the situation did not warrant it. His 0.93 runs scored per game is one of the highest percentages in baseball history.
- Billy Nash starred for the Boston Beaneaters for eleven years, from 1885 to 1895, as one of the key elements in their tight inner defense. He led the National League in fielding average four times, in assists twice, and in double plays three times. The

John McGraw was a member of the famed Baltimore Orioles of the 1890s. He's shown here in 1890 as a member of the Olean, New York, club.

career .275 hitter was also a decent offensive force, carrying 101 runs across the plate for every 154 games played while driving in 92 teammates.
- Denny Lyons, a stocky 5'10", 185-pound infielder, was an offensive threat as opposed to a defensive threat. He was a career .310 hitter with a .407 OBP and a .442 slugging average. He batted over .300 seven times in his career with an average of .367 in 1887 and .354 in 1890. His defense was just adequate, but he did lead the league in double plays twice and set the major league record for putouts in a single season with 255.
- Billy Shindle was a slender 5'8", 155-pound right-handed hitter who excelled both on offense and defense. Although his career batting average was just .269, he was still an offensive threat, averaging 94 runs scored and 72 RBIs during his 13-year career. On defense, he led the league in fielding average once, in assists three times and in double plays twice.
- Arlie Latham was a happy-go-lucky third baseman for the St. Louis Browns when they captured four consecutive American Association pennants in the 1880s. The .269 career hitter's contributions to the Browns' success included a league-leading 152 runs scored in 1886, a league-leading 109 stolen bases in 1888, and two .300+ batting seasons. He led the league's third basemen in both assists and double plays twice.
- Lave Cross played major league baseball for 21 years, compiling 2,651 base hits to become the only nineteenth century third baseman with more than 2,000 base hits. The Milwaukee native batted .292 during his career while averaging 81 runs scored a season. He was also an outstanding defensive third baseman, leading the league in fielding average five times, assists four times, and double plays twice. He ranks fourteenth in career assists with 3,715.

Offensive Ratings

John McGraw and Denny Lyons were the most dangerous offensive third basemen of the nineteenth century. McGraw had a .466 OBP to Lyons' .407, but Lyons had more pop in his bat as evidenced by his 47 extra-base hits compared to Mugsy's 29. Lyons drove in 97 runners a year, McGraw just 65. And Lyons' huge slugging average differential put him over the top. No other third baseman was close to the top two. Lave Cross had a decent .292 batting average but, like McGraw, had little power.

	OBPD	NOBPD	SLGD	NSLGD	Total Points	Final Offensive Ratings
Denny Lyons	+62	0.652	+75	1.000	1.652	1
John McGraw	+108	1.000	+21	0.476	1.476	2

	OBPD	NOBPD	SLGD	NSLGD	Total Points	Final Offensive Ratings
Billy Nash	+18	0.318	−4	0.233	0.551	3
Lave Cross	−13	0.083	+12	0.388	0.471	4
Arlie Latham	−3	0.159	−28	0.000	0.159	5
Billy Shindle	−24	0.000	−18	0.097	0.097	6

Defensive Ratings

Lave Cross' five season fielding average titles were no mirage. His career fielding average differential of +36 topped his closest competitor, Billy Nash, by 16 points. Nash had a better range factor than Cross, but his advantage was not enough to overtake Cross in the final rating. Denny Lyons, the offensive titlist, finished fifth in defense, and John McGraw brought up the rear.

	FAD	NFAD	RFD	NRFD	Total Points	Final Defensive Ratings
Lave Cross	+36	1.000	+13	0.811	1.811	1
Billy Nash	+20	0.484	+22	0.981	1.465	2
Billy Shindle	+12	0.226	+23	1.000	1.226	3
Arlie Latham	+5	0.000	+13	0.811	0.811	4
Denny Lyons	+11	0.194	+1	0.585	0.779	5
John McGraw	+6	0.032	−30	0.000	0.032	6

Final All-Around Ratings

Since third base was considered to be one of the more important defensive positions on a ballclub, the offense-to-defense ratio was set at two-to-one. The offense was the all-determining factor in this race, with the offensive leaders finishing in the same order in the final overall ratings. In fact, even if the offense-to-defense had been rated at one-to-one, Denny Lyons would still have been awarded the title as the nineteenth century's greatest all-around third baseman. The only difference in the final ratings would have been Lave Cross nosing out John McGraw for second place.

	Offense × 2	Defense × 1	Total Points	Final All-Around Ratings
Denny Lyons	3.304	0.779	4.083	1
John McGraw	2.952	0.032	2.984	2

	Offense × 2	Defense × 1	Total Points	Final All-Around Ratings
Lave Cross	0.942	1.811	2.753	3
Billy Nash	1.102	1.465	2.567	4
Billy Shindle	0.194	1.226	1.420	5
Arie Latham	0.318	0.811	1.129	6

Right Field and Left Field

The right field and left field positions were considered to be primarily offensive positions. Therefore, the offense-to-defense ratio was set at four-to-one for those positions. A total of eleven players competed for the title as the nineteenth century's greatest all-around right or left fielder.

- Ed Delahanty had the fourth-highest career batting average in major league history, a sizzling .346. He led the league in doubles five times, triples once, home runs twice, RBIs three times, batting average twice, on-base percentage twice, slugging average five times, and stolen bases four times. He collected 2,597 base hits, with 1,600 runs scored and 1,466 RBIs, in 16 years. He won two batting titles, with a high of .410 in 1899.
- Harry Stovey could hit, hit with power, run, field, and throw. Playing when the plate was only 50 to 55 feet from the mound, Stovey batted .289 while averaging 31 doubles, 16 triples, and 11 home runs for every 550 at-bats. He also was one of the top base stealers of his time, leading the league with 68 stolen bases in 1886 and 97 stolen bases four years later. His 1.00 runs per game scoring average is number three all-time.
- Hugh Duffy, a .326 lifetime batter, has the highest single-season batting average in baseball history, hitting .440 in 1894. The diminutive right-handed hitter became the game's first Triple Crown winner that year, smashing 18 home runs and driving in 145 teammates. He also led the league in base hits (237) and doubles (51). The native of Cranston, Rhode Island, was one of the top defensive outfielders of his era as well.
- Samuel "Big Sam" Thompson was one of the top sluggers of the nineteenth century, pounding the ball at a .341 clip over 15 years, with 31 doubles, 15 triples, 12 home runs, and 119 runs batted in a year. His .505 career slugging average is the second-highest in the nineteenth century. He was also one of the league's best fly-chasers, with a steel trap for a glove and rifle for a throwing arm. He led the league in fielding average and assists twice.

- Pete Browning was strictly an offensive outfielder who batted a torrid .341 over a 13-year career, number twelve all-time and number four in the nineteenth century. He led the league in batting average three times during his career with a high of .378 in 1882. He also had a .403 OBP and a .467 slugging percentage during his career. On the other hand, he was a defensive liability who was nicknamed "the Gladiator" for his fierce battles with fly balls.
- James "Orator Jim" O'Rourke enjoyed a 23-year major league career, from 1872 to 1894, and he made the most of it, batting .310 with 2,304 base hits. The man who was credited with the first base hit in National League history in 1876 batted over .300 thirteen times with a high of .362 in 1877. The loquacious Irishman retired at the age of 43 but came back for one more game when he was 54 years old.
- Mike Tiernan was a .311 career batter for the New York Giants from 1887 to 1899. His .463 slugging average is the fourth-best of the sixteen outfielders in this study. He played on two world championship teams with the Giants, in 1888 and 1889, leading the league in runs scored with 147 in 122 games in 1888. Two years later, he led the National League with 13 home runs and a .495 slugging average.
- Thomas "Oyster" Burns starred for the league champion Brooklyn Bridegrooms in 1889 and 1890, leading the National League with 13 homers and 128 RBIs in 1890. He was a lifetime .300 hitter who averaged 103 runs scored and 99 runs batted in during his eleven-year major league career. The stocky Burns was a decent defensive outfielder with a reliable glove, but his lack of speed was a liability.
- Jesse "the Crab" Burkett tattooed opposing pitchers to the tune of .338 during his 16-year career. He was not a slugger of note, but he batted over .400 twice with a high of .410 in 1896, and he captured three batting titles and led the league in base hits three times and runs scored twice. Burkett's outstanding .415 on-base percentage contributed to his 112 runs scored for every 550 at-bats.
- Billy Hamilton, a .344 career hitter, had an exceptional batting eye that produced an average of 104 bases on balls for every 550 at-bats and that, along with his 189 base hits, contributed to his 1.06 runs scored per game average, the highest such average in the annals of the game. Hamilton's skill at reaching base combined with his blazing speed earned him five stolen-base crowns en route to a career total of 914 stolen bases.
- Willie "Wee Willie" Keeler, a tiny 5' 4", 140-pound left-handed hitter who advised other players to "hit 'em where they ain't," was essentially a singles hitter, but he hit enough of them to produce a .341 career batting average with 110 runs scored a year. Keeler's .424 batting average in 1897

is the fifth-highest average in major league history. The little man led the league in fielding average twice and assists once.

Offensive Ratings

Billy Hamilton's .455 OBP was forty points higher than Jesse Burkett's and 44 points higher than Ed Delahanty's; he easily won the OBPD race, finishing 100 points above the league average. Delahanty, who had a .411 OBP compared to .403 for Pete Browning, lost his spot to Browning when the adjusted OBPs were determined, with Burkett slipping into third place. Sam Thompson easily won the normalized adjusted slugging average category. He was tied with Delahanty for the official slugging average, but when the era adjustments were made, Thompson nosed out Delahanty, +129 to +125. Overall, Pete Browning captured first place in the offensive rating with 2.767 points to 2.391 for Delahanty. Hamilton finished fourth behind Orator Jim O'Rourke, with Thompson nailing down the fifth spot.

Willie Keeler of "Hit 'em where they ain't" fame batted .341 during his 19-year major league career.

Defensive Ratings

Ed Delahanty finished first in the defensive ratings with 1.513 total points. The fleet-footed outfielder covered acres of ground in left field and he kept base runners honest with a powerful throwing arm. His 243 career assists place him ninth all-time in assists per game. Hugh Duffy came in second with 1.255 points and Billy Hamilton was third with 1.076 points.

Final All-Around Ratings

The offensive leader obviously had a huge advantage in the final all-around ratings since the offense was weighted at four times the defense. And, holding true to form, Pete Browning was crowned as the best all-around right-left fielder of the nineteenth century, although Ed Delahanty made a close race of it thanks to his outstanding performance in the defensive ratings, where he beat Browning by 0.835 points. If the offense-to-defense had been rated at two-to-one instead of four-to-one, Ed Delahanty would have finished first.

	Offense × 4	Defense × 1	Total Points	Final All-Around Ratings
Pete Browning	7.068	0.678	7.746	1
Ed Delahanty	6.172	1.513	7.685	2
Billy Hamilton	5.448	1.076	6.524	3
Sam Thompson	5.376	0.999	6.375	4
Harry Stovey	4.636	0.900	5.536	5
Jesse Burkett	4.896	0.510	5.406	6
Mike Tiernan	4.396	0.439	4.835	7
Jim O'Rourke	3.592	0.838	4.430	8
Oyster Burns	3.728	0.579	4.307	9
Willie Keeler	3.120	0.769	3.889	10
Hugh Duffy	2.408	1.255	3.663	11

Center Field

The center-field position, along with the catcher, second baseman, and shortstop, was considered to be one of the keys to a team's defense. The old adage, "To win a pennant, a team has to be strong up the middle," was as true in the nineteenth century as it was in the twentieth century. There were five players competing for the title of the nineteenth century's greatest all-around center fielder. Their offense was weighted at three-to-one over their defense.

- Mike Griffin was an outstanding center fielder for the Brooklyn Dodgers during the 1890s, leading the league in fielding average five times and assists twice. He also led the league with 152 runs scored in 137 games in 1889, and with 36 doubles in 1892. Griffin batted .296 over 12 years, averaging 29 doubles, 10 triples, and four home runs for every 550 at-bats.
- Paul Hines was a 16-year major leaguer who was one of the best all-around center fielders of his era. The husky right-handed hitter, who compiled a career batting average of .301, was an offensive threat who led the league in doubles three times, home runs once, RBIs once, and slugging average once. He also showed the way in fielding average twice and assists once.
- George Gore, another career .301 hitter, batted over .300 eight times in fourteen years, with a high of .360 in 1890 when he won the batting title.

He also led the league in on-base percentage (.399) and slugging average (.463) that year. Gore, who scored over 100 runs seven times, is number two all-time in runs scored per game with 1.01. He averaged 136 runs scored a year, thanks to punching out 166 base hits and drawing 74 bases on balls.
- Steve Brodie was an important cog in the Baltimore Orioles' three consecutive National League pennants from 1894 to 1896. The 5'11", 180-pound left-handed hitter played all 392 games during that span, batting .338 with 71 doubles, 32 triples, and 317 runs scored. During his 12-year major league career, Brodie led the league's outfielders in fielding average three times and assists twice.
- George Van Haltren was a southpaw pitcher during his first three years in the major leagues, going 39–31, but was converted to a strong-armed outfielder who became the pride of New York during the 1890s. Van Haltren put together a .316 career batting average with 112 runs scored, 20 doubles, 11 triples, and five home runs for every 550 at-bats.

Offensive Ratings

There was not much to choose from as far as the offensive statistics of the five center-field candidates were concerned. George Gore nosed out Paul Hines for the number one spot based on his on-base percentage. Both men had a career .301 batting average, but Gore, thanks to his 74 bases on balls a year, built a .386 on-base percentage, while Hines, who drew only 32 walks a year, had to settle for a .343 OBP. In addition, Gore enjoyed a +70 point era adjustment while Hines had to be content with a +40 point adjustment. Hines out-pointed Gore in SLGD, but it was not enough to offset the huge lead Gore had built in OBPD.

Defensive Ratings

Mike Griffin was a sensational all-around outfielder, and he dominated both the fielding average category and the range factor category, compiling a perfect 2.000 point total. His closest rival was Steve Brodie, who finished second in both categories with a 1.689 point total. Paul Hines was a close third in both categories and third overall. George Gore, who had set the pace on offense, came in a miserable fourth for defense.

Final All-Around Ratings

Mike Griffin, who finished a distant third in the offensive ratings, swept the defensive ratings to capture the title as the greatest all-around nineteenth century center fielder, based on a three-to-one offense to defense rating system. His 3.941 point total edged George Gore by a mere 0.008 points. Paul Hines was third with 3.818 points.

	Offense × 3	Defense × 1	Total Points	Final All-Around Ratings
Mike Griffin	1.941	2.000	3.941	1
George Gore	3.132	0.801	3.933	2
Paul Hines	2.406	1.412	3.818	3
George Van Haltren	1.767	0.625	2.392	4
Steve Brodie	0.000	1.689	1.689	5

MAJOR LEAGUE BASEBALL'S NINETEENTH CENTURY ALL-STAR TEAM

	First Team	*Second Team*
Catcher	Buck Ewing	Jack Clements
Pitcher	Bob Caruthers	Kid Nichols
First Base	Dan Brouthers	Roger Connor
Second Base	Fred Dunlap	Hardy Richardson
Shortstop	Hughie Jennings	Jack Glasscock
Third Base	Denny Lyons	John McGraw
Right-Left Field	Pete Browning	Billy Hamilton
	Ed Delahanty	Sam Thompson
Center Field	Mike Griffin	George Gore

Chapter 4

Baseball's Greatest Catchers

There were a total of twenty catchers competing for the title of baseball's greatest all-around catcher.

- Gene Tenace was one of the game's most underrated catchers. He was a solidly built six-footer weighing 190 pounds. A right-handed hitter, Tenace hit with power and had an excellent on-base-percentage. He is often overlooked because his batting average was a mediocre .241, and he struck out 125 times for every 550 at-bats. In his support, he walked 123 times a year, giving him an excellent .388 on-base percentage (OBP) that was significantly higher than the league average. And his power, which produced 25 home runs and 84 RBIs a year, gave him a .429 slugging average that was considerably higher than most other catchers. On defense, Tenace had a better-than-average fielding average and caught-stealing percentage. Unfortunately, shoulder problems curtailed his catching career after 892 games, sending him to first base, where his bad shoulder would not affect his game and where he could still help the team with his big bat.

  Gene Tenace was a member of the 1972–74 world championship Oakland Athletics and, in 1972, he was voted the World Series' Most Valuable Player after smashing four home runs in seven games, driving in nine of the 16 runs the A's scored in the Series, and batting .348.

- Mickey Cochrane was a member of Connie Mack's powerful Philadelphia Athletics, American League champions of 1929–31. The feisty backstop who won two world titles with the A's also won two American League pennants and one world championship with the 1934–35 Detroit Tigers. Cochrane was a tough field general who hated to lose and did whatever it took to leave the field victorious. Over the course of his 13-year major league career, "Black Mike," as he was called, compiled a .320 batting average, the highest career batting average for any major league catcher.

He also had the highest on-base percentage and one of the game's better slugging averages. On defense, he was the field general, positioning players, running the game from behind the plate, and keeping his pitchers focused on the job at hand. His only defensive weakness was a poor throwing arm that left him below the league average in caught-stealing percentage. However, he did lead the league a total of twelve times in the four major defensive categories, fielding average, putouts, assists, and double plays.

- Gabby Hartnett learned the art of catching from his father, a former semi-pro catcher and a tough taskmaster. Hartnett, who caught his father's pitches in the back yard every evening after his father got home from work, was an excellent defensive catcher before the age of fifteen, and he possessed what may be the strongest throwing arm in major league history. During Hartnett's 19-year career with the Chicago Cubs, fans used to go out to the park several hours before game-time just to watch him rifle the ball around the infield. The big catcher had no weaknesses. On offense, he hit for average (.297 career), hit with power (20 homers and 101 RBIs for every 550 at-bats), and he could also advance base runners with well-placed sacrifice bunts if the situation warranted it. And, thanks to his father, Gabby's defense was flawless, even to protecting against passed balls and wild pitches. He was taught to shift his feet and get his body in front of any balls that were wide of the plate rather than trying to backhand balls like Johnny Bench and most of today's catchers do. In addition to his other skills, Hartnett was a fearless gunner who would throw to any base at any time and, as a result, he had one of the highest pickoff averages of all the world-class catchers. During his career he led the league in a combined total of twenty-two of the four major defensive categories. And if a catcher's caught-stealing rating was available as an official statistic, he would have added another ten or more stars to his crown. He is number four all-time in career double plays with 163.
- Bill Dickey was considered by some baseball experts to be the heart and soul of the great New York Yankee teams of the 1930s. He was an outstanding field leader and a great handler of pitchers as well as a durable catcher who established a major league record for catching 100 or more games in 13 straight seasons. In addition to his defensive strengths, he was also a force to be reckoned with on offense, compiling a .313 career batting average, second only to Mickey Cochrane among catchers. He was considered by many opposing players to be the toughest clutch hitter on the Yankee squad, even though he played with such legends as Lou Gehrig, Babe Ruth, and Joe DiMaggio. During his 17-year major league career, Dickey played on eight American League pennant winners and

seven world championship teams. Dickey led the league in a total of fourteen times in the major defensive categories.

- Roy Campanella was the epitome of the baseball catcher. He was a solid offensive presence who was a .300 hitter when he was healthy. He had good plate discipline, seldom struck out, and was capable of coaxing a base on balls. He could also hit for power or sacrifice a runner along with a bunt when needed. But as good as he was on offense, he prided himself on his defensive capabilities. He turned professional at the age of 15, playing with the Baltimore Elites in the Negro leagues. He learned the art of catching under Biz Mackey, arguably the greatest all-around catcher in Negro league history. Campanella's stocky physique gave the mistaken impression that he was a slow runner, but nothing could be further from the truth. A former high school track star, he was fast on his feet, often beating the runner to first base while backing up throws on ground balls to the infield. He also had extremely quick reflexes, whether pouncing on a ball in front of the plate or digging potential wild pitches out of the dirt, so quick, in fact, that New York writers dubbed him "the Cat." His greatest strength was his powerful throwing arm. His arm might not have been as strong as Gabby Hartnett's, but he more than made up for it in accuracy, finishing his career with the highest career caught-stealing percentage in major league history. Over his brief career, he led the league eleven times in the four major defensive categories and, if a catcher's caught-stealing record was available, he would have added another six or more awards to his total.
- Joe Torre enjoyed an 18-year major league career, playing 2,209 games, including 903 games behind the plate. He also played first base and third base. Torre's biggest problem was that he was versatile and cooperative. He was the first-string catcher for the Milwaukee and Atlanta Braves during his first nine years in the National League, and he was a two-time Gold Glove catcher. After he was traded to the St. Louis Cardinals, he played wherever he was needed. When Ted Simmons arrived in St. Louis, Torre moved to third base to make room, and after Ken Reitz arrived, Torre moved across the diamond to first base. But wherever Torre played, he did a superb job defensively, and he always had that big bat to keep him happy. Over his career, he batted .297, with 24 doubles, four triples, 18 home runs, and 83 RBIs for every 550 at-bats. In 1971, he was voted the Most Valuable Player in the National League while leading the league in four categories: batting with a .363 average; base hits with 230; total bases with 352; and runs batted in with 137.
- Darrell Porter was a hard-hitting backstop in the mold of Gene Tenace, except that he batted left-handed. He had a mediocre .247 batting average, but he averaged 91 bases on balls a year to go along with 24 doubles,

Gabby Hartnett, 1938.

five triples, 19 home runs, and 83 RBIs, giving him a fine .354 on-base percentage and a .409 slugging average. His best year at the plate was 1979 when he hit a career-high .291 with 23 doubles, 10 triples, 20 home runs, 101 runs scored, and 112 RBIs. His league-leading 121 bases on balls gave him an outstanding .421 on-base percentage and a .484 slugging average. On defense, the 6', 193-pound Porter was considered to be a good handler of pitchers and an above-average defensive catcher with a strong throwing arm.

- Ernie Lombardi was one of the top offensive catchers in major league history, and one of only five catchers with a career batting average over .300. His .306 average ranks fourth behind Mickey Cochrane, Bill Dickey, and Babe Phelps, who hit .310. Called the "Schnozz" because of his large nose, the affable giant who stood 6'3" and weighed 230 pounds was noted for his powerful line drives that frequently ricocheted off outfield fences around the National League. He had extra-base power similar to Torre and Porter, while averaging 93 RBIs a season. He was also noted for his lack of speed, often leading the league in grounding into double plays. His slowness afoot was so obvious that infielders played back on the grass, challenging him to beat out an infield hit, something he seldom did. But, in spite of his lack of speed, the right-handed slugger won two batting titles, hitting .342 in 1938 and .330 four years later, the only catcher to achieve that honor. Lombardi called a good game and was a good handler of pitchers, but in all other aspects of the game he was an average defensive catcher.

- Johnny Bench was one of the best catchers of the 1960s to 1980s, along with Carlton Fisk, Gary Carter, Jim Sundberg, and Bill Freehan. The fact that Bench is invariably rated as the greatest catcher in baseball history by modern observers can be traced to two things. First, he was one of the more visible players on the Big Red Machine championship teams of the 1970s, and one of the game's first television celebrities. Second, he was the game's biggest self-promoter. Oftentimes, when he was quoted or interviewed, he began the discussion by saying, "Whenever people talk about great catchers, they begin with me." He was also quoted as saying, "I can throw out any man alive." Johnny Bench had many admirable qualities but modesty was not one of them. He was, however, one of the catching profession's greatest power hitters and one of its best defensive players. He is seventh all-time in career putouts with 9,260. During his 17-year career, Bench led the league just five times in the four major defensive categories, the fourteenth-best out of the twenty catchers in the study. He led the league in putouts twice, and in fielding average, assists, and double plays once each.

- Yogi Berra's metamorphosis from an ugly duckling backstop to one of baseball's greatest defensive catchers under the tutelage of New York Yankee legend Bill Dickey was almost miraculous. The stocky youngster from St. Louis could always hit, but when he was promoted to the New York Yankees he was a mediocre outfielder. Manager Casey Stengel, desperately trying to find a position Berra could handle so he could keep his bat in the lineup, eventually converted him to a catcher, a move that looked for awhile like a monumental blunder. Berra looked lost behind the plate. In the 1947 World Series, the Brooklyn Dodgers, with Jackie Robinson, Pee Wee Reese, and company, ran the bases with abandon, stealing seven bases in less than four games and forcing the Yankee manager to bench his protégé in Game Five. Stengel then brought Bill Dickey on board in spring training to teach the 22-year-old backstop the rudiments of the catching position. At the time, Dickey said he thought that Berra could be a good (not great, but good) catcher. Yogi proved him wrong. With an old-time work ethic, lightning-fast reflexes, and a strong throwing arm, Berra soon became one of the greatest defensive catchers in the annals of the sport. He went on to lead the American League in double plays six times while throwing out 49 percent of runners who attempted to steal on him. He was outstanding at calling a game, handling a pitching staff, and blocking balls in the dirt, and he pounced on a bunt as Casey Stengel liked to say, "like it was a dollar bill." Berra is number ten in career putouts with 8,729, and number three in career double plays with 175. He led the league in a total of nineteen of the four major defensive categories, including eight times in putouts and six times in double plays.

- Jim Sundberg was a great defensive catcher who led the American League in fielding percentage, putouts, and assists six times each and in double plays five times, the best defensive record of any catcher in this study. His .993 career fielding average is tied for the highest norm in baseball history, and his 9,414 career putouts rank fifth. He had a powerful throwing arm that discouraged base runners from attempting to steal against him, and he had the quick reflexes required to run down pop fouls or field bunts. And he was durable, catching 140 or more games in six consecutive seasons, and more than 130 games ten times. Sundberg's weakness was his offense. He carried a career batting average of just .248 with only 34 extra-base hits for every 550 at-bats.

- Gary Carter was a 6'2", 215-pound firebrand who starred in the major leagues for 19 years, primarily with the Montreal Expos and New York Mets. The California native could do it all, on defense and offense. He led the National League in fielding percentage twice, in most chances six times, and putouts, assists and double plays five times, a defensive record exceeded by only two other catchers — Jim Sundberg and Gabby Hartnett. He is number one in career putouts with 10,360, number three in games caught with 2,056, and number eight in double plays with 149. He was an expert in blocking balls in the dirt and preventing wild pitches by his pitchers. He once set a record with just one passed ball in 150 games. But unlike many of his peers, Carter could more than hold his own with a bat in his hands. His career total of 324 home runs has been exceeded by only four other catchers. He hit 20 or more home runs nine times

Jim Sundberg was one of the best defensive catchers ever to don the "tools of ignorance" (courtesy of the Texas Rangers).

with a high of 32 homers in 1985, and he drove in more than 100 runs four times with a high of a league-leading 106 RBIs in 1984. Carter is one of the few catchers to accumulate more than 2,000 base hits in his career. In the 1986 World Series with the New York Mets, Carter batted .276 with two home runs and a Series-high nine RBIs in seven games.

- Lance Parrish was another outstanding all-around catcher who starred in the major leagues from 1977 to 1995. He never led the league in fielding average but was consistent from year to year, and his career mark of .991 is number seven all-time, as is his 1,818 games played. And his strong throwing arm cut down enemy base runners at a rate 5 percent above the league average. He had good reflexes and superior range, but he did have one chink in his armor. He had problems with balls in the dirt, and he led the league with 21 passed balls in 1979. Nevertheless, he was a six-time all-star who was a major contributor on offense, batting .252 with 25 home runs and 83 runs batted in for every 550 at-bats. He helped the Detroit Tigers win the 1984 world championship, slamming 33 homers and driving in 98 runs during the regular season, and then hitting .278 with a homer and two RBIs in the World Series against the San Diego Padres. He also kept the Padre runners in check in the Series, allowing only two stolen bases while shooting down three base runners.
- Tony Pena, another of baseball's defensive standouts, had a unique catching style, with one leg straight out when he crouched. The 6', 180-pound native of the Dominican Republic who starred in the major leagues for 17 years was a particular favorite in Pittsburgh, where he played from 1980 to 1986. When he was traded to the St. Louis Cardinals in 1987, he helped Whitey Herzog's team capture the world championship, batting .381 with five runs scored in the NLCS and .409 with four RBIs in the World Series. Pena was a light hitter, compiling a .261 career batting average with 22 doubles, two triples, and nine home runs for every 550 at-bats, but he dominated behind the plate. He was an outstanding glove man. He is number six all-time in games caught, number eight in total chances per game, number four in putouts, and number six in double plays. He led the league in fielding average twice, putouts five times, assists twice, double plays four times, and he won three Gold Gloves.
- Harry Danning was an excellent catcher for the New York Giants in the late 1930s. Unfortunately, his major league career was cut short by World War II. He served in the military from 1943 to the end of the war, and retired from baseball on his return home. During his abbreviated career, Danning showed remarkable expertise in all aspects of the defensive game, from fielding to cutting down would-be base stealers, blocking balls in the dirt, preventing wild pitches, and chasing down foul pop-ups and bunts. The 6'1", 190-pound right-handed hitter compiled a .285 career batting average with 30 doubles, five triples, 11 homers and 73 RBIs a year. Danning was dubbed "Harry the Horse" by the press, either because, as he said, he looked like a horse or worked like one. He did

work like one, that's for sure. Like most old-time ballplayers, Danning had an admirable work ethic and an apparent disregard for pain that allowed him to play through numerous injuries.

- Ray Mueller was one of baseball's top defensive catchers, but also one of its slowest. He had a below-average range factor, and he was always among the league leaders in grounding into double plays. Other than that, he was a standout behind the plate or with a bat in his hand. He had the highest fielding average differential of any catcher in the study (tied with Jim Sundberg), and he had the fourth-highest caught-stealing differential (also tied with Sundberg). He allowed the fewest passed balls per game of any of the twenty catchers, and was number three in the fewest wild pitches allowed (tied with Berra). As a batter, he hit a modest .252 with just 38 extra-base hits for every 550 at-bats.

- Chris Hoiles was a fine all-around catcher during the 1990s, but an unlucky one who spent most of his ten-year career playing with and through injuries. Finally, when the pain from his leg and hip injuries proved to be too restrictive, he graciously retired from the game. But during his brief career, he established himself as one of the game's top catchers, both offensively and defensively. On defense, he had the fewest passed balls and permitted the fewest wild pitches of any catcher in the study. He also had an excellent fielding average and an above-average range factor. His one weakness was his throwing arm that caught just 28 percent of the runners attempting to steal. As a hitter, he averaged 29 home runs for every 550 at-bats, one of the highest rates of any of the twenty catchers. He was also among the leaders in on-base percentage and slugging percentage. In 1993, he became just the fifth American League catcher to bat .300 with at least 25 doubles and 25 homers in a season. Three years later, in a game against the Seattle Mariners, he experienced his most exciting moment. Coming to the plate in the bottom of the ninth inning with the bases full and his team trailing by three runs, he took a full-count pitch downtown, a walk-off, grand-slam home run. And, on August 14, 1998, he had a game to remember, smashing two grand-slam homers in the same game.

- Bill Freehan was a Detroit Tiger mainstay for 15 years, from 1961 through 1976. By the time he retired, he had accumulated numerous records. His .993 career fielding average is tied for the highest career norm for a catcher in baseball history. He led the league in fielding average three times, putouts six times, and double plays once. He is number three all-time in total chances per game with 6.79, and number three in putouts with 9,941. Freehan had quick reflexes and good speed for a big man, and he also had a quick bat. The 6'2", 205-pound right-handed hitter batted .262 over 15 years, with 22 doubles, three triples, and 18 home runs a year. Three times in his career he hit 20 or more home runs with a high of 25 in 1968, the year the Tigers won the world championship. He batted .263 that year with 84 RBIs and 73 runs scored, in support of Gibson, Cash, Horton, and company. The Michigan native was tested continuously by the Cardinal rabbits, who had stolen 110 bases during the regular National League season. They swiped eleven more bases during the Series, including seven by Lou Brock, but Freehan gunned down five of them to keep the games under control.

- Earl Battey was a key factor in the Minnesota Twins' march to the 1965 American League pennant. The California native, a career .270 hitter, stroked the ball at a .297 clip that year, with 60 runs batted in in 394 at-bats. In the World Series he ran into a railing, neck-first, while chasing a pop foul, but like the warrior he was, he shook off the injury and caught the rest of the Series. During his 13-year career, Battey was equally as good on offense and defense. His batting average was supplemented by 16 homers a year, a .351 on-base-percentage, and a .409 slugging average. His adjusted OBP was the sixth-best of the twenty catchers in the study. As noted in *The Ballplayers*, "A three time Gold Glove winner, Battey topped all ML catchers in 1962 with a .280 BA, threw out 24 runners, and picked off 13." The publication also noted that Battey routinely played through injuries that included dislocated fingers, a bad knee, and a goiter problem that occasionally added 60 pounds to his weight. During his career he led the league four times each in putouts and assists, and twice in double plays.

- Carlton Fisk was baseball's most durable catcher, catching a major league record 2,229 games over a memorable 24-year career. He is also number four in putouts with 9,428 and tenth in double plays by a catcher with 147. Fisk was more an offensive catcher than a defensive one, but he called a good game, handled a pitching staff with great skill, and was outstanding in preventing passed balls and wild pitches. At the plate he was one of the best. His .269 career batting average included 2,356 base hits, one of the highest base-hit totals for any catcher in the annals of the game. His 421 career doubles, 376 home runs, 1,276 runs scored, and 1,386 runs batted in also rank with the best. The 220-pound right-handed slugger hit 20 or more home runs six times, with a high of 37 homers in 1985. The image of Fisk that sticks in most people's minds is that of his frantic hand-waving as he tried to steer a high fly ball he had hit to left field into home run territory in Game Six of the 1976 World Series. The pleading worked as his ball ricocheted off the foul pole for a walk-off homer that knotted the Series at three games apiece. Unfortunately, the Cincinnati Reds won Game Seven, 4–3, to claim the world championship.

Mike Piazza, baseball's greatest offensive catcher.

- Two of the foremost world-class catchers were still active when this study was conducted — Ivan "Pudge" Rodriguez and Mike Piazza. Their statistics and ratings were not included in the study, but their potential future ratings were discussed at the end of the section. Rodriguez, through the 2006 season, boasted a .304 batting average and had gunned down 48

Pudge Rodriguez has the major leagues' best throwing arm since Roy Campanella (courtesy Ivan "Pudge" Rodriguez Foundation).

percent of all base runners who dared challenge his arm. Piazza, who was primarily an offensive catcher, batted .309 through 2006, with 35 home runs and 108 RBIs for every 550 at-bats.

Offensive Ratings

The offensive ratings for catchers included on-base percentage (OBP), slugging average (SLG), stolen bases (SB), sacrifice hits (SH), and double plays grounded into (GIDP). The published slugging statistics were first adjusted for the individual player's park factor, then adjusted for the era in which the player played, and finally normalized. The on-base percentages were era adjusted and then normalized, and the SB, SH, and GIDP statistics were all normalized. The two most important offensive statistics for catchers were OBP and SLG. Players in general who had high OBPs also had high runs scored averages, and players who had high SLGs also had high RBI rates; after all, teams that score the most runs win the most games. For this study, NOBPA and NXSLGA were rated at a maximum of twenty points each while NSB, NSH, and NGIDP, were rated at a maximum of one point each, giving a total of 43 points that could be realized by a catcher for his offensive contribution.

Normalized Adjusted On-Base Percentage (NOBPA)

As noted above, some catchers were underrated since their low batting averages caused their overall offensive contributions to be overlooked. A complete measure of a player's offense must include his ability to reach base by drawing bases on balls. The most notable example of a player who fell through the offensive cracks was Gene Tenace, whose mediocre .241 batting average caused him to be disregarded by most baseball experts. However, Tenace had a good batting eye that brought him 123 bases on balls a year, and increased his OBP from a lowly .241 to a healthy .388. Although Tenace's batting average was the lowest in the study, his OBP was the second-highest of the twenty catchers, trailing only Mickey Cochrane, who had a sensational .419 OBP. Cochrane had the highest career batting average at .320, and combined with his 91 bases on balls a year, it helped him retain his top spot in the OBP category. Another catcher who was helped by his keen batting eye was Darrell Porter, who hit just .247 but drew 90 walks a year to give him one of the top adjusted on-base percentages in the study. Gene Tenace's on-base percentage, adjusted to the era in which he played (OBPA), was .392, second to

Cochrane's .401. Other catchers who had excellent OBPAs included Bill Dickey (.368), Joe Torre (.363), the aforementioned Darrell Porter (.362), and Earl Battey (.359). The leader in OBPA, Mickey Cochrane, posted the maximum point total of 20.000 for the normalized adjusted on-base percentage (NOBPA). Gene Tenace's normalized point total was .392/.401 × 20 = 19.551. He was followed by Bill Dickey (18.354), Joe Torre (18.105), Darrell Porter (18.055), and Earl Battey (.17.905). Bringing up the rear was Tony Pena, whose .298 OBPA gave him a normalized point total of 14.863, Ray Mueller, whose .308 OBPA resulted in a 15.362 point total, and Lance Parrish, whose .309 average gave him 15.411 points.

Normalized Adjusted Slugging Average (XSLGA)

The catchers with the highest career slugging averages were Roy Campanella, who sported a fancy .500 career slugging average, Gabby Hartnett (.489), Bill Dickey (.486), and Yogi Berra (.482). Jim Sundberg held down the bottom spot with a career slugging average of .348, and he was closely followed by Tony Pena at .364 and Ray Mueller at .368. They were the only three catchers in the study with career slugging averages under .400. When the slugging averages were adjusted for individual park factors and the era in which the player was active, there were some minor changes to the slugging ratings. For instance, Johnny Bench, thanks to a favorable era adjustment of 17 points, overtook Roy Campanella to claim the top spot in the adjusted slugging average ratings with a XSLGA of .302 compared to .283 for Campanella, who lost eight points in the era adjustment. Gene Tenace, with a favorable seven-point era adjustment, slipped past Gabby Hartnett into third place, with Hartnett fourth and Darrell Porter fifth. Bill Dickey was hurt by his highly unfavorable park factor that saw him hit 24 home runs for every 550 at-bats at home compared to just 11 home runs on the road. And he was further penalized by a three-point negative era adjustment.

Normalized Stolen Bases (NSB)

Catchers, for the most part, are not noted for their base-stealing skills, but occasionally a catcher comes along who brings with him a very aggressive base running game, including the ability to steal bases. Carlton Fisk was such a catcher. He ran the bases with abandon and in the process stole an average of eight bases for every 154 games played, the highest total for any of the twenty catchers evaluated in this study. Mickey Cochrane and Tony Pena with seven stolen bases and Gene Tenace and Johnny Bench with five were the only other catchers with more than four stolen bases a year.

Normalized Sacrifice Hits (NSH)

Catchers, for whatever reason, were not very adept at laying down sacrifice hits. That situation was partially caused more by philosophical changes in baseball strategy as opposed to incompetence on the part of the catchers. However, the statistic is part of the offensive evaluation for all players, so it may be that some players were penalized through no fault of their own. Catchers of long ago, like Mickey Cochrane with 16 sacrifice hits a year and Gabby Hartnett with 10 sacrifice hits a year, were not only dangerous hitters, they were also skilled in the art of laying down a sacrifice bunt to move a runner along at a critical juncture in the ball game. Over the past sixty years, only one catcher has averaged more than four sacrifice hits a year. Jim Sundberg had eleven.

Normalized Double Plays Grounded Into (NGIDP)

As most people know, catchers have never been noted for their blazing speed and, as a result, they have recorded some of the highest frequencies for grounding into double plays of any players at any position. Not surprisingly, Ernie Lombardi, long recognized as one of the slowest men ever to play the game, grounded into an average of 25 double plays for every 154 games played. Ray Mueller with 21 double plays grounded into and Tony Pena with 20 were close behind. At the other end of the spectrum, Mickey Cochrane, Gene Tenace, and Darrell Porter grounded into only ten double plays a year. Of the active players, Mike Piazza averages 19 GIDPs a year and Ivan Rodriguez averages 14.

Final Offensive Ratings

Mickey Cochrane led all catchers in three important offensive categories — NOBPA, NSH, and NGIDP — and he was a close second in NSB. Cochrane was no better than twelfth in NXSLGA, and his lack of power allowed Gene Tenace to overtake him for the number one spot in the final offensive ratings. Tenace, whose 123 bases on balls a year gave him a second-place finish in the NOBPA category, was also number one in NGIDP.

Name	NOBPA × 20	NXSLGA × 20	.05NSB × 20	.05NSH × 20	.05NGIDP × 20	Total Points	Final Offensive Ratings
Tenace	19.551	17.748	.625	.188	1.000	39.112	1
Cochrane	20.000	14.371	.875	1.000	1.000	37.246	3
Hartnett	17.257	17.417	.625	.938	.167	36.404	6

Name	NOBPA × 20	NXSLGA × 20	.05NSB × 20	.05NSH × 20	.05NGIDP × 20	Total Points	Final Offensive Ratings
Dickey	18.354	14.901	.375	.250	.167	34.047	10
Campanella	17.506	18.742	.375	.250	.132	37.005	4
Torre	18.105	16.623	.250	.063	.125	35.166	8
Porter	18.055	17.086	.500	.125	1.000	36.768	5
Lombardi	17.506	16.159	.125	.125	.100	34.015	11
Bench	17.207	20.000	.625	.063	.179	38.074	3
Berra	17.257	16.821	.375	.063	.227	34.743	9
Sundberg	16.259	9.007	.250	.625	.167	26.308	18
Carter	16.808	16.026	.375	.125	.208	33.542	13
Parrish	15.411	15.695	.250	.125	.167	31.648	15
Pena	14.863	9.404	.875	.375	.125	25.642	19
Danning	15.960	6.755	.250	.250	.147	23.362	20
Mueller	15.362	10.596	.375	.125	.119	26.577	17
Hoiles	17.756	15.695	.125	.125	.192	33.893	12
Freehan	17.656	13.974	.250	.188	.208	32.276	14
Battey	17.905	11.788	.250	.375	.132	30.450	16
Fisk	17.207	17.020	1.000	.125	.192	35.544	7

Defensive Ratings

The defensive ratings for catchers were determined by comparing fielding average (FA), caught stealing percentage (CS), passed balls (PB), wild pitches by the pitching staff (WP), range factor (RF), and assists other than caught stealing assists (ASSA). FA, CS, RF, WP, and ASSA were compared to the league average and the difference was normalized. PB were normalized. Unfortunately, many of a catcher's defensive responsibilities cannot be measured directly, such as calling a game, handling a pitching staff, and backing up bases, but verbal evidence presented by baseball experts, historians, and former players indicates that all the world-class catchers, particularly those in the top ten, were rated high in all the intangible categories. For this study, NFAD, NCSD, and NRFD were rated at a maximum of twenty points each, NASSAD was rated at ten points, NPB was rated at six, and NWPD was rated at 1.5, for a total maximum of 77.5 points.

Normalized Fielding Average Differential (NFAD)

Jim Sundberg, long noted as one of the game's foremost defensive catchers, led the way in fielding average differential with a +8 differential, his .993

career fielding average being eight points above the .985 league average. He was joined in the top spot by Ray Mueller, whose .988 career fielding average was eight points above the .980 league average. Most catchers had fielding averages that were better than the league average. The exceptions were Darrell Porter, whose .982 career fielding average was two points below the league average, and Ernie Lombardi, whose .979 average fell one point short of the league average. The fielding average differentials (FAD) were adjusted upward by two points to bring Porter's fielding average differential to zero before calculating NFAD.

Normalized Caught-Stealing Percentage Differential (NCSD)

Roy Campanella was head and shoulders above all other world-class backstops when it came to gunning down would-be base stealers. His career caught-stealing percentage of 58 percent does not begin to do justice to his skill in that area. During his first five years in the National League, his caught-stealing percentage (CS) was a glittering 63 percent. One time he went 52 games without allowing a stolen base, and another time he threw out 13 consecutive runners who tested his powerful throwing arm. Injuries over his last five years reduced his career averages, but he still retained his number one rating, and he averaged 18 percent better than the league average. Gabby Hartnett, who may have had baseball's strongest throwing arm, could not match Campanella in quickness or accuracy. Still, he finished second to Campy with a 53 percent CS and a 12 percent caught-stealing differential (CSD). Johnny Bench's numbers were 44 percent CS versus a 35 percent league CS, for a 9 percent CSD. Jim Sundberg and Ray Mueller, both with a 6 percent CSD, trailed the three leaders. Ivan "Pudge" Rodriguez, who is still active, may give Campanella a run for his money by the time he retires. Through the 2006 season, baseball's latest hired gun enjoyed a 49 percent caught-stealing percentage and a healthy 17 percent caught-stealing differential. The caught-stealing differentials (CSD) were all adjusted upward by four points to bring Chris Hoiles' four-point negative differential to zero before calculating the NCSD.

Normalized Passed Balls (NPB)

Ray Mueller and Chris Hoiles, two of the game's best defensive catchers, were charged with just five passed balls a year, giving them the maximum total of six points. Gary Carter and Harry Danning, two other outstanding glove men, were charged with six passed balls. Lance Parrish was one of baseball's top defensive catchers, but he was weak on passed balls, piling up an average of 19 passed balls a year. And Ernie Lombardi, who was recognized as an outstanding offensive catcher, had 15 passed balls for every 154 games played.

Normalized Wild Pitch Differential (NWPD)

Many baseball experts claim that catchers who are among the leaders in preventing passed balls are also among the leaders in minimizing wild pitches by their pitching staffs. That does seem to be the case, generally speaking, and wild pitches by a team's pitching staff was included in this study, and was compared to the average wild pitches in the league in order to measure the catcher's ability to minimize that misadventure. Since a catcher has a limited effect on the team's wild pitches, it was only weighted at a maximum of 1.5 points. Carlton Fisk, who was proficient at preventing passed balls, was sensational in minimizing his team's wild pitches. Fisk's teams were guilty of throwing only 23 wild pitches a year compared to the league average of 39, a solid 16 wild pitches below the average. Chris Hoiles matched Fisk's efficiency in preventing wild pitches, but they were the only catchers whose teams were more than seven wild pitches below average. Yogi Berra's teams were seven wild pitches below average, while Johnny Bench's teams and Gary Carter's teams were five wild pitches better than average.

Normalized Range Factor Differential (NRFD)

Roy Campanella, who had been a track star in high school, and had catlike reflexes, compiled a career range factor of 4.66, a full 1.32 points better than the league average. Bill Freehan, another backstop with quick reflexes, had a range factor of 5.68, 1.06 better than the league average. And, as might be expected, Yogi Berra, Mickey Cochrane, Bill Dickey, and Gary Carter were among the elite in that category. Johnny Bench, a superior defensive catcher who was not blessed with quick reflexes or outstanding speed, was no better than 15th in range factor differential after all the results were normalized.

Normalized Other Assists Differential (NASSAD)

Catchers can compile assists in a variety of ways, such as throwing out runners attempting to steal, picking runners off base, throwing out a batter after dropping the third strike, throwing out a batter on a bunt or a topped ball, or by participating in a rundown. Most catcher assists are the result of throwing out would-be base stealers, but the other assists are equally important. This category subtracted the caught-stealing assists from a catcher's total assists, and compared the result to the league average in order to measure a catcher's proficiency in the other areas. Surprisingly, only seven of the twenty catchers in the study had other assists that exceeded the league average. The reason for that is unknown. Gabby Hartnett, who had a reputation for throwing to any base at any time in an effort to pick runners off base, led the group with a +6 differential in other assists. Johnny Bench at +4, Gary Carter at +3, Lance Parrish at +2, and Jim Sundberg, Tony Pena, and Ray Mueller at +1 were the other catchers who exceeded the league average.

Final Defensive Ratings

The usual suspects finished at the top of the defensive catcher ratings. In another close race, Roy Campanella nosed out Gabby Hartnett, the pride of Millville, Massachusetts, by a score of 60.380 to 56.420. Campanella's big lead in the caught-stealing category clinched the victory for him. Jim Sundberg, the greatest catcher in Texas Ranger history, came in third, thanks to his excellent showing in the fielding average category and the range factor category. He was followed by Gary Carter, who was strong in almost all categories, and Lance Parrish, who also was strong in most categories with the exception of passed balls and wild pitches prevented. Bill Dickey was sixth, but some of the other favorites finished far down the list, including Johnny Bench (10th), Yogi Berra (12th), and Mickey Cochrane (13th). Gene Tenace was a decent though not outstanding defensive catcher and his 18th-place finish in the final defensive ratings would cost him dearly in the final all-around ratings.

Name	NFAD × 20	NCSD × 20	NPB × 6	NWPD × 1.5	NRFD × 20	NASSAD × 10	Total Points	Final Defensive Ratings
Tenace	8.000	4.545	2.308	.071	0	2.000	16.924	18
Cochrane	14.000	1.818	3.333	.094	14.611	2.000	35.856	13
Hartnett	16.000	14.545	2.727	.094	13.054	10.000	56.420	2
Dickey	16.000	4.545	4.286	.088	14.491	3.333	42.743	6
Campanella	12.000	20.000	4.286	.094	20.000	4.000	60.380	1
Torre	8.000	5.455	1.998	.075	4.671	3.333	23.532	17
Porter	0.000	5.455	2.308	.083	2.275	2.000	12.121	20
Lombardi	2.000	3.636	1.998	.088	5.629	3.333	16.684	19
Bench	10.000	10.000	3.750	.125	6.707	8.667	39.249	10
Berra	8.000	8.182	4.286	.150	14.731	1.333	36.681	12
Sundberg	20.000	9.091	2.727	.079	11.497	6.667	50.061	3
Carter	14.000	7.273	5.000	.125	14.251	8.000	48.649	4
Parrish	14.000	8.182	1.875	.079	12.575	7.333	44.044	5
Pena	12.000	6.364	3.750	.088	12.575	6.667	41.444	8

Name	NFAD × 20	NCSD × 20	NPB × 6	NWPD × 1.5	NRFD × 20	NASSAD × 10	Total Points	Final Defensive Ratings
Danning	14.000	5.455	5.000	.075	9.581	6.000	40.111	9
Mueller	20.000	9.091	6.000	.150	.599	6.667	42.507	7
Hoiles	12.000	0.000	6.000	1.500	11.617	4.000	35.117	14
Freehan	16.000	0.909	3.000	.100	16.886	0.000	36.895	11
Battey	6.000	7.273	2.308	.100	10.539	6.000	32.220	15
Fisk	8.000	0.909	3.333	1.500	9.940	4.667	28.349	16

Final All-Around Ratings

The Final All-Around Ratings were determined by adding the Offensive Point Totals to the Defensive Point Totals in a one-to-one ratio since a catcher's defense was considered to be equal to his offense in this study. In my book, *Backstop*, which compared the top fifty world-class catchers for both their offensive and defensive skills, a catcher's offense was rated at twice his defense for identifying baseball's greatest all-around catcher, Gabby Hartnett. This study differed from that study in two important aspects. First, the catcher's offense and defense were rated equal in this study. Second, this study was slightly more sophisticated and more accurate than the previous study. It measured not only who was better or worse in a particular category, but by how much better or worse. The previous study did not measure the magnitude of difference between players. As a result, this study identified Roy Campanella as baseball's greatest all-around catcher, edging Gabby Hartnett in a close race, 1.640 to 1.575. A few other players also changed their positions significantly from that study to this. For instance, Gary Carter catapulted from 13th place to third place, Johnny Bench moved up from seventh place to fourth place, and Jim Sundberg improved his position from 35th (out of 50) to ninth. On the other hand, Yogi Berra lost four places, to eighth place, Joe Torre fell from ninth to 17th place, and Gene Tenace plummeted from eighth place to 15th place.

Name	Offense Divided by 43	Defense Divided by 77.5	Total Points	Final All-Around Ratings	HOF
Tenace	.910	.218	1.128	15	
Cochrane	.866	.463	1.329	6	*
Hartnett	.847	.728	1.575	2	*
Dickey	.792	.552	1.344	5	*
Campanella	.861	.779	1.640	1	*

Name	Offense Divided by 43	Defense Divided by 77.5	Total Points	Final All-Around Ratings	HOF
Torre	.818	.304	1.122	17	
Porter	.855	.156	1.011	19	
Lombardi	.791	.215	1.006	20	*
Bench	.885	.506	1.391	4	*
Berra	.808	.473	1.281	8	*
Sundberg	.612	.646	1.258	9	
Carter	.780	.628	1.408	3	*
Parrish	.736	.568	1.304	7	
Pena	.596	.535	1.131	14	
Danning	.543	.518	1.061	18	
Mueller	.618	.548	1.166	13	
Hoiles	.788	.453	1.241	10	
Freehan	.751	.476	1.227	11	
Battey	.708	.416	1.124	16	
Fisk	.827	.366	1.193	12	*

Note: HOF denotes a member of the National Baseball Hall of Fame through the Class of 2007.

THE TOP TEN

Offense	Defense	Baseball's Greatest All-Around Catchers
1. Gene Tenace	1. Roy Campanella	1. Roy Campanella
2. Johnny Bench	2. Gabby Hartnett	2. Gabby Hartnett
3. Mickey Cochrane	3. Jim Sundberg	3. Gary Carter
4. Roy Campanella	4. Gary Carter	4. Johnny Bench
5. Darrell Porter	5. Lance Parrish	5. Bill Dickey
6. Gabby Hartnett	6. Bill Dickey	6. Mickey Cochrane
7. Carlton Fisk	7. Ray Mueller	7. Lance Parrish
8. Joe Torre	8. Tony Pena	8. Yogi Berra
9. Yogi Berra	9. Harry Danning	9. Jim Sundberg
10. Bill Dickey	10. Johnny Bench	10. Chris Hoiles

Pudge Rodriguez and Mike Piazza were still active as of 2007. Their statistics were reviewed during this study but their ratings were not tabulated since their ratings will more than likely decline as their careers wind down. At this point in his career, Mike Piazza has an excellent chance to be one of the top five offensive catchers of all-time after he retires, and he may finish as high as number three, behind Gene Tenace and Mickey Cochrane. If he had retired after the 2006 season, he might even have captured the number one spot. His weak showing on defense, however, might cost him a spot in baseball's top ten all-around catchers when he finally calls it a day. Pudge Rodriguez, on the other hand, has made a strong showing on both offense and defense, and he has a good chance to finish in the top ten all-around, possibly as high as number seven.

CHAPTER 5

Baseball's Greatest Pitchers

There were a total of twenty-two pitchers competing for the title of baseball's greatest all-around pitcher.

- Walter Johnson is almost always selected as baseball's greatest pitcher in any poll conducted by baseball experts, the media, or fans. One exception was Major League Baseball's infamous All-Century team selected by baseball fans across the country in 1999 that placed Johnson in sixth place, behind Nolan Ryan, Roger Clemens, and Bob Gibson. "The Big Train," as he was called, came out of the California oil fields in 1907 to dominate the American League for 21 years. He won 417 games during his career, a total that would have been much higher if he had pitched for a contender instead of the Washington Senators, who were the doormats of the league, finishing in the second division ten times, including five seventh-place finishes and two basement finishes. Walter Johnson and Nolan Ryan are the only pitchers in the study whose teams had a winning percentage below .500. The 6'1", 200-pound right-hander threw a blazing fastball with an easy sidearm motion that came by way of third base and instilled fear into the hearts of the right-handed batters. Even the great Ty Cobb, a lefty, confessed to being intimidated by him. Johnson left many records behind when he retired, including the major league career record of 3,509 strikeouts in an era when batters considered it a disgrace to strike out. The next highest strikeout total was Cy Young's 2,803 strikeouts. Johnson also owned the major league record for throwing 56 consecutive scoreless innings and 110 shutouts, twenty more than the closest competitor. And he held the American League record for 16 consecutive victories. During his illustrious career, Johnson led the league in victories six times, winning percentage twice, complete games six times, shutouts seven times, innings pitched five times, strikeouts twelve times (including eight years in a row) and earned run average five times. He is second all-time in career victories, fourth in complete games with 531 out of 666 games started (80 percent), third in innings pitched (5,914), and seventh in ERA (2.17).

- Grover Cleveland "Old Pete" Alexander, a contemporary of Walter Johnson, pitched for the Philadelphia Phillies, Chicago Cubs, and St. Louis Cardinals from 1911 to 1930, winning 373 games against 208 losses. He led the league in victories six times, with a high of 33 victories in 1916. He also led the league in complete games six times, with a high of 38 complete games in 1916, innings pitched seven times, strikeouts five times, and ERA five times. The tall, lanky right-hander was plagued with epilepsy and alcoholism throughout his career, but that rarely affected his work on the mound as he won more than 20 games a year nine times and pitched more than 300 innings a year nine times. He threw with an easy three-quarter overhand motion, relying almost exclusively on a live fastball and a sharp-breaking curveball to retire batters. His impeccable control — just 1.65 walks a game — allowed him to keep the ball low and on the outside corner of the plate, making him almost unhittable. Alexander's greatest moment in baseball came in the twilight of his career, after he helped pitch the St. Louis Cardinals into the 1926 World Series. Old Pete was handed the ball in Game Two after New York had taken the opener by a 2–1 margin, and he handcuffed Miller Huggins' team, winning 6–2 with 10 strikeouts. He came back to beat the Yankees again in Game Six, winning 10–2. Then in the finale the following day, he was called into the game in the seventh inning to face Tony Lazzeri with two men out, the bases loaded, and the Cardinals clinging to a 3–2 lead. The crafty 39-year-old veteran worked the count to 1–2 and then gave the Yankee rookie a sweeping, low outside curveball that had Lazzeri lunging for it and coming up with nothing but air. Alexander went on to blank the Yankees for two more innings, earning the save as the Cardinals claimed the world championship. Even though he retired nearly 80 years ago, he remains third all-time in career victories, twelfth in complete games with 437, second in shutouts with 90, and tenth in innings pitched with 5,190.
- Christy Mathewson, "Big Six," according to *The Ballplayers*, "looked like the classic American hero: tall, blond, and blue-eyed, with a reputation for clean living and good sportsmanship that was often held up as a splendid example for the nation's youth." The Pennsylvania native attended Bucknell University before becoming a professional baseball player in 1899. He became an icon almost overnight, and was idolized by millions of baseball fans, men and women alike, throughout his major league career. The New York Giants bought him from Norfolk in the Virginia League after he had dazzled the Virginians with a 20–2 record.

Christy Mathewson excelled in all phases of the game — pitching, batting, and fielding.

Mathewson had a brief learning curve, where he went a combined 34–34 his first two years in New York, but then exploded. Using a complete pitching repertoire that included his famous fadeaway pitch, he went 30–13 in 1903 and 33–12 the following year. The 6'1", 190-pound right-hander also had near-perfect control, walking only 1.59 men a game while striking out 4.7 men. He set a record in the 1905 World Series that will probably never be broken. Over a period of six days, Big Six tossed three shutouts at Connie Mack's Philadelphia Athletics, winning by scores of 3–0, 9–0, and 2–0. He held the A's to just 14 base hits in 27 innings while striking out 18 against a single walk. Mathewson is third all-time in career victories, seventh in winning percentage, thirteenth in complete games with 434, third in shutouts with 79, and fifth in ERA with 2.13. America's hero died of tuberculosis in 1925 at the age of 47.

- Lefty Grove was arguably baseball's greatest southpaw pitcher, and may have been baseball's all-time greatest all-around pitcher. The hot-tempered Maryland native pitched for the Philadelphia Athletics and Boston Red Sox from 1925 to 1941, winning 20 or more games eight times. His best year was 1931 when he went 31–4 with a 2.06 ERA, a full 2.32 earned runs per game below the league average. Grove led the league in many categories that year, including wins, winning percentage (.886), complete games (27), shutouts (four), strikeouts (175), and ERA. The legendary lefty, who was noted for his temper tantrums, hated to lose. One of his teammates said he hated to go into the clubhouse after Grove had lost a game because there would be clothing, bats, stools, and buckets flying all over the room. Fortunately, the 6' 3", 190-pound southpaw did not lose that often as his 300–141 record showed. He pitched in three World Series for the A's between 1929 and 1931, going 4–2 with a 1.74 earned run average. During his career he led the league in victories four times, winning percentage five times, complete games and shutouts three times each, strikeouts his first seven years in the major leagues, and ERA nine times. He is fourth all-time in winning percentage (.680), and number one in adjusted ERA, a measure of how a pitcher's ERA compares to the league average ERA.

- Sandy Koufax is frequently ignored by all-time rating systems because his 12-year career was really two separate and distinct careers: the first six years one of a pitcher trying to find himself, and the second six years one as baseball's greatest pitcher. From 1955 through 1960, Koufax won 36 games and lost 40, with 22 complete games in 103 starts, while continually struggling with his control, walking five men a game with a 4.00+ ERA. Once he learned to control his fastball, he was almost unbeatable. From 1961 through 1966, Koufax went 129–47, with 115 complete games in 201 starts. And from 1963 to 1966, he was even more dominant, going 97–27 with a sparkling 1.85 ERA, 1.60 earned runs below the league average. He averaged 298 innings pitched a year, with 307 strikeouts and just 65 bases on balls. The smooth-throwing southpaw set the major league record for strikeouts in a season with 382 in 1965. He also threw no-hitters in four consecutive years, including a 1–0 perfect game against the Chicago Cubs in 1965. Koufax was at his best in his last two years, going 26–8 in 1965 and 27–9 in 1966. His combined totals included 54 complete games in 82 starts (a 66 percent completion rate), 699 strikeouts in 658 innings pitched, and a brilliant 1.89 ERA. He led the league in ERA in each of his last five years with the Dodgers. Unfortunately, he was forced to retire after the 1966 season because of arthritis in his pitching elbow. His career ERA of 2.76 is the third best all-time in the lively ball era. Koufax pitched in four World Series, going 4–3 with a miniscule 0.95 ERA and 61 strikeouts in 57 innings, including 15 strikeouts in a 5–2 win over the New York Yankees in 1963.

- Bob Feller pitched against the St. Louis Cardinals in an exhibition game when he was only 17 years old, and he struck out eight Redbirds in three innings. He made his major league debut the same year and fanned 15 St. Louis Browns. Later he fanned 17 Philadelphia Athletics before returning to high school to finish his junior year. The fireballing right-hander went 5–3 that year, upped his record to 9–7 the next year, went 17–11 with a league-leading 240 strikeouts as a 19-year-old, then exploded in 1939 when he went 24–9 and led the American League in victories, complete games (24), innings pitched (296), and strikeouts (246). He also posted a 2.85 earned run average. Feller led the league in victories the following two years with 27 and 25, respectively. The 6', 185-pound pitcher, now known as "Rapid Robert," stood on the threshold of greatness. He had compiled a record of 107–54 with 1,233 strikeouts—and he had yet to celebrate his 23rd birthday. But then fate took a hand. World War II began on December 7, 1941, and Feller was one of the first major leaguers to enlist. He spent most of the next four years in the United States Navy, serving in the Pacific theatre of war where he earned eight battle stars before returning to baseball in time to post a 5–3 slate at the end of the 1945 season. Feller went on to enjoy three more 20-victory seasons, throw three no-hitters and 12 one-hitters, and set a major league season strikeout record of 348. The Van Meter, Iowa, native completed a memorable 18-year career with 266 victories against 162 losses, with 2,581 strikeouts. He probably lost 100 or more victories because of his military service, but he never complained about his lost time. He was a patriot and he was honored to serve his country. In his career, he led the league in victories six times, complete games three times, innings pitched five times, ERA once, and strikeouts seven times.

- Warren Spahn was a graceful, smooth-throwing southpaw who looked like he would pitch forever. He completed a notable 21-year major league career in 1965 at the age of 44. During his career, most of which he spent with the Boston and Milwaukee Braves, the master of consistency won 20 or more games in 13 different seasons, with a high of 23 in 1953. Spahn, like all of the old-time pitchers, took pride in finishing what he started,

Warren Spahn was one of baseball's greatest southpaw pitchers, winner of 363 games.

tossing 382 complete games in 665 starts, with many of his starts going 14 innings or more. One of his finest efforts ended in a loss in 1952 when he dropped a tough 2–1 decision to the Chicago Cubs. He struck out 18 batters in the 15-inning game and gave his team its only run with a homer, all to no avail. Spahn was a role model for older ball players, tossing three no-hitters, all after the age of 39, and leading the National League in victories five consecutive years from age 36 to 40. The classy 6', 175-pounder, who relied primarily on a fastball and a curve early in his career, led the league in victories eight times, complete games nine times, innings pitched and strikeouts four times each, and ERA three times. His long career put him in elite company. His 363 victories are fifth all-time, and the most wins ever recorded by a southpaw. He is eleventh in games started, eighth in innings pitched (5,243), and sixth in shutouts (63). He also holds the National League record for the most career home runs by a pitcher, with 35. He was elected to the National

Baseball Hall of Fame in Cooperstown, New York, in his first year of eligibility in 1973.

- Dizzy Dean was like a comet streaking across the evening sky. He lit up the heavens for a brief moment, and then he was gone. The Arkansas hillbilly's career, much like that of Sandy Koufax, was cut tragically short by an injury after just five-and-a-half years. After going 18–15 in his rookie season, the 23-year-old right-hander compiled a record of 102–50 over the next four years, leading the league in victories twice, complete games three times (107 complete games in 137 starts), and strikeouts three times. In the 1934 World Series against the Detroit Tigers, the brash youngster, coming off a scintillating 30–7 season, bragged about how he would tame the ferocious Tigers, and then he went out and beat them twice, including an 11–0 thrashing in Game Seven. Shortly thereafter, disaster struck. Dean was hit by a line drive off the bat of Earl Averill in the 1937 All-Star game, fracturing his toe. When he tried to come back too soon, he injured his pitching arm, effectively ending his career. He finished 1937 with a record of 13–10, and then struggled for another three years, winning 16 games against eight losses before hanging up his glove for good. He did have one more brief moment of glory. Pitching for the Chicago Cubs in 1938, Dean, relying primarily on a slow curveball, helped pitch the Cubs to the pennant with a 7–1 record and a 1.81 ERA. Manager Gabby Hartnett selected Dean to pitch the key game of the season, a late–September matchup against the first place Pittsburgh Pirates. And the great one responded, pitching brilliantly for 8⅔ innings in a 2–1 Cubs victory. His effort gave the Cubs the momentum they needed to sweep the Pirates and claim the top spot.

    Dean, who quit school in the third grade so he could go to work to help out the family, was illiterate, but he was not dumb. In fact, he was smart enough to market himself successfully throughout his life. He used racial epithets at the drop of a hat, but he was not a bigot. It was just the way he was raised. Dizzy loved everyone, and he was a friend to everyone. During the 1930s he and his major league all-star team toured the country with Satchel Paige and Paige's Negro league all-stars, and the two teams played each other four or five times a week, with the two adversaries pitching a couple of innings against each other in the afternoon before hitting the pubs together every night. Dizzy liked and admired Satch, at one time saying that if he and Satch pitched on the same team, they would win the pennant by July and then go fishing the rest of the year.

- Bob Gibson was one of baseball's greatest money pitchers. If the pennant or the World Series were on the line, and one pitcher was needed who could almost guarantee a victory, Gibson's name would be at the top of the list. The 6'2", 195-pound right-hander with the blazing fastball and an intimidating mean streak pitched in three World Series, starting nine games, completing eight, and racking up a 7–2 record. He holds the World Series career strikeout record with 92 in 81 innings. He also holds World Series records for the most strikeouts in a game with 17 and the most strikeouts in one Series with 35. In season play, Gibson won 20 or more games five times en route to a career record of 251–174. His greatest season was 1968 when he went 22–9 with 13 shutouts and a miniscule 1.12 earned run average, the fourth-lowest ERA in major league history, and the lowest season ERA since 1914. Gibson's career would have been even more impressive if not for the injuries he had to play through, including a broken leg, knee surgery, and a strained elbow. When he was healthy, he owned the plate and he demanded it, pitching inside frequently to keep the batter loose. One time a reporter suggested that Gibson would even hit his own mother, to which Gibson replied, "I would if she crowded the plate."

- Tom Seaver, or "Tom Terrific" as New York fans called him, was a hard-working right-handed pitcher who possessed a blazing fastball and outstanding control over his 20-year major league career. The handsome Californian reeled off five 20-win seasons while leading the league in victories three times, strikeouts five times, and ERA three times. He pitched the New York Mets to their first National League pennant and first world championship in 1969 when he compiled a 25–7 record with a league-leading .781 winning percentage and a 2.21 ERA. He went 1–1 with a 3.00 ERA in the Series, winning Game Four 2–1 in ten innings. Four years later, he posted a 2.40 ERA in the World Series but lost his only decision by a 3–1 score. Seaver had many memorable moments over his career. On April 22, 1970, he struck out 19 batters in a nine-inning game, including the last ten men in succession. Eight years later, on June 16, 1978, he hurled a no-hitter at the St. Louis Cardinals, winning 4–0. He also tossed three one-hitters during his career. By the time he retired in 1986, Seaver had 311 victories to his credit against 205 losses, with 231 complete games in 647 starts. He is seventh all-time in career shutouts (61), sixth in strikeouts (3,640), and 12th in games started. He was the National League Rookie of the Year in 1967, an eleven-time all-star, and a three-time Cy Young Award winner.

- Jim Palmer, a high-kicking right-hander with a wide assortment of pitches and good control, rebounded from two years of arm problems to become the biggest winner in Baltimore Oriole history. The 6'3", 195-pound New Yorker began his major league career in 1965 at the age of 19, and one year later he became the youngest pitcher to hurl a complete-game victory in the World Series, defeating Sandy Koufax and the Los

Tom Seaver, a career 311-game winner, struck out 19 San Diego Padres in 1970, including ten in a row to end the game (courtesy New York Mets).

Angeles Dodgers, 6–0, in the Orioles' shocking four-game sweep of the National League champions. Palmer's bubble burst the next spring when his arm went dead, dashing his dreams of a long, successful career. He missed most of the next two seasons before arm surgery gave him a second chance, and he made the most of it. Shortly after he returned to action, he pitched an 8–0 no-hitter against the Oakland Athletics, en route to a dream-like 16–4 season. From there, his career took off. He won 20 or more games eight times over the next nine seasons, sparking Earl Weaver's team to five American League pennants and two more world championships. He appeared in six World Series overall, going 4–2 with a 3.20 ERA. And he added a 4–1 record with a 1.96 ERA in the LCS. The three-time Cy Young Award winner compiled a 268–152 won-lost record over his 19-year career, with 221 complete games in 521 starts, a 40 percent completion rate. Jim Palmer's 2.86 ERA is the fourth-lowest ERA since the lively ball was introduced in 1920, trailing only Hoyt Wilhelm, Whitey Ford and Sandy Koufax.

- Juan Marichal, another high-kicking flamethrower, was the mainstay of the San Francisco Giants' pitching staff during the 1960s and early 1970s. Back in the days when men were men and major league pitchers took pride in completing their starts, the big right-hander threw 244 complete games in 457 starts, a 53 percent completion rate. Marichal, whose vast pitching repertoire included a curve, slider, and screwball in addition to his heater, was a control artist who walked less than two men per nine innings, while striking out six. He won 20 or more games six times in his career, with a high of 26 in 1968, when he led the league in wins, complete games (30 in 38 starts, or 79 percent), and innings pitched (326). Five years earlier, he had put together a brilliant 25–8 mark, leading the league in victories and innings pitched (321). Two of his more memorable games were pitched that year. On June 15, he no-hit the Houston Colt .45s, 1–0, and a little more than two weeks later he hurled 16 innings to defeat Warren Spahn of the Milwaukee Braves, 1–0, in one of the game's great pitching duels. Overall, Marichal won 242 games against 142 losses in his 16-year major league career, with a 2.89 career ERA, number six all-time in the lively ball era. He was enshrined in the Baseball Hall of Fame, joining the other immortals, in 1983.

- Steve Carlton's 329 career victories are second to Warren Spahn for the most victories ever recorded by a left-handed pitcher. The hard-throwing Floridian was a menacing presence on the mound, standing 6'4" tall, and weighing a solid 210 pounds. He threw smoke whenever he needed a strikeout, but he was more than just a one-pitch pitcher. He also had a decent curveball and a devastating slider. He broke upon the major league stage in 1965 at the age of 20, pitching in 15 games with no decisions, and he became a regular starter two years later when he won 14 games against nine losses with a 2.98 earned run average. Carlton spent his first seven years with the St. Louis Cardinals before a salary dispute ended with his being traded to the Philadelphia Phillies, one of the worst trades in Cardinal history. Lefty had just won 20 games with St. Louis in 1971, and in his first year in the City of Brotherly Love, he led the National League with 27 victories, 30 complete games, 346 innings pitched, 310 strikeouts, and a miniscule 1.97 ERA. Overall, he led the league in victories four times, complete games three times, innings pitched and strikeouts five times, and ERA once. Carlton pitched in four World Series, going 2–2 with a 2.56 ERA. In the 1980 Fall Classic, he defeated the Kansas City Royals twice, including a 4–1 victory in the deciding seventh game. He is eleventh all-time in career victories, fifth in games started with 709, fourteenth in shutouts with 55, ninth in innings pitched with 5,217, and fourth in strikeouts with 4,136.

- Eddie Plank was one of Connie Mack's money pitchers during Philadelphia Athletics' glory days between 1910 and 1914, when they won four American League pennants and three world championships. Plank pitched in three of the World Series, but he was a hard-luck pitcher, winning just two games against five losses in spite of a brilliant 1.32 ERA. In the 1911 Series, he defeated the New York Giants, 3–1, in Game Three, then lost Game Five in relief. Two years later he lost a heartbreaking 3–0 game to Christy Mathewson and the Giants, a 10-inning thriller that saw Mathewson single in the winning run. Plank had the last laugh, however, when he out-pitched Mathewson, 3–1, in Game Seven to give the A's the world championship. In 1914, the year of the miracle Boston Braves, he lost another heartbreaker, a 1–0 decision to Bill James. "Gettysberg Eddie," as he was known, spent all but three years of his 17-year major league career in Philadelphia, winning 20 games eight times, on his way to a career record of 326-194. He is number 11 in career victories, number 15 in complete games with 410 in 529 games started, a 78 percent completion rate, number five in shutouts with 69, and number 13 in ERA with 2.35. He is a 1946 inductee into the Baseball Hall of Fame.
- Whitey Ford, the "Chairman of the Board," was Casey Stengel's secret weapon during the New York Yankees' historic pennant runs in the 1950s and 1960s. Ford pitched for the Yankees for 16 years, winning 11 American League pennants and six world championships. In Series play, he won 10 games against eight losses, the most World Series victories by any pitcher. In regular-season play he was dominant, winning 236 games against 106 losses, a .690 winning percentage, tied with Dave Foutz for the highest career winning percentage in major league history. Ford had a season winning percentage of more than .700 on seven occasions. In his rookie season, he went 9–1 for a .900 winning percentage. Three years later, he was 18–7, .720, and the next year he led the league with a .760 winning percentage on the basis of a 19–6 record. His greatest season was 1961, when he went 25–4, leading the league in wins, winning percentage (.862), and innings pitched (283). He wrapped up his career season by going 2–0 in the World Series, with a perfect 0.00 ERA in 15 innings. Ford's 2.75 career ERA is the second-lowest major league ERA since 1920, trailing only Hoyt Wilhelm. The only chink in Ford's armor was his lack of stamina that often prevented him from pitching nine innings.

He completed only 36 percent of his starts in an era when the top major league pitchers were completing at least half of their starts. Warren Spahn, for instance, completed 57 percent of his starts, Bob Lemon completed 54 percent of his starts, and Robin Roberts completed 50 percent of his starts. One year, when a reporter asked Ford if he thought he could win 20 games that year, Ford said, "I think I can if Arroyo's arm holds out," referring to the New York fireman, Luis Arroyo.

- Addie Joss, one of baseball's greatest pitchers, had his career cut short by tubercular meningitis in 1911 at the age of 31. But during his brief nine-year career, the slim 6'3", 185-pound right-hander proved his greatness, so much, in fact, that the Veterans Committee in 1978 bypassed the Hall of Fame's minimum 10-year requirement for induction and welcomed him into the prestigious bastion of baseball's legendary players. Joss began his major league career with the Cleveland Naps (later the Indians) of the American League in 1902, and he tossed a one-hitter en route to a 17–13 season. He pitched for the Naps through the 1910 season, winning 20 or more games four times, with a high of 27 in 1907. His greatest game was unquestionably the October 2, 1908, contest that matched him against "Big Ed" Walsh in the heat of the pennant race. Joss responded to the challenge by throwing a perfect game at the Chicago White Sox, winning 1–0. Walsh tossed a four-hitter and struck out 15 Naps in the loss. Joss no-hit the White Sox again in 1909. His health began to decline that year and he finished the season at 14–14, followed by a 5–5 year in 1910 when he pitched in just 13 games. He died on Opening Day, April 14, 1911. Addie Joss compiled a record of 160–97 during his career, with 234 complete games in 260 starts, an amazing 90 percent completion rate. His 1.89 career ERA is second all-time behind Ed Walsh, who had a 1.82 ERA, and his 1.16 ERA in 1908 is the eighth-lowest season ERA in major league history.
- Ed Walsh, known as "Big Ed," was a spitball artist who was the ace of the Chicago White Sox's staff from 1906 through 1912, winning 168 games over that period, an average of 24 wins a year. He paced the White Sox to the American League pennant in 1906, his first full year in the league. He went 17–13 during the season, pitching 278 innings. Then, in the World Series against their cross-town rivals, the Chicago Cubs, he won two games without a loss, including a 3–0 shutout in Game Three. Two years later, he put together a career season, winning 40 games, second only to Jack Chesbro's 41 wins for the most single-season wins in the twentieth century. Big Ed led the American League in many pitching categories that year, including victories, winning percentage (.727), games pitched (66), complete games (42), shutouts (11), saves (six), innings pitched (464), and strikeouts (269). Walsh's career, like Joss', was rela-

tively short. He had only nine years in which he pitched more than 100 innings. Supposedly, his spitball was easy on the arm and allowed him to pitch over 400 innings twice during his career and over 367 innings three other years. But the wear and tear on his arm took its toll, and in 1909 he threw just 230 innings. Then, after three more heavy-duty seasons of 369, 368, and 393 innings pitched, his arm went dead. He struggled through five more years, winning just 13 games total, before retiring in 1917. Walsh retired with 195 victories against 126 losses and baseball's all-time lowest ERA, a dazzling 1.82.

- Mordecai "Three Finger" Brown lost his right forefinger and mangled his middle finger in a farm accident when he was just seven years old. As it turned out, it might have been a blessing in disguise because he developed a sharp-breaking curveball that rolled off his damaged fingers, leading to an outstanding 14-year major league career, primarily with the Chicago Cubs. Brown, who was noted for his vigorous training regimen, paced the Cubs to four National League pennants and two world championships between 1906 and 1910. The 1908 pennant race became legendary when New York Giant first baseman Fred Merkle failed to touch second base after an apparent game-winning hit, forcing a playoff between the Giants and Cubs to determine the pennant winner. Three Finger Brown out-pitched Christy Mathewson by a 4–2 count in the playoff game to send the Cubbies to the Series. The Cubs faced the Chicago White Sox, known as "the Hitless Wonders" in the 1906 Fall Classic, with the White Sox coming out on top in six games. In 1907, the Tinker-to-Evers-to-Chance combination took the measure of the Detroit Tigers and their sensational 20-year-old batting champion, Ty Cobb, in five games. Brown won the deciding game, 2–0, while holding Cobb to a single in four at-bats. In a rematch the next year, the Cubs came out on top again in five games, with Brown winning Game One in relief before blanking the Bengals, 3–0, in Game Four. After falling to second place in 1909, Chicago roared back in 1910 to win the pennant by a whopping 13 games over the New York Giants. This time, they lost to the Philadelphia Athletics in five games, with Brown going 1–2, including a 7–2 thrashing in Game Five.

Brown was a workhorse for the Cubs for ten years as both a starter and reliever. He pitched in relief 149 times during his career in addition to starting 332 games. He led the National League in saves for four consecutive years, 1908 through 1911, on his way to a major league record 49 saves, a record that lasted until 1926. His overall won-lost record was 239–130, giving him a .648 winning percentage. He had 271 complete games, an 82 percent completion rate, 55 shutouts, and a 2.06 career ERA. He stands fifteenth all-time in winning percentage, fourteenth in shutouts, and third in ERA. He is enshrined in the National Baseball Hall of Fame in Cooperstown, New York.

- Denton True "Cy" Young was the first of the great modern-day pitchers. Young was a 36-game winner in 1892 when the distance from the mound to home plate was just 55' but when the distance was extended to its present-day distance of 60'6", the 26-year-old right-hander did not miss a beat, winning 34 games. Young, who was given the nickname of Cyclone, or Cy for short, because of his blazing fastball, was a star from the first day he put on a major league uniform. He spent nine years with the Cleveland Spiders, including eight full seasons in which he won more than 20 games every year, and more than 30 games three times. In 1901, Young joined the Boston Pilgrims of the fledgling American League, pitching them to the pennant in 1903, when he led the league in victories (28), winning percentage (.757), complete games (34), shutouts (7), and innings pitched (341). In the World Series that year, a best-of-nine Series, the 6'2", 210-pound flamethrower pitched in four games, including three complete-game starts and one relief appearance. He went 2–1 in 34 innings pitched, as the Pilgrims persevered in eight games. When Young retired after the 1911 season, completing an historic 22-year major league career, he left behind many records that may never be broken. He is number one all-time with 511 career victories, 316 career losses, 815 games started, 749 complete games, 7,356 innings pitched, 15 years with 20 or more victories, and five years with 30 or more victories. He is number four all-time with 76 shutouts and number nine with 906 games pitched. He was one of the original members of the Baseball Hall of Fame, elected in 1938.

- Nolan Ryan, dubbed by the media "the Ryan Express," was arguably the greatest strikeout pitcher in the history of the game, sending 5,714 batters back to the bench talking to themselves. The 6'2", 195-pound Texan, another disciple of a rigid physical fitness regimen, showcased his tremendous skills for 27 years, from 1966 through 1993. He might be considered a modern miracle. He never had a sore arm in spite of the fact that he relied on his fastball a high percentage of the time, and considering the fact that he was frighteningly wild, fanning 9.5 batters a game while walking 4.7 batters a game. He often threw in excess of 150 pitches a game in a complete-game effort, of which he threw 222 in his career. Ryan had twenty years where he won 10 or more games, but he posted 20-win seasons on only two occasions. He was a great power pitcher but essentially a .500 pitcher overall, with 324 career victories against 292 losses for a .524 winning percentage. He struck out a total of 5,714 batters in his career, more than 1,000 ahead of the runner-up, Roger Clemens. But he also walked a career total of 2,795 batters, 50 percent

Randy Johnson is the most dominant strikeout pitcher the game has ever produced. He struck out an average of 10.8 batters per game through the 2007 season (courtesy James R. Madden, Jr.).

more than any other pitcher in the history of the game. When his fastball was humming, the Ryan Express was unhittable, leading the league in strikeouts eleven times, including four consecutive years after he turned forty years of age. In 1973, he set the major league single-season strikeout record with 383, one more than Sandy Koufax. In 1989, he became the oldest pitcher ever to strikeout 300 batters in a season, fanning 301 men at the age of 42. Ryan also threw an unbelievable seven no-hitters, two of which came after he turned 43. He also had a record 12 one-hitters, a total tied with Bob Feller. The native of Alvin, Texas, is number 12 in career victories, number three in career losses, number two in games started, number seven in shutouts, number five in innings pitched, number one in bases on balls, and number one in strikeouts. He was elected to the Baseball Hall of Fame in his first year of eligibility in 1999.

- Wes Ferrell was baseball's greatest hitting pitcher, smashing 38 career home runs, an average of 18 homers for every 550 at-bats, while knocking in 97 runs and posting a .280 career batting average. Ferrell was part of one of baseball's most famous brother acts, pitching to his brother, catcher Rick Ferrell, on the Boston Red Sox for four years. Rick Ferrell was elected to the Baseball Hall of Fame in 1984. Brother Wes is still waiting, but hopefully the Veterans Committee will see fit to let him join Rick in the Hall in the near future. Wes Ferrell was a big, strong 6'2", 195-pound North Carolina farmboy who pitched in his first major league game in 1927 at the age of 19. Two years later, he was a 20-game winner, going 21–10 for the Cleveland Indians. He won 20 games in each of the next four years and, after two sub-par years caused by a sore arm, the former fireballer bounced back with a new-found curveball to lead the American League in victories with 25, in complete games with 31, and in innings pitched with 322. Ferrell was called a prima donna and a hothead by the media, and he was that. He hated to lose, and he took it out on himself and everything around him after a tough loss. But he was also a winner, who won 193 games against 128 losses during his 15-year career.

- Carl Hubbell, a.k.a. "King Carl," was the ace of the New York Giant pitching staff for 16 years, during which time he pitched the Giants into three World Series. When Bill Terry's team took the measure of the Washington Senators in 1934, King Carl won two of the five games, winning 4–2 in the opener and taking Game Four by a 2–1 count in 11 innings. Overall, Hubbell went 4–2 in the three World Series with a 1.79 ERA. The lanky, left-handed screwball artist won more than 20 games in five consecutive seasons, from 1933 through 1937, leading the league in victories and ERA in three of those years. He is best remembered for his 1934 All-Star Game performance when he fanned five American Leaguers in succession — Ruth, Gehrig, Foxx, Simmons, and Cronin. He also won 24 consecutive games over two seasons, winning his last 16 games in 1936 and his first eight games in 1937. Over the course of his career, the 6', 170-pound hurler compiled a record of 253–154 with an excellent 2.98 ERA.

Other former pitchers who were reviewed but who did not make the top 22 included Hoyt Wilhelm and Don Sutton.

There are several world-class pitchers who are still active and are candidates for the all-time all-star team, including Roger Clemens, Pedro Martinez, Greg Maddux, Randy Johnson, and Tom Glavine. Their statistics through 2007 are impressive. Roger Clemens, who at the age of 44 is a six-time Cy Young Award winner, was still pitching in 2007. He has won 354 games against just 184 losses, for a sensational .658 winning percentage. Pedro Martinez, a three-time Cy Young Award winner, has an even better winning percentage of .692 based on 209 victories against 93 losses. Greg Maddux, a four-time Cy Young Award winner, has a 347–214 won-lost record with an excellent 3.11 ERA. Randy Johnson, a five-time Cy Young Award winner, including four in a row between 1999 and 2002, has 284 victories against 150 losses, and is the most terrifying pitcher of his era, averaging 10.8 strikeouts per game. Tom Glavine, a two-time Cy Young Award winner, with 303 victories against 199 losses, joined his former teammate, Greg Maddux, as a 300-game winner in 2007.

Pitching Ratings

The pitching position was the most difficult position of all to evaluate from one era to another because of the many changes made to the game over the past century that had a significant effect on the position. To begin with, there have been many changes to the size of the strike zone, the use of foreign substances on the ball, the size of the ballparks, the height of the mound, and the construction of the baseball. However, these changes could all be accounted for satisfactorily in the formulas. The changes that complicated the evaluation of the pitching position from one era to another were the strategic alterations regarding the position. Perhaps the single biggest strategic change has been the use of relief pitchers. Prior to 1900, 80 percent or more of the games played were complete-game efforts by the starting pitcher. When the twentieth century got underway, a relief pitcher was nothing more than a mop-up man, someone who came into the game when the starting pitcher was being hit hard and the game was hopelessly lost. He was usually a former starting pitcher whose career was essentially over, or a rookie just breaking in. John McGraw, the manager of the New York Giants, changed all that when he began to use a designated relief pitcher, someone who could come into the game in the late innings and save the game for a tired or embattled starting pitcher. His first designated relief pitcher was Otis "Doc" Crandall, so named because he "cured the team's ills." Crandall was primarily a relief pitcher from 1909 through 1913, with 142 relief appearances and 24 saves against 56 starts over that period. It was common practice in the early part of the century for a team to use its best starting pitcher for late-inning relief when the game was still in doubt. Mordecai "Three Finger" Brown of the Chicago Cubs was the league's number one save pitcher during the first decade of the twentieth century. He was the ace of the Cubs' staff who between 1906 and 1911 won 20 or more games each year, throwing 154 complete games in 182 starts. But, in addition to his heavy starting pitching workload, he also relieved in 81 games, accumulating 38 saves. He led the league in saves four consecutive years, from 1908 to 1911. Ed Walsh of the Chicago White Sox was another one-man team, starting 315 games and relieving in 115 others during his career. He had 34 saves in 14 years and led the American League in saves five times. Grover Cleveland Alexander had 96 relief appearances with 32 saves in 20 years and Walter Johnson had 136 relief appearances in 21 years, with 34 saves.

As the game entered the third decade of the century, relief pitching began to evolve into a specialized responsibility, with names like Firpo Marberry, Wilcy Moore and Johnny Murphy appearing in the box scores frequently. The Yankee-Dodger rivalry dominated the 1940s, and their firemen, Joe Page and Hugh Casey, made the figure a sport's celebrity. Page, in particular, popularized the position. He pitched in four of the seven games in the 1947 World Series, with one win and one save, and he held the powerful Dodgers to a single base hit over the final five innings of the finale, as New York prevailed, 5–2. He was often photographed wearing a fireman's helmet and climbing over the low bullpen fence on his way to putting out another fire. Through the 1950s and 1960s, firemen became more and more important to the fortunes of the team, with relievers like Ron Perranoski pitching as many as six innings in a game. The single most important baseball event in the twentieth century was probably the abolition of the reserve clause and the birth of free agency that gave players the opportunity to negotiate with any team after fulfilling their contractual responsibilities to their original team. That decision, made by arbitrator Peter Seitz, set in motion a chaotic era that continues to this day, with skyrocketing salaries caused by teams bidding for the services of the best players. Free agency also resulted in the appearance of player agents, who helped their clients negotiate more lucrative contracts. As a result of free agency and the new salary scale, club owners and player agents alike began to be more protective of their valuable property. Over the next two decades, starting pitchers pitched fewer and fewer complete games as owners, who were concerned about possible injuries to a pitcher's multi-million dollar arm, did not want to overwork them. Relief pitchers were brought into a game earlier and earlier each decade. As a result, relief pitching became more specialized, developing to the point in which today every team has long relievers, situational pitchers, setup men, and closers who normally pitch only one inning in a game and seldom pitch two consecutive games.

Originally, pitchers were evaluated based only on their pitching contributions, their won-lost percentage, the number of complete games they pitched, the number of innings per game they pitched, and their earned run average. As the game has evolved, other more equitable means of comparing pitchers had to be found. In the first place, pitchers had to be evaluated, not only for their pitching skills but also for their batting and fielding skills. After all, many pitchers have won their own games by making a key base hit or by making a sensational fielding play. From a pitching standpoint, a pitcher's won-lost percentage, per se, could not be used, as noted earlier, because a pitcher on a winning team would normally have a better won-lost percentage than a pitcher on a losing team. It was finally decided that the most equitable statistics for comparing pitchers was their won-lost percentage above or below their team's overall won-lost percentage, and their adjusted ERA.

This study does not include relief pitchers, primarily because the role of the relief pitcher has been in a constant state of flux since the nineteenth century. As noted above, starting pitchers handled the chore during the first two decades of the twentieth century. Then the firemen arrived, led by Joe Page and Hugh Casey, and they handled the relief assignments for the better part of four decades, often pitching as many as six innings in a game. Now, over the past two decades, the game has evolved to the point where there are relief specialists for every conceivable situation, with the man designated as the closer assigned to pitch no more than one inning in an effort to save the game. There is some question already about the need for a closer who pitches only one inning. It is possible that in the near future the game could return to the firemen days of forty years ago. Only time will tell.

Normalized Won-Lost Percentage Differential (NWLPD)

Whitey Ford had the highest won-lost percentage of any pitcher in the study, a fancy .705 for seasons of 100 or more innings pitched, but his team, the New York Yankees, were the most successful team of his era, with a winning percentage of .616, giving Ford a winning percentage differential of +.089. Walter Johnson, who toiled in relative obscurity with the hapless Washington Senators during most of his career, had a winning percentage of .599, which when compared to his team's .492 winning percentage gave him a differential of +.107. Of the 22 pitchers in the study, only Ford had a winning percentage of more than .700, while four of them — Johnson, Warren Spahn, Steve Carlton, and Nolan Ryan — had winning percentages between .525 and .599. The rest of the pitchers had winning percentages between .600 and .680. Ford was also the only pitcher to play with a team that had a winning percentage of more than .600. Two pitchers, Walter Johnson and Nolan Ryan, pitched for teams with a losing percentage, and the remainder of the pitchers played for teams that had winning percentages between .502 and .597.

When the pitcher's winning percentages were compared to the team's winning percentages and the differences were normalized, Grover Cleveland

Alexander finished first in the category with a +.108 differential and the maximum 45.000 point total. Walter Johnson came in second with a +.107 differential and a point total of 44.583. He was followed closely by Sandy Koufax, who had a differential of +.105 and a point total of 43.750. Whitey Ford, who had the highest winning percentage of any pitcher, finished eighth with a +.089 differential and a 37.083 point total. Jim Palmer was last in the category with a winning percentage differential of +.049 and a point total of 20.416.

Normalized Adjusted Earned Run Average (NAERA)

The Adjusted ERA was arrived at by comparing the pitcher's ERA to the league average ERA and then factoring in the pitcher's home park factor. The unadulterated ERAs of the 22 pitchers ranged from 1.82 for Ed Walsh to 4.04 for Wes Ferrell. Naturally the lowest ERAs belonged to pitchers whose careers spanned the dead ball era, between 1902 and 1917 — Ed Walsh and Addie Joss. The highest ERA of 4.04 belonged to Wes Ferrell, who pitched in the first high ERA era, between 1929 and 1938, when the league ERA fluctuated between 4.04 and 5.04, with an average in the 4.50 range. That era also defined the greatness of Lefty Grove, whose career paralleled that of Wes Ferrell. While the rest of the American League was showing an ERA of about 4.50, Grove was sensational with a career ERA of 3.06.

Grove, not surprisingly, compiled an adjusted ERA of 1.48 that won him first place with a normalized point total of 45.000. Walter Johnson (2.17 ERA) and Ed Walsh (1.82 ERA) finished in a tie for second place with a point total of 44.088. Steve Carlton finished 21st with an adjusted ERA of 1.15 and a point total of 34.966. Nolan Ryan was 22nd with an adjusted ERA of 1.12 and a point total of 34.054.

Final Pitching Ratings

The final pitching ratings are shown below. The point totals for pitching accounted for 90 percent of the pitchers' final all-around point totals. A pitcher's offense accounted for 6 percent of his final point totals and his fielding accounted for 4 percent of the total.

Name	NWLPD × 45	NAERA × 45	Total Points	Final Pitching Ratings
Walter Johnson	44.583	44.088	88.671	1
Lefty Grove	42.500	45.000	87.500	2

Name	NWLPD × 45	NAERA × 45	Total Points	Final Pitching Ratings
G.C. Alexander	45.000	41.047	86.047	3
Cy Young	42.500	41.959	84.459	4
Sandy Koufax	43.750	39.831	83.581	5
Tom Seaver	42.500	38.615	81.115	6
Christy Mathewson	36.667	41.351	78.018	7
Whitey Ford	37.083	40.439	77.522	8
Dizzy Dean	34.583	39.527	74.110	9
Nolan Ryan	40.000	34.054	74.054	10
Carl Hubbell	32.389	39.527	71.916	11
Ed Walsh	26.667	44.088	70.755	12
Mordecai Brown	27.500	41.959	69.459	13
Juan Marichal	31.250	37.095	68.345	14
Addie Joss	24.167	43.176	67.343	15
Wes Ferrell	30.000	35.574	65.574	16
Bob Gibson	26.667	38.615	65.282	17
Warren Spahn	27.917	35.878	63.795	18
Bob Feller	23.750	37.095	60.845	19
Eddie Plank	22.500	37.095	59.595	20
Jim Palmer	20.416	38.007	58.423	21
Steve Carlton	22.083	34.966	57.049	22

Offensive Ratings

Pitchers from the early days of the game, from 1893 to the 1920s and beyond, were expected to excel in the offensive and defensive categories compared to their more modern counterparts. In the early days, with limited rosters, players had to be more versatile and were expected to help the team with their bat and glove. Jack Stivetts, for instance, one of the aces of the Boston Beaneater championship teams of the 1890s, played outfield in 192 games, plus every infield position, while pitching in 388 games with a 203–132 won-lost record. Walter Johnson played the outfield in California before he joined the Washington Senators, and he even played 13 games in the outfield for the Senators. And Wes Ferrell played 13 games in the outfield in 1933 for the Cleveland Indians to take advantage of his big bat. He also fielded 1.000 that year. One pitcher, Smoky Joe Wood, even reinvented himself as an outfielder after his arm went dead in 1913. The fireballing right-hander, who sparked the Boston Red Sox to the world championship in 1912 when he went 34–5, saw his pitching career crumble after his sensational season. Instead of retiring, however, Smoky Joe went back to the drawing board and, thanks to his all-around baseball skills, he returned to the major leagues after an absence of almost two years as an outfielder for the Cleveland Indians. He played five more years, batting .298 over that span with 35 doubles, nine triples, and seven home runs for every 550 at-bats, finally retiring in 1922 to become the baseball coach at Yale University. The ultimate hitting pitcher, of course, was Babe Ruth, who won 89 games against 46 losses with a 2.28 ERA during his pitching career in Boston. Over that same period, he batted a nifty .308, averaging 41 doubles, 15 triples, and 25 home runs for every 550 at-bats — and that was during the dead ball era! Needless to say, Ruth became a full-time outfielder in 1920, and a legend was born.

Pitchers in this study were rated on their on-base percentage normalized to the league average, with a maximum point total of three, and their slugging average normalized to the league average, with a point total of three. Offense accounted for 6 percent of a pitcher's all-around rating.

Normalized Adjusted On-Base Percentage (NOBPA)

Some pitchers were decent hitters, including Walter Johnson, Grover Cleveland Alexander, and Whitey Ford, but Wes Ferrell was by far the most dangerous pitcher with a bat in his hands. His .351 on-base percentage was a full 77 points higher than his nearest competitor, Walter Johnson. Hitting seems to be a lost art among pitchers in the major leagues in recent years. Only Bob Gibson (.243 OBP) and Whitey Ford (.256 OBP) had OBPs above .225, while several of them, most notably Sandy Koufax (.145 OBP), Juan Marichal (.191 OBP), and Nolan Ryan (.148 OBP), fell below the Mendoza line. Of the active pitchers, only Roger Clemens can boast of his batting skills. His .241 OBP is 45 points higher than Greg Maddux, 90 points higher than Randy Johnson, and 110 points higher than Pedro Martinez. Wes Ferrell claimed the number one spot for OBP with a point total of 3.000. Christy Mathewson was second with an OBP of .272, an OBP differential of –57, and a point total of 2.109. At the other end of the spectrum, Nolan Ryan, in 21st place, had a –173 differential and a point total of 0.120, and Sandy Koufax brought up the rear with a –180 differential and a point total of 0.000.

Normalized Adjusted Slugging Average (NXSLGA)

Pitchers in general were not power hitters. The exception to the rule was Wes Ferrell, who had a .446 slugging average, 17 points higher than the league average. Only three other pitchers had slugging averages above .300. They were Walter Johnson (.342), Dizzy Dean (.301) and Bob Gibson (.301). Of course, slugging averages have been on the increase in recent times because of the lively ball and the smaller ballparks. When Addie Joss pitched, the league slugging average was just .334, and during Walter Johnson's career, it was .359. It spiked to .402 in the 1930s, fell as low as .339 in 1968, bounced back to the .370s and .380s in the 1980s, and then exploded to about .430 after the Costa Rican rabbit ball was introduced in 1993. In 2006, the league slugging averages were .420 in the American League and .409 in the National League. Today's pitchers, however, have not kept pace with the league. In general, they are a sorry lot with a bat in their hands. Of the four active pitchers who were reviewed in this study, only Roger Clemens (.212) and Greg Maddux (.212) had slugging averages above .200. Randy Johnson was at .157, and Pedro Martinez could do no better than .114.

Final Offensive Ratings

It was strictly no contest for the game's greatest offensive pitcher. Wes Ferrell was number one for both NOBPA and NXSLGA by wide margins. Walter Johnson and Christy Matheson finished second and third, respectively, while Sandy Koufax and Carl Hubbell anchored the list.

Name	NOBPA × 3	NXSLGA × 3	Total Points	Final Offensive Ratings
W. Johnson	1.989	2.658	4.647	2
G.C. Alexander	1.389	1.755	3.144	10
C. Mathewson	2.109	2.067	4.176	3
L. Grove	0.393	0.621	1.014	19
S. Koufax	0.000	0.000	0.000	22
B. Feller	0.789	0.942	1.731	18
W. Spahn	1.440	1.707	3.147	9
D. Dean	1.218	1.776	2.994	11
B. Gibson	1.560	1.887	3.447	6
T. Seaver	1.218	1.095	2.313	15
J. Palmer	0.960	1.173	2.133	16
J. Marichal	0.789	0.963	1.752	17
S. Carlton	1.200	1.515	2.715	12
E. Plank	1.818	1.827	3.645	4
W. Ford	1.782	0.882	2.664	13
A. Joss	1.113	1.374	2.487	14
E. Walsh	1.440	2.088	3.528	5

With a near .700 winning percentage, Pedro Martinez will go down in baseball lore as one of the greatest pitchers in the history of the game (courtesy Julie Cordeiro).

Name	NOBPA × 3	NXSLGA × 3	Total Points	Final Offensive Ratings
M. Brown	1.491	1.857	3.348	7
Cy Young	1.251	1.947	3.198	8
N. Ryan	0.120	0.402	0.522	20
W. Ferrell	3.000	3.000	6.000	1
C. Hubbell	0.717	0.108	0.825	21

Defensive Ratings

As noted above, pitchers from the early days were expected to dominate the defensive statistics because they were schooled in all aspects of the game in order to be able to make a major contribution to the team's success. A pitcher's defensive skills accounted for 4 percent of his overall rating in this study. Over the years there have been many outstanding defensive pitchers, such as Wes Ferrell, Jim Palmer, and Tom Seaver, but again the moderns were left in the dust by their ancient counterparts. Almost without exception, the top pitchers in the early days far exceeded the league average fielding averages. For instance, Grover Cleveland Alexander had a career fielding average of .985 compared to a league average of .955. Wes Ferrell had a career fielding average of .975, Eddie Plank had a career fielding average of .971, and Christy Mathewson had a career fielding average of .972. Greg Maddux, who may be the best fielding pitcher of his generation, has a fielding average of .969, and Roger Clemens has a fielding average of .975, but most of the other modern pitchers are near average or below average.

Normalized Fielding Average Differential (NFAD)

Grover Cleveland Alexander had a fielding average of .985, a full 30 points above the league average. Christy Mathewson's fielding average of .972 was 29 points above the league average, and Eddie Plank's .971 average was 28 points above the league average. They finished one, two, three in the fielding average differential category. Nolan Ryan was by far the worst fielding pitcher in the study. His .895 fielding average was 57 points below the league average.

Normalized Range Factor Differential (NRFD)

Many of the world-class pitchers had quick reflexes and outstanding instincts that permitted them to get to more ground balls than the average pitcher and also allowed them to react to infield grounders between first and second base in time to cover first, beating the runner to the bag and taking the throw from the first baseman or the second baseman for the out. The oldtimers were well schooled in the fundamentals and generally had range factors above the league average. Ed Walsh was the leader of the pack, with a range factor of 3.35 that was 1.11 points above the league average. Addie Joss had a range factor .94 points higher than the league average, while Sandy Koufax finished .93 points below the league average and Dizzy Dean was .66 points below the average.

Final Defensive Ratings

The final defensive ratings favored the old-timers, with only Whitey Ford, who finished in eighth place, and Jim Palmer, who finished ninth, able to crack the top ten.

Name	NFAD × 2	NRFD × 2	Total Points	Final Defensive Ratings
W. Johnson	1.839	0.451	2.290	13
G. C. Alexander	2.000	1.137	3.137	5
C. Mathewson	1.977	1.461	3.438	3
L. Grove	1.287	0.461	1.748	19
S. Koufax	1.310	0.000	1.310	21
B. Feller	1.471	0.422	1.893	17
W. Spahn	1.264	0.922	2.186	14
D. Dean	1.333	0.265	1.598	20
B. Gibson	1.218	0.735	1.953	16
T. Seaver	1.471	0.941	2.412	11
J. Palmer	1.540	1.001	2.541	9
J. Marichal	1.195	1.147	2.342	12
S. Carlton	1.310	0.471	1.781	18
E. Plank	1.954	0.461	2.415	10
W. Ford	1.425	1.196	2.621	8
A. Joss	1.793	1.833	3.626	2
E. Walsh	1.770	2.000	3.770	1
M. Brown	1.770	1.000	2.770	6
Cy Young	1.632	1.108	2.740	7
N. Ryan	0.000	1.127	1.127	22
W. Ferrell	1.793	1.490	3.283	4
C. Hubbell	0.628	1.558	2.186	14

Final All-Around Ratings

The pitching skills of the competitors were by far the determining factor in the final all-around pitcher ratings. There were minor changes that resulted from the batting and fielding ratings, such as Lefty Grove dropping from second place to fourth place, Sandy Koufax falling from fifth place to seventh place, and Wes Ferrell, who was number one in batting and number four in fielding, moving up from number fifteen overall to number thirteen.

Nevertheless, the ratings demonstrated without a doubt that the individual's pitching skills far outweighed any other skill the pitcher might have had.

Name	NPitching × 90	NOffense × 6	NDefense × 4	Total Points	Final All-Around Ratings	HOF
W. Johnson	88.671	4.647	2.290	95.608	1	*
G. Alexander	86.047	3.144	3.137	92.328	2	*
Cy Young	84.459	3.198	2.740	90.397	3	*
Lefty Grove	87.500	1.014	1.748	90.262	4	*
Tom Seaver	81.115	2.313	2.412	85.840	5	*
C. Mathewson	78.018	4.176	3.438	85.632	6	*
Sandy Koufax	83.581	0.000	1.310	84.891	7	*
Whitey Ford	77.522	2.664	2.621	82.807	8	*
Dizzy Dean	74.110	2.994	1.598	78.702	9	*
Ed Walsh	70.755	3.528	3.770	78.053	10	*
Nolan Ryan	74.054	0.522	1.127	75.703	11	*
M. Brown	69.459	3.348	2.770	75.577	12	*
Carl Hubbell	71.916	0.825	2.186	74.927	13	*
Wes Ferrell	65.574	6.000	3.283	74.857	14	
Addie Joss	67.343	2.487	3.626	73.456	15	*
Juan Marichal	68.345	1.752	2.342	72.439	16	*
Bob Gibson	65.282	3.447	1.953	70.282	17	*
Warren Spahn	63.795	3.147	2.186	69.128	18	*
Eddie Plank	59.595	3.649	2.415	65.659	19	*
Bob Feller	60.845	1.731	1.893	64.469	20	*
Jim Palmer	58.423	2.133	2.541	63.097	21	*
Steve Carlton	57.049	2.715	1.781	61.545	22	*

Note: HOF denotes a member of the National Baseball Hall of Fame.

One question remained to be addressed and resolved before the ratings could be finalized. Several polls over the years have selected Sandy Koufax as the greatest pitcher of all-time, but in this study, based on a player's entire career, Koufax finished in seventh place. The great Dodger southpaw actually had two distinct and separate careers, as noted earlier. Between 1961 and 1966, he completely dominated the National League, leading the league in ERA five times, strikeouts four times, victories three times, winning percentage twice, complete games twice, shutouts three times, and innings pitched twice. In an effort to clarify Koufax's place in pitching history, his statistics were re-evaluated using only his last six years, his "Hall of Fame" years, to determine his rating. When that was done, Koufax did finish number one all-around. However, that comparison obviously did not provide a level playing field for the other candidates since they were rated on their entire careers, not only their best years. In order to better understand Koufax's position in the pitching hierarchy, several other pitchers, Lefty Grove, Grover Cleveland Alexander, and Walter Johnson, were re-evaluated using only their six best consecutive years. When those calculations were completed, Koufax was no longer number one. He might have been able to sneak past Lefty Grove on the basis of his won-lost differential, but he trailed Johnson and Alexander in both the won-lost differential and the adjusted ERA. This exercise confirmed the fact that Sandy Koufax was one of the great pitchers of all-time, but definitely not the number one man. It also justified the case for comparing pitchers on their entire careers, not only their five or six best years.

Pete Palmer developed a formula for measuring a pitcher's overall value to a team. It is called the Pitcher Wins (PW), and represents the number of wins a pitcher is worth to his team compared to the average pitcher, including pitching, batting, fielding, and base stealing. Like other Palmer ratings, it is a value rating, meaning that a player's length of service is a significant factor in determining his overall rating. For the following comparison, Pete Palmer's Pitcher Wins (PW) was converted to a skill system by converting the pitcher's PW rating to a 20-year basis.

Name	PW	PW per 20 Years	PW Rating	McNeil Rating
W. Johnson	89.9	85.6	1	1
G.C. Alexander	62.9	62.9	5	2
C. Mathewson	56.3	66.2	4	6
L. Grove	59.1	69.5	3	4
S. Koufax	22.3	37.2	13	7
B. Feller	31.6	35.1	17	20
W. Spahn	51.4	49.0	10	18
D. Dean	22.3	37.2	13	9
B. Gibson	44.9	52.8	8	17
T. Seaver	49.1	49.1	9	5
J. Palmer	34.3	36.1	15	21
J. Marichal	27.5	34.4	18	16
S. Carlton	33.2	27.7	19	22
E. Plank	30.3	35.6	16	19
W. Ford	37.2	46.5	12	8
A. Joss	23.0	51.1	8	15
E. Walsh	37.7	53.9	6	10
M. Brown	32.7	46.7	11	12

Name	PW	PW per 20 Years	PW Rating	McNeil Rating
C. Young	77.0	70.0	2	3
N. Ryan	21.5	15.9	20	11
W. Ferrell	31.1	62.2	6	14
C. Hubbell	38.8	51.7	8	13

The active pitchers noted at the beginning of this chapter were also evaluated for their pitching, batting, and fielding skills, using the same formulas as were used above. Their Pitching Wins (PW) was also reviewed, and by either method, at least three of them — Pedro Martinez, Roger Clemens, and Randy Johnson — gave indications that, when they retire, they could be rated in the top ten all-time. Pedro Martinez has an outside chance of challenging Walter Johnson as the greatest pitcher in baseball history, but depending on the severity of Martinez's downside as his career comes to a close, he may fall short of the top spot. Greg Maddux may not make the top ten because of his low ratings for both his won-lost differential and his adjusted ERA. Tom Glavine may also fail to make the top ten for the same reasons, and will probably fall somewhere below Maddux.

Chapter 6

Baseball's Greatest First Basemen

There were a total of 20 first basemen competing for the title of baseball's greatest first baseman.

- Lou Gehrig was an outstanding pitcher in college, once striking out 17 men in a game against Williams College. Like Ruth and other pitchers who carried a big bat, he was converted to an everyday player, a first baseman, when he entered professional baseball. The husky 6', 200-pound left-handed slugger was one of the game's great hitters, but he was never more than an average defensive first baseman in spite of the many hours he worked on his fielding. Gehrig was one of baseball's most durable players. Called "the Iron Horse," he set a major league record by playing in 2,130 consecutive games, a record that lasted fifty years until Cal Ripken, Jr., broke it. Gehrig's career was filled with highlights. In 1927, when the entire American League hit 439 home runs, Babe Ruth hit 60 for the Yankees and Gehrig was right behind him with 47. The next-highest home run total was 18 hit by teammate Tony Lazzeri. In 1935, Lou Gehrig won the Triple Crown, batting .363 with 49 home runs and 165 RBIs. In all, the Iron Horse led the league in home runs three times and in runs batted in five times. His 0.92 RBIs per game is the highest average in modern major league history. And like most of the great hitters of the early days, he was a contact slugger, rarely striking out. During his career, Gehrig averaged 34 homers for every 550 at-bats, while striking out only 54 times and walking 103 times. He was elected to the Baseball Hall of Fame in 1939.
- Jimmie Foxx was a rarity, a catcher who was versatile enough to play most any position on the field. When he arrived in Philadelphia in 1925, Connie Mack already had a catcher, a young man named Mickey

Lou Gehrig (left) and Hank Greenberg were two of the most devastating sluggers of the 1930s.

Cochrane. Cochrane had been tried at several other positions and had been found wanting. Foxx, on the other hand, was a talented and skillful outfielder and third baseman, and he played third base for a short time. When injuries finally ended Joe Hauser's career, the affable Foxx moved across the diamond to first base, where he became one of the greatest first basemen in major league history. In addition to his slugging prowess, leading the league in batting twice, on-base percentage three times, home runs four times, slugging average five times, and runs batted in three times, he also led the league in fielding percentage three times. The solidly built farm boy from Sudlersville, Maryland, with the unsettling nickname "the Beast," packed 195 pounds of muscle on his six-foot frame, and he tortured opposing pitchers for 20 years, driving extra-base hits to all parts of the ballpark, off the fences and over them, while compiling a .325 career batting average. Foxx entered the Baseball Hall of Fame in 1951.

- Hank Greenberg was one of baseball's great clutch hitters, averaging 0.92 runs batted in per game, just behind Lou Gehrig. The 6'3", 210-pound right-handed hitter was also one of the game's first free swingers, averaging 85 strikeouts a game in an era when most players felt it was humiliating to strike out. "Hammerin' Hank," as he was called, led the American League in RBIs four times, doubles twice, home runs four times, bases on balls twice, slugging percentage once, and fielding percentage once. The New York native was one of the first players to enlist in the U.S. military in World War II, entering the army in the spring of 1941 while at the peak of his baseball career. He served his country for four years, being discharged in 1945. He retired after the 1947 season at the age of 36. Some of Greenberg's feats were otherworldly. For instance, he slammed 63 doubles in 1934, the fourth-highest total of all-time. Three years later, he drove in 183 runs, the third-highest total in baseball history, and in 1938 he hit 58 home runs, second to Babe Ruth at the time. When Hank Greenberg began his professional career in 1930, he was considered to be clumsy and uncoordinated, but through countless hours of hard work, he became a better-than-average defensive first baseman with a reliable glove and good range. He is a 1956 member of the Baseball Hall of Fame.

- Harmon Killebrew was a powerful six-foot tall, 215-pound right-handed slugging machine from Payette, Idaho, who starred for the Washington Senators and Minnesota Twins, beginning in 1954 before playing for Kansas City in his final season in 1975. During the peak of his career, from 1959 through 1971, the man they called "Killer" terrorized American League pitchers, averaging over 40 home runs a year. He hit more than 40 home runs eight times, with a high of 49 homers in both 1964 and

Johnny Mize was one of baseball's greatest clutch hitters in the 1940s.

1969. He led the league in home runs six times, in RBIs three times, and in bases on balls four times. Killebrew averaged 39 home runs, 107 RBIs, and 87 runs scored over a 22-year span. And despite his bulk, he was also a decent defensive first baseman, although not one of the world-class members. As can be seen from his peak years noted above, Killebrew did not have any career years. He was consistent, year in and year out, as he helped the Twins to three American League pennants and one World Series.

- Johnny Mize was another of baseball's great clutch hitters. He was so respected that, at the age of 36, an age when most players were retired, the New York Yankees obtained his services, and he played in Yankee Stadium for five years, helping Casey Stengel's team capture five consecutive world championships. In the 1952 Series, won by the Yankees in seven games over the Brooklyn Dodgers, Mize stung the ball at a .400 clip with a double, three homers, and six RBIs in 15 at-bats. "The Big Cat" was a decent fielder, but his forte was hitting the cover off the ball, as evidenced by his .312 career batting average and his 31 doubles and 31 homers for every 550 at-bats. Still, the graceful left-handed hitting Mize, like many of the other big sluggers of his day, also had a good batting eye, striking out only 43 times a season, while walking 73 times and driving in 114 runs. He batted over .300 nine times in twelve years and drove in more than 100 runs eight times. He led the league in batting once, home runs four times, doubles once, triples once, runs batted in three times, and slugging percentage four times. He hit 51 home runs in 1947, when hitting 51 home runs meant something, and he hit three home runs in a Game Six times. Johnny Mize was elected to the Baseball Hall of Fame in 1981.

- George Sisler was a smooth-swinging left-handed contact hitter with little power. He had a .340 career batting average, number 14 all-time, and he struck out only 22 times a season. At the same time, he had only 46 extra-base hits, including six home runs, and he walked only 31 times, giving him a .379 on-base percentage and a .468 slugging average. Known as "Gorgeous George," the 5'11", 170-pound first sacker was considered to be one the top two first basemen in baseball history during the first thirty years of the twentieth century, but his standing has slipped somewhat with the emergence of the big sluggers who now dominate the position. Sisler twice batted over .400, leading the league in batting in 1920 with an average of .407 and repeating in 1922 when he hit .420. In the former year, he set a major league record of 257 base hits that stood for more than eighty years until it was broken by Ichiro Suzuki. In 1922, he also led the league with 134 runs scored, 246 base hits, and 18 triples. *The Ballplayers* noted that "In the field Sisler was fast, adroit, and graceful, a combination that gave elegance to his execution of plays." Sisler's 1,528 career assists rank third all-time behind Eddie Murray and Keith Hernandez. He was elected to the Baseball Hall of Fame in 1939.
- Willie "Stretch" McCovey, standing an imposing 6'4" tall and weighing a powerful 210 pounds, struck fear into the hearts of opposing pitchers. The left-handed slugger enjoyed a 22-year career in the major leagues, most of it with the San Francisco Giants, where in 1962 he came within an inch or two of becoming a legend. In the World Series that year, the Giants were trailing the New York Yankees, 1–0, in the bottom of the ninth inning of Game Seven, when they put the potential tying and winning runs on second and third with two men out. Yankee pitcher Ralph Terry faced McCovey, who had tripled in his previous at bat. Terry worked the count to 1–1 when McCovey, a dead pull hitter, tied into a pitch and sent a screamer toward right-center field. Yankee second baseman Bobby Richardson moved slightly to his left, threw his glove into the air, and snatched the ball, ending the Series and McCovey's dream

of glory. The big first baseman, who was noted for his bat and not his glove, averaged 35 home runs for every 550 at-bats, one of the highest home run averages in major league history. He led the league in home runs three times, RBIs twice, and slugging average three times. He was a 1986 entry to the Baseball Hall of Fame.

- Eddie Murray, at 6' 2" tall and weighing 220 pounds, was one of the game's greatest switch-hitters, and one of its best all-around first basemen. His 22-year major league career produced 3,255 base hits, 504 home runs, 1917 RBIs, and a .993 fielding average. He was voted the American League's Rookie of the Year in 1977, when he was used as a designated hitter. Later, after becoming Baltimore's first baseman, he won three consecutive Gold Gloves. Murray, who accumulated 560 doubles, 35 triples, and 504 home runs in his notable career, is one of the few major league hitters to accumulate more than 1,000 extra-base hits. He is eighth all-time in games played, fifth in at-bats, 11th in base hits, 13th in doubles, 15th in home runs, ninth in total bases, eighth in RBIs, third in putouts, first in assists, and second in double plays. His outstanding all-around play earned him election to the Baseball Hall of Fame in 2003.

- Keith Hernandez was another of the outstanding all-around first basemen that thrilled baseball fans across the country during the twentieth century. The handsome Californian played major league baseball for seventeen years, including nine years with the St. Louis Cardinals and six years with the New York Mets. He helped both teams win world championships, the Cardinals in 1982 and the Mets four years later. Hernandez's teams won 15 games against eight losses in post-season play, including the National League Championship Series, and although he batted a modest .263, he drove in 16 runs. During his career, the smooth-swinging lefty batted a cool .296, averaging 32 doubles, four triples, and 12 home runs for every 550 at-bats. In 1979 he tied for the National League's Most Valuable Player award, while leading the league in batting (.344), runs scored (116), doubles (48), and on-base percentage (.421). On defense, Hernandez had no equal. He won eleven straight Gold Gloves and set a major league record for the most consecutive seasons leading the league in double plays with six. He led the National League in fielding average twice, assists five times, and putouts four times. He is tied for ninth all-time in career fielding average, sixth in career double plays, and second in career assists.

- Norm Cash was a long ball-hitting first baseman who also excelled in the field. He had a career season with the bat in 1961, leading the American League in batting with an average of .361, in base hits with 193, and in on-base percentage with .488 (number 33 all-time). He also slugged 41 home runs that year, scored 119 runs, drew 124 bases on balls, and drove in 132 teammates. Over his 17-year career, Cash hit more than 30 home runs in a season five times and more than 20 home runs a season eleven times. He helped the Detroit Tigers capture the world championship in 1968, batting .385 with five RBIs in seven games, and he ignited the winning rally in Game Seven by ripping a two-out single off Bob Gibson that led to a three-run seventh inning, breaking up a scoreless pitching duel between Gibson and Mickey Lolich. Detroit went on to win the game and the championship by a 4–1 score. Cash was as good in the field as he was at the plate. He led all American League first basemen in fielding twice, en route to a career fielding average of .992. His 1,317 career assists are eighth all-time.

- Bill Terry is the last National Leaguer to bat .400 in a season, accomplishing that feat in 1930 when he compiled an average of .401. He batted over .300 eleven times in 14 years, including four years above .350. He also led the league that year with 254 base hits, while cracking 39 doubles, 13 triples, and 20 home runs with 139 runs scored and 129 runs batted in. Terry scored 100 or more runs in a season seven times, and drove in more than 100 runs six times. When he retired in 1936, he left behind a .341 career batting average, number 13 all-time, a .393 on-base percentage (number 63) and a .506 slugging average (number 45). Terry was also a star on defense. He led the league in fielding percentage twice, putouts five times, assists five times, and double plays three times. He had excellent range, with a .992 career fielding average and 10.91 total chances per game (number eight all-time). He was elected to the Baseball Hall of Fame in 1954.
- Will "the Thrill" Clark began his major league career with the San Francisco Giants in 1986, retiring in 2000 after fifteen distinguished seasons. He was Mr. Consistency with the bat, hitting between .282 and .308 for eleven of those years. He batted .333 in 1989, .329 in 1994, .326 in 1997, and .319 in 2000. He never batted below .282. Clark's major league career got off to a rousing start when he homered off Nolan Ryan in his first major league at-bat. The smooth-swinging lefty was a terror in postseason play, posting a torrid .441 average, with six doubles, one triple, three home runs, and eleven runs batted in in 59 at-bats. But Clark was more than a solid hitter. He was also dependable on defense with a good glove and good range.
- Vic Power was one of the greatest defensive first basemen of all-time. He was a flashy, energetic fielder who did everything with a special flair. During his twelve-year major league career, he won seven Gold Gloves,

while leading the league in fielding average three times, double plays three times, putouts twice, and assists six times. In 1959, he led all American League first basemen in games played, innings played, fielding average, putouts, assists, and double plays. The following year he led the league in all categories except putouts. His .994 career fielding average is number nine all-time. But the 5'11", 195-pound right-handed hitter was more than just a defensive player. He was also a contact hitter who struck out only 22 times for every 550 at-bats and compiled a career batting average of .284. He batted over .300 three times, including .312 in 1958, when he led the league with 10 triples, while also hitting 37 doubles and 16 home runs with 80 RBIs. Although Power was a good contact hitter, he was also impatient at the plate, and he walked only 27 times a year, giving him a mediocre .317 on-base percentage.

- Boog Powell was a mighty hulk of a man, standing 6'4" tall and weighing a muscular 240 pounds. The left-handed slugger, Baltimore's cleanup hitter for the better part of thirteen years, was an imposing figure as he stood at the plate. His handsome, freckled face, topped with a shock of red hair, was a disarming visage that often led to serious difficulty for the opposing pitcher. Powell averaged 27 homers and 92 RBIs a year during his 17-year career. His best years were 1966 (34 homers and 109 RBIs), 1969 (when he stroked the ball at a .304 clip with 37 homers and 121 RBIs), and 1970 (35 homers and 114 RBIs). The Orioles won pennants in each of those years, and they added world championships to the 1966 and 1970 American League titles. They also won the American League pennant in 1971 when Powell hit 22 homers and drove in 92 runs. In addition to his slugging prowess, Powell was also a decent fielder who saved his infielders numerous errors by scooping their low throws out of the dirt. He led the league in fielding average in 1975 with a .997 fielding percentage.

- Orlando Cepeda, "the Baby Bull," patrolled first base for the San Francisco Giants for eight years and the St. Louis Cardinals for three years during his 17-year major league career. He was another powerful slugger at 6'2", 210 pounds, and he tattooed opposing pitchers to the tune of .297 with 26 home runs and 95 RBIs a year. Unlike Boog Powell, who was a patient hitter who averaged 101 strikeouts and 82 bases on balls a year, Cepeda walked only 42 times and struck out 81 times for every 550 at-bats. The native of Puerto Rico, whose nickname was derived from his father's nickname, Perucho, ("the Bull"), compiled ten .300+ seasons with a high of .317 in 1959. His best season was 1961 when he batted .311 while leading the National League with 46 home runs and 142 runs batted in. He was also a competent, if not spectacular fielder.

- Jeff Bagwell, recently retired, was in the upper echelon of first basemen, both offensively and defensively. His 15-year career produced a .297 batting average with 32 home runs a year, 107 runs scored and 108 runs batted in. He also averaged 110 strikeouts and 99 bases on balls. Bagwell and teammate Craig Biggio were known as "the Killer Bees," the heart and soul of the Houston Astro lineup. But Bagwell was more than a big bat. He was also one of the league's top fielding first basemen, with a .993 fielding average. He led the league in games played three times, innings played four times, assists five times, and double plays once.
- Jack Clark was primarily an offensive first baseman. The right-handed power hitter averaged 27 home runs and 95 runs batted in for every 550 at-bats. His .267 batting average was supplemented with 101 bases on balls a year, giving him an excellent .383 on-base percentage. He led the league in walks three times, with a high of 136 in 1987. He was a member of the 1985 and 1987 pennant-winning St. Louis Cardinals, but he was held to a .240 batting average in the 1985 World Series, and an ankle injury kept him out of the 1987 Fall Classic. His greatest day in baseball occurred in the 1985 NLCS against the Los Angeles Dodgers when he blasted a three-run homer deep into the left-field stands at Dodger Stadium with two men out in the top of the ninth inning, giving his team a 7–5 victory and a National League pennant
- Don Mattingly was a slick-fielding first baseman who could also hit for average and with significant power. From 1984 through 1989, the slim left-handed slugger batted .327 while averaging 38 doubles, 24 home runs and 101 RBIs a year. He led the league in base hits twice during that period, doubles three times, and RBIs once. Unfortunately, Mattingly injured his back in a locker-room accident in 1987 and it continued to bother him the rest of his career. It eventually sapped his strength to the point where he was reduced to being a slap hitter who batted just .288 with 11 homers and 70 RBIs a year over his final six years. Another potential Hall of Fame career was short-circuited by injuries. Still, the classy Hoosier continued to outshine his peers on defense, leading the league in fielding average seven times overall, including three times near the end of his career. The five-time Gold Glove winner also led the league in putouts once and double plays twice.
- Gil Hodges, after forty years of being ignored by the baseball community, is still looking to take his rightful place alongside the other greats of the game in Cooperstown. The Indiana native was arguably the best all-around first baseman in the National League during the 1950s, but being a typical strong, silent type on a team that included Jackie Robinson, Pee Wee Reese, Duke Snider, and Roy Campanella, he was often overshad-

owed by his more colorful teammates. But when the chips were down, Hodges delivered. He drove in more than a hundred runs a season for seven consecutive years, and hit more than thirty home runs in a season six times. His best year was 1954 when he hit .304 with 42 home runs, 130 runs batted in, and a .995 fielding average. He was regarded as the league's best defensive first baseman during his career, leading the league in fielding average three times and winning three Gold Gloves. He was noted for his big hands, his graceful moves around the bag, and his quick footwork.

- Fred McGriff was a superior all-around first baseman from 1986 to 2004. He was in the top twenty in both offense and defense during his career, batting .284 with 31 home runs and 97 RBIs a year. Although the lanky, left-handed power hitter led the National League in home runs twice, he was a patient hitter who walked frequently and went down on strikes even more, averaging 82 bases on balls and 118 strikeouts for every 550 at-bats. He played for the Atlanta Braves in two World Series, batting a combined .279 with four home runs and nine RBIs in 12 games. In the field, he led the league in putouts once, fielding average once, and double plays twice.

Active Players

There are an unusually high number of first basemen who are still active that might challenge the candidates for places on the legendary all-time all-star team. Albert Pujols, at the age of 26, completed his sixth full season as the St. Louis Cardinals' first baseman in 2006. He has a hefty .332 career batting average with 39 homers and 114 RBIs for every 550 at-bats. It is within the realm of possibility that Pujols could pass Barry Bonds' career home run totals before he retires and perhaps even challenge the magic 800 home run barrier. Todd Helton of the Colorado Rockies is another big bopper, sporting a .333 batting average with 31 homers and 107 RBIs a year over his ten-year career. Jim Thome, a husky 6'4", 220-pound left-handed slugger, passed the 500 home run mark in 2007. He is a career .282 hitter over 16 years, and averages 41 homers and 112 RBIs a year. Paul Konerko completed ten years of major league service in 2006 with a .280 batting average, 30 home runs, and 97 RBIs. His career has a long way to go as he just celebrated his 31st birthday on March 5, 2007. Frank Thomas, known affectionately as "the Big Hurt," stands 6'5" tall and weighs a hefty 257 pounds. The 39-year-old right-handed hitter, who is nearing the end of his career, passed the 500 homer mark in 2007. His batting average for 17 years is .305, and he has averaged 36 homers and 117 RBIs for every 550 at-bats.

Albert Pujols is quickly becoming a legend in the game of baseball after just seven years in the major leagues.

Offensive Ratings

The offensive statistics that were evaluated to determine baseball's greatest offensive first basemen were on-base percentage (OBP), slugging percentage (SLG), stolen bases (SB), sacrifice hits (SH), and double plays grounded into (GIDP).

Normalized Adjusted On-Base Percentage (NOBPA)

At .447, Lou Gehrig had the highest official career OBP of any of the first base candidates in the study, followed by Jimmie Foxx at .428 and Hank Greenberg at .412. At the other end of the spectrum, Vic Power had only a .315 OBP and Orlando Cepeda had a .350 OBP. The adjusted on-base percentage (OBPA) penalized the players who were active in the 1920s and '30s because that era was dominated by great hitters with higher than normal league average OBP's. In the top three, Lou Gehrig lost 20 points because of the era adjustment, while both Jimmie Foxx and Hank Greenberg lost 16 points. George Sisler, who played a significant part of his career in the dead ball era, lost 13 points, but Norm Cash, who played from 1958 to 1974, gained 14 points, giving him a fifth-place finish in the category.

Normalized Adjusted Slugging Average (NXSLGA)

The first step in arriving at the normalized slugging average (NXSLGA) was to determine the player's individual park factor. For players who were active after 1956, the home and away splits are readily available. Norm Cash's splits were:

	AB	H	S	D	T	HR	SB	SH	GIDP
(H)	3285	907	565	112	16	214	21	8	68
(A)	3412	911	594	129	25	163	22	9	69

When broken down into a 550 at-bat season, the following results emerged.

	AB	H	S	D	T	HR	SB	SH	GIDP
(H)	550	152	97	19	3	36	4	1	11
(A)	550	147	95	21	4	27	4	1	11

During the time Norm Cash played in the major leagues, the number of teams in the American League varied from eight to 12. He played two years when there were eight teams in the league, eight years when there were 10 teams, and six years when there were 12 teams; therefore, the weighted average of that data gave:

$(2 \times 12) + (8 \times 10) + (6 \times 12) = 168/16$ years = 10.5 Equivalent Teams

Cash's home ballpark accounted for just one of the 10.5 equivalent teams, while the away ballparks accounted for the other 9.5 teams.

Norm Cash's adjusted park factor, based on 10.5 equivalent teams, was:

Adjusted base hits = $(147 \times 9.5) + (152 \times 1)$ =
$1548.5/10.5$ = 147 adjusted base hits.

The same procedure was followed for all the stats, giving these adjusted stats:

AB	H	S	D	T	HR	SB	SH	GIDP
550	147	95	21	4	27	4	1	11

It is obvious that a player's away statistics were much more important in determining his adjusted stats, simply because they were heavily weighted for the number of teams in the league. In Cash's case, his adjusted stats were identical to his away stats.

Before calculating Norm Cash's adjusted slugging average, the data had to be modified to eliminate the total base hits (his singles plus one base from each of his extra-base hits) since those stats were already accounted for in the OBPA calculation and the use of them again would be double-dipping.

The 147 base hits were subtracted from the 550 at-bats during a normal season to give an adjusted at-bat figure of 403.

Cash's XSLG = (A + B + C)/D = (21 + 8 + 81)/403 = .273

Where:

> XSLG = Slugging Average adjusted for park factor
> A = Cash's doubles (X1) – 21
> B = Cash's triples (X2) – 4
> C = Cash's home runs (X3) – 27
> D = Cash's adjusted at-bats – 403

Next, Cash's XSLGA, his slugging average adjusted for the era in which he played, had to be calculated.

XSLGA = XSLG – (E – F) = .273 – (.372 – .388) = .289

Where:

> XSLG = Slugging Average adjusted for park factor = .273
> E = League Slugging Average during Cash's career = .372.
> F = Base Point Slugging Average (1960) = .388.

The normalized slugging average was determined by comparing Cash's XSLGA with the highest XSLGA in the study, in this case, Lou Gehrig's XSLGA, which was .421. The ratio was weighted at a maximum of 20 points. Lou Gehrig's NXSLGA was 20.000.

Norm Cash's NXSLGA = .289/.421 × 20 = 13.729.

For players whose careers took place prior to 1957, a different procedure was necessary since there were no detailed splits available for those players, with a few exceptions like Yogi Berra and Bill Dickey. There were home run factors (HRF) available for all players, as noted previously, so the player's home and away home runs were known, but it was necessary to make several assumptions to arrive at the other stats. A study of the modern player's splits indicated that, in general, a player's doubles changed by the same amount as a player's home runs, but in the opposite direction. Therefore, if a player averaged 35 home runs and 35 doubles, and if his home runs at home were 37 and away were 33, then his doubles at home would be 33 and away would be 37. A study of the splits also indicated that the other stats, like triples, stolen bases, sacrifice hits, and grounded into double plays, were the same at home and away. At-bats were approximately 5 percent higher on the road than they were at home, since players often do not bat in the bottom of the ninth inning in their home park. So, if a player had 550 at-bats, and the difference between his home at-bats and his away at-bats was 5 percent, then his home at-bats would be 550/1.025 = 537 and his away at-bats would be × 1.025 = 564.

The calculations for determining a player's normalized slugging average were then made the same way as they were for Norm Cash above.

Normalized Stolen Bases (NSB)

First basemen, in general, did not steal many bases. They were primarily run producers who were expected to drive the ball to the deepest recesses of the ballpark for extra bases or to put the ball out of the park for a home run. George Sisler, who played much of his career during the dead ball era, when one run was still important and 1–0 games were commonplace, averaged 25 stolen bases a year between 1915 and 1930. Of the modern players, only Jeff Bagwell with 14 stolen bases a year and Orlando Cepeda with 10 stolen bases a year produced in double figures. Naturally, Sisler was a runaway winner in the stolen base category with 1.000 point, the maximum point total for the category. Bagwell's normalized point total was 0.560 and Cepeda's was 0.400.

Normalized Sacrifice Hits (NSH)

First basemen were also not proficient at laying down a strategic sacrifice bunt. Once again, they had their sights set on bigger things. George Sisler was the leader in this category as well as the stolen base category. He averaged 15 sacrifice bunts a year, followed by Bill Terry with 12. No other first baseman averaged more than seven sacrifice hits a year.

Normalized Double Plays Grounded Into (NGIDP)

First basemen were, in general, big men who usually lacked speed and were susceptible to grounding into double plays. In this study, only two men, Johnny Mize and Will Clark, grounded into fewer than 10 double plays a year.

Final Offensive Ratings

The maximum offensive rating of 43 points for first basemen consisted of 20 points maximum each for NOBPA and NXSLGA, and one point maximum each for NSB, NSH, and NGIDP.

Name	NOBPA × 20	NXSLGA × 20	.05NSB × 20	.05NSH × 20	.05NGIDP × 20	Total Points	Final Offensive Ratings
Gehrig	20.000	20.000	.280	.470	.800	41.550	1
Foxx	19.297	18.622	.240	.330	.421	38.910	2
Greenberg	18.548	18.290	.240	.270	.500	38.848	3
Mize	18.126	16.770	.080	.130	1.000	36.106	4
Sisler	17.143	9.359	1.000	1.000	.670	29.172	17
McCovey	17.658	15.629	.080	.000	.670	34.037	6
Murray	16.815	12.637	.200	.000	.530	30.181	16
Hernandez	18.033	9.264	.280	.070	.670	28.317	18
Cash	18.173	13.729	.160	.070	.727	32.859	9
Terry	17.611	11.496	.200	.800	.727	30.834	13
W. Clark	17.799	11.401	.200	.070	.889	30.359	14
H. Killebrew	15.222	17.910	.040	.000	.471	33.643	7
V. Power	15.035	8.171	.160	.470	.615	24.451	20
B. Powell	17.330	14.062	.080	.130	.571	32.143	10
O. Cepeda	16.581	14.347	.400	.000	.530	31.858	11
Bagwell	18.689	14.490	.560	.000	.500	34.198	5
J. Clark	17.845	14.347	.240	.070	.571	33.073	8
Mattingly	16.768	9.739	.040	.070	.500	27.117	19
Hodges	16.534	12.637	.200	.270	.615	30.256	15
McGriff	17.096	13.397	.200	.000	.571	31.264	12

Lou Gehrig was rated as the greatest offensive first baseman in baseball history, which is no surprise. It is also no surprise that Jimmie Foxx and Hank Greenberg finished second and third, respectively, although there might be some healthy discussions over the other positions. Johnny Mize was number four, a strong showing by Bagwell in NOBPA rewarded him with a fifth-place finish, and strong performances in both NOBPA and NXSLGA by both Willie McCovey and Harmon Killebrew earned them a fifth-place finish and a sixth-place finish, respectively. Some active players were also evaluated to see where they might fall in the offensive ratings. Paul Konerko would have been about number 20, with Jim Thome and Frank Thomas both about number five. Todd Helton was about number eight, and Albert Pujols was number four. Konerko and Pujols, who are both in the prime of their careers, may see their ratings rise, and for Pujols, the sky is the limit. Thome, Thomas, and Helton, who are in decline, will probably see their ratings drop by the time they retire.

As can be seen from the above table, the players with a high NOBPA were those players who had a decent batting average plus a knack for drawing bases on balls. Lou Gehrig, with a .340 batting average and an average of 105 bases on balls for every 550 at-bats, and Jimmie Foxx, with a .325 batting average and 98 walks, finished first and second, respectively. Another player who had a good NOBPA was Keith Hernandez, who batted .296 and drew 80 bases on balls. Sluggers like Gehrig, Foxx, and Greenberg dominated the NXSLGA category, while players with less power, like Don Mattingly, Vic Power, George Sisler, and Keith Hernandez, brought up the rear. Not surprisingly, most first basemen stole very few bases with the exception of George Sisler, who averaged 25, Jeff Bagwell, who averaged 14, and Orlando Cepeda, who averaged 10. The sacrifice hit category is a sign of the times. In the old days, prior to 1960, many first basemen were capable of laying down a well-executed sacrifice bunt now and then, but in today's game the first baseman is counted on to hit a home run in that situation. George Sisler averaged 15 sacrifice hits a year, Bill Terry averaged 12, and even Lou Gehrig averaged seven. In today's world Fred McGriff never sacrificed in his major league career, while Jeff Bagwell laid down only three. Not unexpectedly, most first basemen, being big sluggers, hit into a fair amount of double plays. Only Johnny Mize with eight and Will Clark with nine grounded into fewer than 10 double plays a year.

Defensive Ratings

Normalized Fielding Average Differential (NFAD)

The fielding average of the candidates was compared to the league fielding average during the player's career, and the differential was normalized, with a maximum point total of 20. Don Mattingly had the highest fielding average differential, and was awarded 20 points. Vic Power, an outstanding defensive first baseman from 1954 to 1965, had a career fielding average of .994 compared to a league average of .991, giving him 17.500 points. Keith Hernandez, Gil Hodges, Bill Terry, Johnny Mize, and Jimmie Foxx, all of whom had a fielding average that was two points above the league average, earned 15.000 points for their defensive prowess.

Normalized Adjusted Fielding Runs (NAFR)

Range Factor was not considered to be a good measuring stick for first basemen since most of their putouts resulted from handling throws on infield grounders, which, for the most part, were routine. Also, putouts by a first baseman were significantly affected by the number of batters struck out by the pitchers on his team. Obviously, the more batters struck out by his team's pitchers, the fewer ground ball outs would be recorded at first base; a first baseman on a team whose pitchers had a high number of strikeouts versus the league average would suffer in the range factor category. Gil Hodges, one of the league's best fielding first basemen, is a good example. His team, the Brooklyn Dodgers, had a pitching staff that routinely led the National League in strikeouts during his career, a situation that had nothing to do with Hodges' fielding skills, but would have had a significant negative effect on his Range Factor rating. It was finally decided to use Pete Palmer's Fielding Runs (FR) formula, after modifying it from a value system to a skill system by converting the result to a 2,000 game basis. Pete Palmer's FR formula subtracts the effect of a team's strikeouts from the formula, putting all first basemen on a level playing field. The FR formula is:

$$FR = PFR/(PO - SO \text{ for team}) - LFR/(PO - SO \text{ for league}) \times \text{player innings}$$

Where:

$$PFR = \text{Player fielding rate for first base} = .2 \times (2 \times A - E)$$
$$LFR = \text{League fielding rate.}$$

The Fielding Runs result was then normalized with a maximum point total of 20.

The defensive ratings for first basemen are:

Name	NFAD × 20	NAFR × 20	Total Points	Final Defensive Ratings
Gehrig	12.500	05.300	17.800	15
Foxx	15.000	11.356	26.356	6
Greenberg	12.500	10.978	23.478	10
Mize	15.000	08.265	23.265	11
Sisler	05.000	14.763	19.763	12
McCovey	00.000	09.968	09.968	19
Murray	12.500	12.240	24.740	9
Hernandez	15.000	17.098	32.098	2
Cash	12.500	12.681	25.181	8
Terry	15.000	14.511	29.511	3
H. Killebrew	12.500	4.101	16.601	17
W. Clark	10.000	07.823	17.823	13
V. Power	17.500	20.000	37.500	1

Name	NFAD × 20	NAFR × 20	Total Points	Final Defensive Ratings
B. Powell	10.000	07.571	17.571	14
O Cepeda	10.000	06.246	16.246	18
Bagwell	10.000	17.539	27.539	4
J. Clark	05.000	04.606	09.606	20
Mattingly	20.000	07.444	27.444	5
Hodges	15.000	10.852	25.852	7
McGriff	10.000	07.319	17.319	16

Vic Power, Keith Hernandez, and Bill Terry rank first, second and third, respectively, as baseball's greatest defensive first basemen.

Final All-Around Ratings

The final ratings for baseball's greatest all-around first baseman are shown below. The offense was rated at four times the defense.

	Offense Divided by 43 × 4	Defense Divided by 40	Total Points	Final All-Around Ratings	HOF
Gehrig	3.865	0.445	4.310	1	*
Foxx	3.620	0.659	4.279	2	*
Greenberg	3.521	0.587	4.108	3	*
Mize	3.359	0.582	3.941	4	*
Sisler	2.714	0.494	3.208	20	*
McCovey	3.166	0.249	3.415	13	*
Murray	2.808	0.619	3.427	12	*
Hernandez	2.634	0.802	3.436	10	
Cash	3.057	0.630	3.687	6	
Terry	2.868	0.738	3.606	7	*
H. Killebrew	3.130	0.415	3.545	8	*
W. Clark	2.824	0.526	3.350	15	
V. Power	2.275	0.938	3.213	18	
B. Powell	2.990	0.439	3.429	11	
O. Cepeda	2.964	0.406	3.370	14	*
Bagwell	3.181	0.688	3.869	5	
J. Clark	3.077	0.150	3.227	17	
Mattingly	2.523	0.686	3.209	19	

	Offense Divided by 43 × 4	Defense Divided by 40	Total Points	Final All-Around Ratings	HOF
Hodges	2.815	0.646	3.461	9	
McGriff	2.908	0.433	3.341	16	

Note: HOF denotes a member of the National Baseball Hall of Fame.

Lou Gehrig beat out Jimmie Foxx by the slightest of margins for the title of baseball's greatest all-around first baseman. Foxx's excellent defensive rating almost wiped out the advantage Gehrig had built up on offense. Actually, the difference in the final point total between the two superstars, less than 1 percent, might in many cases be declared too close to call. The two legends were, in many ways, mirror images of each other, as their season averages show.

	ABs	H	D	T	HR	RBI	BB	BA	FA	FRs/ 2000 G.
Lou Gehrig	550	187	37	11	34	137	104	.340	.991	−55
Jimmie Foxx	550	179	31	8	36	130	98	.325	.992	41

Hank Greenberg and Johnny Mize, although a level below Gehrig and Foxx, nevertheless showed they belong in the elite upper echelon of the top five first basemen.

	ABs	H	D	T	HR	RBI	BB	BA	FA	FRs 2000 G.
H. Greenberg	550	172	40	8	35	135	90	.313	.991	35
Johnny Mize	550	172	31	7	31	114	73	.312	.992	−8

The big surprise in the study was the showing of Jeff Bagwell, who finished in fifth place. His high rating was based on his sensational all-around performance. He finished in fifth place on offense and fourth place on defense. The former Houston Astro was solid in all phases of the game.

	ABs	H	D	T	HR	RBI	BB	BA	FA	FRs 2000 G.
Jeff Bagwell	550	163	34	2	32	108	99	.297	.993	132

Although the defense was only rated one to four to the offense, the excellent defensive rating of Keith Hernandez moved him up from 18th on offense to ninth all-around. Similar improvements were made by Norm Cash, who jumped from number eight to number six, Eddie Murray, who moved up from number 16 to number 11, and Gil Hodges, who moved up from number 15 to number eight.

These ratings will surely change as current active players retire. At this early juncture, it appears as if Albert Pujols may pose a serious challenge to Lou Gehrig as the greatest first baseman in baseball history, assuming he stays healthy and maintains the high standard he has set. His offensive production placed him in the top three through 2006, even though he was penalized by a negative 30-point era adjustment for slugging average. Frank Thomas, Todd Helton, Jim Thome, and Paul Konerko could also finish in the top ten based on their current statistics, although all of them face a 30- to 41-point negative era adjustment for slugging average.

Bill Buckner, Steve Garvey, Joe Adcock, Ted Kluszewski, and Tony Perez were originally included in the study, but they were later dropped since only 20 players were listed. Kluszewski and Perez were the highest rated of the five players.

There could be other changes in the ratings of first basemen if Mark McGwire and Rafael Palmeiro become eligible. McGwire, a 6'5", 225-pound behemoth, holds the all-time career home run frequency record with 52 home runs for every 550 at-bats to go along with 125 RBIs. Babe Ruth averaged 47 homers for every 550 at-bats, and Barry Bonds averages 42. McGwire broke Roger Maris' single-season home run mark when he lofted 70 balls into orbit in 1998. Palmeiro, a smooth-swinging left-handed hitter, batted .288 and hit 569 homers over a 20-year career, averaging 30 homers and 98 RBIs a year. If McGwire and Palmeiro eventually join the study, they may both be in the top ten all-around, with McGwire estimated to be about number four and Palmeiro estimated to be about number eight.

CHAPTER 7

Baseball's Greatest Second Basemen

There were a total of seventeen players competing for the title of baseball's greatest all-around second baseman.

- Jackie Robinson was one of the most important figures ever to play the game of baseball. His fantastic success in the major leagues opened the door for people of all races and nationalities to play our National Pastime. And, in spite of the intense pressure he endured as the first black player to play major league baseball in the twentieth century, he dominated his sport, compiling a career .311 batting average and reviving the lost art of base running. He led the league in stolen bases twice, with 29 steals in 1947 and 37 in 1949, modest totals by today's standards but respectable numbers in the 1940s. His 19 career steals of home were the most in the National League since World War I. In the 1955 World Series, his steal of home against the New York Yankees in Game One paved the way for Brooklyn's first and only world championship. But stolen bases were just a part of his legendary base running repertoire. He completely disrupted opposing pitchers with his dancing leads off base, a strategy that frequently led to a stolen base or a balk. And he ran the bases with abandon, taking extra bases on hits and often decoying a harried outfielder into throwing to the wrong base. On those occasions when he was caught in a rundown between bases, it was fifty-fifty that he would escape the trap safely. He was the National League Rookie of the Year in 1947 and its Most Valuable Player two years later when he led the league in batting with a .342 average. But Robinson was more than just a batting and base running star. He also excelled on defense, leading the league in fielding percentage three times and double plays six consecutive years.

- Rogers "Rajah" Hornsby has the second-highest career batting average in major league history, at .356. The husky right-handed slugger, whose leaky glove kept him from making a runaway of the second base competition, hit for power as well as average, with 36 doubles, 11 triples, 20 home runs, and 107 RBIs for every 550 at-bats. He won seven batting titles between 1920 and 1928, three times hitting over .400, with a high of .424 in 1924. His combined batting average from 1921 to 1925 was an astronomical .402. Rajah also led the league in runs scored five times, base hits four times, doubles four times, triples twice, home runs twice, runs batted in four times, on-base percentage eight times, and slugging percentage nine times. He was, in fact, during most of his 23-year career a one-man wrecking crew. As suspicious as his defense was, however, he did lead the league in fielding average in 1922, and he led the league in putouts twice, assists twice and double plays four times. Hornsby could handle any ball he could reach. His problem was his lack of foot speed that prevented him from getting to balls that the majority of major leaguers could reach, and that deficiency left him in last place in range factor among the seventeen second basemen in the study.
- Joe Morgan was a compact 5'7", 160-pound left-handed hitter who was a key element in Cincinnati's Big Red Machine of the 1970s. During his tenure in Cincinnati, he played on five division champions, three National League pennant winners, and two world champions. Little Joe had a keen batting eye that helped him coax an average of 111 bases on balls a year out of opposing pitchers, but he could also hit with power, averaging 27 doubles, six triples, and 16 home runs for every 550 at-bats. The speedy infielder, who averaged 41 stolen bases and 110 runs scored a year, led the league in walks four times, OBP four times, and slugging average once. His 1,865 career walks are the fifth-highest total in major league history, and his 1,650 runs scored are number twenty-seven. But Morgan was not only an offensive player; he also paced the league in fielding average three times. He is number two all-time in career games played at second base with 2,527, number three in assists with 6,967 and number six in double plays with 1,505.
- Napoleon "Nap" Lajoie, considered by many baseball experts to be the game's greatest all-around second baseman, played major league baseball from 1896 to 1916. The powerful right-handed slugger, who towered over his peers at 6'1" tall, and who packed 195 pounds of muscle on his lithe body, was certainly the best second baseman of his era. A native of Woonsocket, Rhode Island, he led the league in runs scored once, doubles five times, home runs once, RBIs three times, batting average three times (with a high of .426 in 1901), OBP twice, and slugging average four times. As powerful as he was with a bat in his hands, he was just as grace-

ful wearing a glove. He led the league in fielding average six times, putouts five times, assists three times, and double plays six times. Lajoie is number eighteen all-time in career batting (.338), number five in doubles (657), number twelve in base hits (3,242), number nineteen in RBIs (1,599), number ten in total chances per game (6.00), number five in career putouts (5,496), number six in putouts per game (2.71), and number seven in career assists (6,262). Lajoie could do it all.

- Edward "Eddie" Collins, a 25-year major leaguer with a career .333 batting average, hit over .300 seventeen times, with a high of .369 in 1920. The 175-pound Collins was strictly a singles hitter, but he hit enough of those to score an average of 101 runs a year. And he was fast enough to lead the league in steals four times, on his way to a career total of 741 stolen bases, number eight all-time. On defense, the slick-fielding infielder, who was known as "Cocky" because of the confidence he had in his ability, had few peers. He led the league in fielding average nine times, assists three times, and double plays four times. His 7,630 career assists are the most in baseball history. The Columbia University graduate, who played on six American League pennant winners and four world championship teams, was one of the few Chicago White Sox players who played to win on the infamous 1919 Black Sox team that conspired to throw the World Series to the Cincinnati Reds, although he hit a miniscule .226 in the eight games. *The Ballplayers,* in reviewing the legendary infielder, noted he was a superlative fielder, adding, "He was an adroit bunter, a slashing, left-handed batting hit-and-run man, and a brilliant base runner."

- Charlie Gehringer, called "the Mechanical Man" because he made everything look so easy, was another all-around second baseman who hit for average and power, and who covered the infield like a blanket. One of Gehringer's teammates was quoted as saying, "You wind him up on opening day, turn him off at the end of the season, and in between he hits .340 to .350." He batted over .300 thirteen times in his 19-year career, and three times hit over .350. His best year may have been 1937 when he tattooed the ball at a league-leading .371 clip and paced all second basemen with a .986 fielding average. Over his long career he compiled a .320 batting average, with 110 runs scored, 36 doubles, nine triples, 11 home runs, and 89 RBIs for every 550 at-bats. He led the league in runs scored twice, base hits twice, doubles twice (with 45 doubles in 1929 and 60 doubles in 1936), triples once, and stolen bases once. He also showed the way in fielding percentage seven times, putouts three times, assists seven times, and double plays four times. The Mechanical Man is seventeenth in career runs scored (1,774) and fifteenth in career doubles (574). His fielding average of .976 was eight points higher than the league average, his 5,369 career putouts are sixth all-time, his 7,068 career assists rank second, and his 1,444 double plays are fifth. The Mechanical Man made everything look easy, on both offense and defense.

- Ryne Sandberg was probably the greatest second baseman in Chicago Cubs history. He was a dazzling defensive second baseman who could also contribute with a bat in his hand. He is the all-time leader in career fielding average with a sensational .989 average, and he is number eight in career assists with 6,363. He established the National League record for highest season fielding percentage (.994) and fewest errors in a season (5) in 1986. The eight-time Gold Glove winner led the league in fielding percentage four times, assists seven times, and double plays once. On offense he was the third major leaguer to steal 50 bases and hit 25 home runs in the same season, and he led the National League in home runs in 1990 with 40. In perhaps his greatest offensive season, in 1984, the 6'2", 180-pound right-handed hitter batted .314, with a league-leading 114 runs scored, 200 base hits, 36 doubles, a league-leading 19 triples, 19 home runs, and 32 stolen bases. And he also led the league in fielding that year with a .993 average. Over his career, he averaged 86 runs scored, 26 doubles, five triples, 18 home runs, and 70 RBIs for every 550 at-bats.

- Rod Carew was one of the greatest hitters of his era. His .328 career batting average is number thirty all-time. The smooth-swinging left-handed hitter led the American League in hitting seven times, with a high of .388 in 1977 when he flirted with the magical .400 mark for most of the summer before tailing off. That year, he led the league in batting, runs scored (128), base hits (239), triples (16), and on-base percentage (.449). In addition to his sensational 1997 batting average, he also compiled season averages of .366, .350, .364, and .359. Carew's secret was his superior bat control, his use of the entire field, and his outstanding speed that kept the third baseman honest. He hit over .300 for fifteen consecutive years, beginning when he won his first batting title at the age of 23. Carew was also recognized as one of the game's best base runners, averaging 21 stolen bases a year, and routinely taking an extra base on lackadaisical outfielders. His defense was above average, but not up to that of his world-class rivals.

- Roberto Alomar, a native of Ponce, Puerto Rico, was an outstanding all-around second baseman who batted over .300 nine times on his way to a career .300 batting average, and who led the American League in fielding percentage three times. The 6', 180-pound switch-hitter averaged 90 runs scored, 30 doubles, five triples, 13 home runs, and 29 stolen bases for every 550 at-bats. He was at his best in post-season play where he hit a cool .313 in 58 games, including .347 in two World Series, both won by his Toronto Blue Jays. In the field, he was sure-handed with quick reflexes

Frankie Frisch, "the Fordham Flash," played in eight World Series, batting .294 in fifty games.

and excellent range. His .984 career fielding average is one of the highest in major league history, and his 6,525 career assists and 1,408 career double plays are both number six all-time. The ten-time Gold Glove winner set the American League record for most consecutive errorless games at 104 and the most errorless chances with 482.
- Frankie Frisch, "the Fordham Flash," had a keen batting eye and speed to

burn. The tall, lanky infielder batted a cool .316 over a 19-year career, averaging 92 runs scored, 28 doubles, eight triples, six home runs, 44 bases on balls, 75 RBIs, and 25 stolen bases a year while striking out just 16 times. He was a proven winner who batted over .300 thirteen times with a high of .348 in 1923, and who played on eight National League pennant winners and four world championship teams. He batted .294 in fifty World Series games with the New York Giants and St. Louis Cardinals, with 10 doubles, three triples, and 10 RBIs. In the field, he led the National League in fielding average three times and putouts, assists, and double plays once each. In 1928, he set National League season records for assists with 641 and total chances accepted with 1,059. He is still number 13 in career assists with 6,026 and number eight in chances per game with 6.05.

- Craig Biggio, whose playing career concluded in 2007, was added to the list because he deserves to be recognized with the best, and his career numbers, as far as second basemen are concerned, are complete. Biggio, one of the Houston Astros' "Killer B's" along with Jeff Bagwell, was converted from a catcher to a second baseman by the Astros after four years behind the plate. He spent the next eleven years guarding the keystone sack before being sent to the outfield in 2003 to save wear and tear on his aging body, but after "resting" in the outfield for two years, he returned to second base in 2005. Biggio, an expert at "taking one for the team," was hit by pitches 283 times through 2006, leading the league in that category five times. He also rapped the ball at a .287 clip during that period, with 96 runs scored, 33 doubles, 14 homers, and 65 RBIs for every 550 at-bats. In 2007 he became the fourth second baseman in baseball history to accumulate more than 3,000 base hits. Biggio led the league in runs scored twice and doubles three times, and he led the pack in putouts six times, assists six times, and double plays once. His .984 career fielding average is number eight all-time.

- Louis "Lou" Whitaker, along with shortstop Alan Trammell, formed an outstanding double-play combination for the Detroit Tigers from 1977 to 1995, a total of nineteen years. Whitaker, a 5'11", 160-pound left-handed batter, had surprising power for a little man, averaging 16 home runs a year to go along with 27 doubles and four triples, driving in 70 runs and scoring 85. He enjoyed his best season in the major leagues in 1983, pounding the ball at a .320 clip with 40 doubles, six triples, 12 home runs, and 17 stolen bases. And his glove was as dependable as his bat. He led the American League in fielding average twice, putouts once, assists twice, and double plays once. His .984 career fielding average was three points higher than the league average, and his 4.95 range factor was 36 points higher than the league average.

- Joe "Flash" Gordon, who played in the major leagues for eleven years, from 1938 to 1950, with two years out for World War II, was a member of six American League pennant winners and four world championship teams with the New York Yankees and Cleveland Indians. He led the Yankees at bat in two Series, slugging the ball at a .400 clip in 1938 with two doubles, a homer, and six RBIs in four games before hitting .500 with a double, a triple, a homer, and five RBIs in five games in 1941. In 1942 he was voted the American League's Most Valuable Player as he led the Yankees into the World Series, batting .322 with 18 homers and 103 RBIs. He also led all second basemen in double plays with 121. Six years later he helped the Cleveland Indians win the pennant, hitting .280 with 32 home runs and 124 runs batted in. Over his career, Gordon averaged 25 doubles, 24 home runs, 88 runs scored, and 94 RBIs for every 550 at-bats.
- Robert "Bobby" Doerr was recognized as one of the greatest all-around second basemen in the history of the game, even as his career progressed. He came out of California in 1937 at the age of 19 to give the Boston Red Sox unsurpassed second base play as well as a bat loaded with dynamite. In his eleven years with Boston, Doerr led the American League in fielding average four times, assists three times, putouts four times, and double plays five times. His .980 career fielding average was nine points higher than the league average, the third-widest margin in baseball history. And at the plate, the husky right-handed hitter tattooed opposing pitchers to the tune of .288, with 85 runs scored, 30 doubles, seven triples, 17 home runs, and 97 runs batted in for every 550 at-bats. In the pennant-winning year of 1946, Doerr batted .271 with 18 homers and 116 RBIs, and followed that up by ripping the ball at a .409 clip with a homer and three RBIs in the World Series' loss to the St. Louis Cardinals. Doerr was a force to be reckoned with, both offensively and defensively.
- Bobby Grich, at 6'2", and 190 pounds, was one of the biggest second basemen in this study, but also one of the quickest. The five-time Gold Glove winner led the American League in fielding average twice, putouts four times, assists three times, and double plays three times. His .995 fielding average in 1973 set a major league record, and after that record was broken, he set another one with a brilliant .997 season in which he committed only two errors. His career fielding average of .984 is number ten all-time. Grich was not a one-dimensional player, however. He also carried a dangerous bat to the plate, averaging 26 doubles, three triples, and 18 home runs a year, with 82 runs scored and 69 RBIs. In 1979, he hit .294 with 30 home runs and 101 runs batted in. Two years later, in the strike-shortened 1981 season, he hit .304 and led the American League with 22 home runs and a .543 slugging average.
- Nellie Fox played in the major leagues for 19 years, at one point setting

the record for the most consecutive games played at second base, with 798. The diminutive, tobacco-chewing infielder led the league in fielding average six times, putouts ten times, assists six times, and double plays five times, and his quick reflexes produced an outstanding 5.43 range factor, fifty-four points higher than the league average. His 6,090 career putouts rank third all-time, his 6,373 assists are eighth, and his 1,619 double plays are second only to Bill Mazeroski. He was no slouch with the bat, either. He had outstanding bat control, averaging just 13 strikeouts a year and leading the league in fewest strikeouts eleven times. His .288 career batting average was mostly of the one-base variety, but he scored 76 runs a year, while leading the league in base hits four times. He batted over .300 six times, with a high of .317 in 1957, and he scored more than 100 runs four times.

- Bill Mazeroski has been called the greatest defensive second baseman of all-time by many baseball experts. He was certainly in the upper echelon, leading the National League in fielding average three times, putouts five times, assists nine times, and double plays eight times. He is number one all-time in career double plays with 1,706, number five in career assists with 6,685, and number seven in career putouts with 4,974. The eight-time Gold Glove winner was not much with the bat, hitting only .260 over his career, but it is with the bat that he is most remembered. His dramatic walk-off home run off Ralph Terry in the bottom of the ninth inning of Game Seven of the 1960 World Series gave the Pittsburgh Pirates their first world championship since 1925. Overall, the 5'11", 183-pound right-handed hitter tattooed Yankee pitchers to the tune of .320 with two doubles, two homers, and five RBIs in that Series.

Active Players

Unlike first base, where there were a number of future candidates for a position on the legendary all-time all-star team, there is only one other active second baseman, in addition to Craig Biggio, who could challenge the candidates for a spot on the team. Jeff Kent has had an outstanding major league career as he nears retirement, particularly on offense. His 15-year career includes a .289 batting average with 25 homers and 100 RBIs a year.

Offensive Ratings

Normalized Adjusted On-Base Percentage (NOBPA)

Baseball's best-hitting second basemen from a batting average standpoint were Rogers Hornsby, Eddie Collins, Nap Lajoie, and Rod Carew. But

Bobby Doerr was one of the game's top defensive second basemen.

when it came to on-base percentage, which also took into account bases on balls, the OBP leaders were Hornsby (.434), Collins (.424), Jackie Robinson (.409), and Charlie Gehringer (404). Lajoie, who walked only 30 times a year, and Carew, who walked 60 times, fell back into the pack. Carew, however, profited from the era adjustment that increased his OBP from .393 to

.402, joining Hornsby and Collins as the only second basemen with OBPAs over .400. Hornsby and Collins tied for the top spot in NOBPA at .422, followed by Carew, Robinson, Joe Morgan, Nap Lajoie, and Gehringer, in that order.

Normalized Slugging Average (NXSLGA)

Rogers Hornsby was head-and-shoulders above all other second basemen when it came to slugging. He was the only candidate with a slugging average above .480, his .577 slugging average giving him a healthy 97-point lead over his nearest rival, Charlie Gehringer. Even after the park factor and era adjustments were made, the Rajah retained his huge lead. His adjusted slugging average (XSLGA) of .335 gave him a 57-point advantage over Joe Gordon and a 95-point lead over the number three man, Nap Lajoie, who came in at .240. By comparison, Jackie Robinson's XSLGA was .220, as was Bobby Grich's. Gehringer's lack of home-run punch relegated him to eighth place with an XSLGA of .217. Eight players finished with XSLGAs in the .100s, and Nellie Fox was dead last with an XSLGA of .086.

Normalized Stolen Bases (NSB)

There were several second basemen who had good speed on the bases and stole more than their share of bases. The leader, not surprisingly, was Eddie Collins, who averaged 41 stolen bases a year over his 25-year career. Close behind Collins was Joe Morgan, who also averaged 41 stolen bases a year. Roberto Alomar averaged 29 stolen bases, Frankie Frisch averaged 25, and Jackie Robinson averaged 24. Conversely, both Nellie Fox and Bill Mazeroski averaged only two stolen bases a year, followed by Bobby Doerr with four, and Joe Gordon and Rogers Hornsby with nine each.

Normalized Sacrifice Hits (NSH)

All early-day players were capable of laying down a sacrifice bunt whenever called upon, and most of them had a significant number of sacrifice bunts to their credit. But over the years, with the advent of the lively ball, teams played more for the home run and the big inning, and the sacrifice bunt was almost forgotten. The leaders were players whose careers ended prior to 1965. Eddie Collins, a lifetime .333 hitter, still sacrificed an average of 28 times a year. And Rogers Hornsby, the most proficient slugger in second-base history, was credited with 15 sacrifice hits a year. Frankie Frisch was next with 14, followed by Lajoie with 13, Jackie Robinson with 12, and Nellie Fox with 10. On the flip side, Ryne Sandberg sacrificed just two times a year, Joe

Morgan laid down three bunts a year, and Joe Gordon and Bill Mazeroski had four sacrifice hits a year to their credit.

Normalized Double Plays Grounded Into (NGIDP)

Second basemen were among the faster players on the team and, as a result, they hit into few double plays. Unlike the catchers, who hit into as many as 25 double plays a year, second basemen only hit into between six and 17 double plays a year. They were led by Joe Morgan with six and Craig Biggio with seven, followed by Lou Whitaker and Ryne Sandberg with nine each and Nellie Fox with 10. Rogers Hornsby, Joe Gordon, and Frankie Frisch grounded into 17 double plays each to bring up the rear.

Final Offensive Ratings

In the final offensive ratings, Rogers Hornsby's huge lead in the on-base percentage and slugging average categories were more than enough to earn him the title of the game's greatest offensive second baseman. Joe Morgan finished in second place, nosing out Nap Lajoie thanks to his outstanding speed that gave him important point advantages in both the stolen base and the grounded into double plays categories. Joe Gordon's second-place finish in the slugging category was enough to give him fourth place in the final offensive ratings, just ahead of Jackie Robinson.

Name	NOBPA × 20	NXSLGA × 20	.05 NSB × 20	.05 NSH × 20	.05 NGIDP × 20	Total Points	Final Offensive Rating
J. Robinson	18.863	13.134	0.585	0.429	0.462	33.473	5
R. Hornsby	20.000	20.000	0.220	0.536	0.353	41.109	1
J. Morgan	18.720	13.612	1.000	0.107	1.000	34.439	2
N. Lajoie	18.341	14.328	0.537	0.464	0.462	34.132	3
E. Collins	20.000	10.388	1.000	1.000	0.462	32.850	6
C. Gehringer	18.294	12.955	0.268	0.321	0.545	32.383	7
R. Sandberg	16.303	11.761	0.561	0.071	0.667	29.363	12
R. Carew	19.052	9.791	0.512	0.286	0.462	30.103	10
R. Alomar	17.156	10.507	0.707	0.321	0.462	29.126	13
F. Frisch	16.777	9.313	0.610	0.500	0.353	27.553	15
C. Biggio	17.156	11.284	0.561	0.179	0.857	30.037	11
L. Whitaker	17.251	10.448	0.220	0.214	0.667	28.800	14
J. Gordon	16.398	16.597	0.220	0.143	0.353	33.711	4
B. Doerr	16.635	13.552	0.098	0.321	0.375	30.981	9

Name	NOBPA × 20	NXSLGA × 20	.05 NSB × 20	.05 NSH × 20	.05 NGIDP × 20	Total Points	Final Offensive Rating
B. Grich	17.820	13.134	0.195	0.321	0.462	31.932	8
N Fox	16.114	5.134	0.049	0.357	0.600	22.254	17
B. Mazeroski	13.934	7.821	0.049	0.143	0.428	33.375	16

Defensive Ratings

Most of the second basemen in this study were outstanding defensive players, as well they should have been since they were the cream of the crop at that position. They were rated on their Normalized Fielding Average Differential (NFAD) and their Normalized Range Factor Differential (NRFD).

Normalized Fielding Average Differential (NFAD)

The early guardians of the keystone sack, Nap Lajoie and Eddie Collins, led the way in the fielding average category. Lajoie enjoyed a 14-point advantage over the league average, while Collins' fielding average was 12 points higher than the league average. The other leaders included Bobby Doerr and Frankie Frisch at +9 each, and Jackie Robinson, Charlie Gehringer, and Ryne Sandberg at +8 each. Nellie Fox and Bill Mazeroski were next at +7. Even Rogers Hornsby was on the plus side at +1, but Joe Gordon (–1) and Rod Carew (–4) failed to hold their own in the competition.

Normalized Range Factor Differential (RFD)

Bill Mazeroski, who seemed to be all over the infield when he played, had the highest range factor differential in the study, a full .86 points above the league average. It is not surprising he won eight Gold Gloves with that kind of quickness. Bobby Grich gave Mazeroski a run for his money, finishing second with a differential range factor of +.76. The only second baseman with a negative range factor differential was Rogers Hornsby, whose 5.36 range factor was 0.15 points below the league average. Some of the more impressive range factor differentials included Nap Lajoie at +.69, Ryne Sandberg at +.63, and Nellie Fox at +.54.

Final Defensive Ratings

The old-timer still showed the way in the overall defensive ratings. Nap Lajoie, whose career ended in 1916, finished first in NFAD and third in NRFD, giving him a total of 36.634 points, narrowly edging out Bill Mazeroski, who finished tied for eighth in NFAD and first in NRFD, for a total of 32.222 points. Ryne Sandberg (28.779 points), Bobby Grich (28.020 points), and Nellie Fox (27.387 points) fought a spirited battle for third, fourth, and fifth place.

Name	NFAD × 20	NRFD × 20	Total Points	Final Defensive Rating
J. Robinson	13.333	7.723	21.056	9
R. Hornsby	5.556	0.000	5.556	17
J. Morgan	8.889	9.703	18.592	12
N. Lajoie	20.000	16.634	36.634	1
E. Collins	17.778	7.723	25.501	8
C. Gehringer	13.333	6.931	20.264	10
R. Sandberg	13.333	15.446	28.779	3
R. Carew	0.000	9.505	9.505	16
R. Alomar	7.778	9.505	17.283	14
F. Frisch	14.444	11.089	25.533	7
C. Biggio	7.778	12.475	20.253	11
L. Whitaker	7.778	10.099	17.877	13
J. Gordon	3.333	6.931	10.264	15
B. Doerr	14.444	11.881	26.325	6
B. Grich	10.000	18.020	28.020	4
N. Fox	12.222	15.165	27.387	5
B. Mazeroski	12.222	20.000	32.222	2

Final All-Around Ratings

The final all-around ratings were determined by giving the offense a two-to-one weight advantage over the defense. Once again, Lajoie came in ahead of the pack. His first-place finish in defense combined with his third-place finish in offense to give him the title of baseball's all-time greatest second baseman. Bobby Grich, one of the modern-day fielding magicians, provided enough offense with his strong showings in both the on-base competition (NOBPA), where he finished eighth, and the slugging competition (NXSLGA), where he finished tied for sixth, to give him enough points when combined with his fourth-place finish in defense to guarantee him a second-place finish in the all-around competition. Eddie Collins, who finished sixth in offense and eighth in defense, accumulated enough points to nail down third place, while Bobby Doerr, another all-around all-star, combined his ninth-place finish in offense with a sixth-place finish in defense to give him fourth place overall. Bill Mazeroski's poor showing in the offensive areas, a sixteenth-place finish against seventeen rivals, cost him dearly in the overall ratings, but his second-place finish in the defensive categories allowed him to finish 13th overall.

Name	Offense Divided by 43 × 2	Defense Divided by 40 × 1	Total Points	Final All-Around Ratings	HOF
J. Robinson	1.557	0.526	2.083	6	*
R. Hornsby	1.912	0.139	2.051	8	*
J. Morgan	1.602	0.465	2.067	7	*
N. Lajoie	1.588	0.916	2.504	1	*
E. Collins	1.528	0.638	2.166	3	*
C. Gehringer	1.506	0.507	2.013	9	*
R. Sandberg	1.366	0.719	2.085	5	*
R. Carew	1.400	0.238	1.638	17	*
R. Alomar	1.355	0.432	1.787	14	
F. Frisch	1.282	0.638	1.920	10	*
C. Biggio	1.397	0.506	1.903	11	
L. Whitaker	1.340	0.447	1.787	14	
J. Gordon	1.568	0.257	1.825	12	
B. Doerr	1.441	0.658	2.099	4	*
B. Grich	1.485	0.701	2.186	2	
N. Fox	1.035	0.685	1.720	16	*
B. Mazeroski	1.041	0.806	1.847	13	*

Jeff Kent has a slight chance to crack the top ten all-around when he retires, although he is presently on the bubble. His rating through 2006 is estimated to be number three on offense, number 14 on defense, and number 10 all-around. He is hampered on defense by a negative fielding average differential, and like the other modern era players, he has a significant negative era adjustment for slugging average.

CHAPTER 8

Baseball's Greatest Shortstops

Fifteen players competed for the title of major league baseball's greatest all-time, all-around shortstop.

- Cal Ripken was one of the game's most amazing players. He became baseball's "Iron Man" on September 6, 1995, when he broke Lou Gehrig's record of playing in 2,130 consecutive games. He added another 502 games to that record before he took himself out of the lineup on September 20, 1998, setting a major league mark that may never be broken — 2,632 consecutive games played. But Ripken was more than somebody who played every day. He was also one of baseball's greatest shortstops, both offensively and defensively. He was a .276 hitter who averaged 32 doubles, 21 home runs, and 81 RBIs for every 550 at-bats. He leads all shortstops in at-bats (11,551), is second to Ernie Banks in home runs (431), second to Honus Wagner in base hits (3,184) and RBIs (1695), and third to Luis Aparicio and Ozzie Smith in games played at shortstop (2,302). On defense, the 6' 4", 225-pound Ripken led the league in fielding average five times, putouts six times, assists seven times, and double plays eight times. His .979 career fielding average is the fifth-highest fielding average in the history of the game. He is number seven in assists (6,977) and number two in double plays (1,565). According to his peers, he was unmatched in positioning himself in the field according to the game strategy, the score, the pitch count, as well as who the pitcher and batter were. He always seemed to be in the right place at the right time.
- Honus Wagner has been called the greatest shortstop that ever lived by most baseball experts and with good reason. "The Flying Dutchman," as he was called, was one of baseball's first superstars. He was a big, rugged right-handed batter who dominated the shortstop game for

more than a dozen years, leading the league in batting average eight times, doubles seven times, triples three times, RBIs five times, slugging average six times, stolen bases five times, fielding average four times, and double plays four times. The husky 5'10", 200-pound shortstop leads all his rivals in career batting average (.328), base hits (3,420), doubles (643), triples (252), RBIs (1,733), and stolen bases (722). Wagner played for the Louisville Colonels for three years and the Pittsburgh Pirates for seventeen years before retiring in 1917. The modest, good-natured Flying Dutchman had long arms and big hands and, although he looked clumsy, he always made the play. Wagner scooped balls out of the ground, dirt and all, like his Negro league counterpart, John Henry Lloyd, before unleashing his throw to first base. His kind may never be seen again.

- Ozzie Smith dazzled baseball fans with his defensive acrobatics for 19 years as a member of the San Diego Padres and St. Louis Cardinals. He thrilled crowds by racing out to his position at the start of an inning and doing a back flip as he reached shortstop. The slick-fielding Smith led the National League in fielding average eight times, putouts twice, assists eight times, and double plays five times. He is tied with Lou Boudreau and Luis Aparicio for the most times leading in fielding average, and is the leader in the most times leading in assists. He is number six all-time in career fielding average (.978), number one in assists (8,375), number eight in putouts (4,249), and number one in double plays (1,590). Ozzie Smith was not much of an offensive threat but he is best remembered for something he did with the bat. In the fifth game of the 1985 National League Championship Series against the Los Angeles Dodgers, with the series tied at two games apiece and Game Five tied 2–2, Smith smashed a walk-off home run off Tom Niedenfuer in the bottom of the ninth inning, his first home run hit while batting left-handed in more than 4,000 at-bats.

- Pee Wee Reese was the heart and soul of the legendary "Boys of Summer" that represented Brooklyn in the late 1940s and 1950s. The Little Colonel led his Dodger compatriots to seven National League pennants in 16 years, and he was a key part of Brooklyn's first and only world championship team in 1955. Reese, like many of his all-star rivals, contributed to his team's success, both with his bat and his glove. He was a career .269 hitter who averaged 91 runs scored, 23 doubles, five triples, nine home runs, 83 bases on balls, 60 RBIs, and 16 stolen bases a year. His .359 OBPA is eighth best of the 15 shortstops in this study. Reese led the league with 132 runs scored and a .977 fielding average in 1949, with 104 base on balls in 1947, and 30 stolen bases in 1952. He also led the league in putouts and assists once each and double plays twice. Reese is

number ten all-time in career putouts (4,040), number twenty-two in assists (5,891), and number ten in double plays (1,246).
- Phil "Scooter" Rizzuto, a contemporary of Reese and a frequent World Series rival of the Little Colonel, was the leader of the great New York Yankee teams of the 1940s and 1950s. During Rizzuto's memorable 13-year career, New York won ten American League pennants and an unprecedented eight world championships, including five in a row between 1949 and 1953. Rizzuto was a pesky hitter who compiled a .273 career batting average with 83 runs scored, 62 bases on balls, 14 stolen bases, and 53 RBIs for every 550 at-bats. He led the league in fielding average twice, putouts twice, assists once, and double plays three times. His best year was 1950 when he ripped the ball at a .322 clip with 125 runs scored, 200 base hits, 36 doubles, 66 RBIs, 92 walks, and a league-leading .982 fielding average.
- Arky Vaughan played major league baseball for 14 years, from 1932 to 1948, with three years out for personal reasons between 1944 and 1946. Vaughan was an outstanding offensive player and a decent defensive player. He had a .318 career batting average, the second-highest career batting average of the fifteen shortstops in this study. He batted over .300 twelve times during his 14-year career, including his first ten years in the major leagues. He is also number one in career on-base percentage (.406) of the fifteen candidates, number two in career triples (128), and number seven in career slugging average (.453). Vaughan paced the National League in batting with a stratospheric .385 in 1935. He also led the league in runs scored, triples, and bases on balls three times each, in putouts and assists three times, and in double plays once. Vaughan played most of his career in spacious Forbes Field, limiting his home run totals to eight a year, but he made the most of the huge outfield by averaging 30 doubles and 11 triples for every 550 at-bats. Sadly, the forty-year-old Vaughan drowned in a boating accident in 1952, just four years after his retirement from the game.
- Robin Yount was one of the greatest players ever to represent the Milwaukee Brewers, the only team he played for during his notable 20-year career. Yount, who joined the Brewers as an 18-year-old shortstop in 1974, held down the key infield position for the Brewers for eleven years before moving to the outfield. During his tenure at shortstop, he led the league in fielding average, putouts, assists, and double plays once each. His fielding percentage was at the league average, but he had outstanding range, his 4.99 range factor being .83 points above the league average, a range factor differential exceeded only by Ozzie Smith. Yount batted over .300 six times, with a high of .331 in 1982. That year, he led the American League in base hits (210), doubles (46) and slugging average (.578).

Ernie Banks was the first shortstop in history to hit more than 500 career home runs.

He also scored 129 runs, hit 12 triples, 29 homers, and drove in 114 runs as the Brewers captured the American League pennant. The 6', 170-pound right-handed batter hit a resounding .414 in the World Series, with three doubles, a home run, and six RBIs as the Brewers dropped a tough seven-game Series to the St. Louis Cardinals.
- Ernie Banks, the greatest shortstop in Chicago Cubs history, was one of the first Negro league players to enter the major leagues, joining the Cubs

in 1953 after two years with the Kansas City Monarchs of the Negro American League. Banks, who quickly became one of the top sluggers in the big leagues, was a lithe 6'1", 180-pound bundle of energy. As a 23-year-old rookie in 1954, the man who would earn the sobriquet of "Mr. Cub" smashed 19 home runs and drove in 79 runs, a major accomplishment for the youngster. The next year he exploded, batting .295, hammering 44 homers, driving in 117 teammates, and leading the National League with a .972 fielding percentage. During the six-year period from 1955 to 1960, Banks slugged 248 home runs, more than any other major leaguer, including Mickey Mantle (236) and Willie Mays (214). From there his career blossomed into a 19-year love affair with the game he cherished. He was famous for walking into the Cubs' locker room with a big smile on his face and joyfully pleading, "Let's play two today." Ernie Banks retired in 1971 with 512 career home runs, the most home runs ever hit by a shortstop. He also hit 407 doubles and 90 triples for a total of 1,009 extra base hits, number 24 all-time. In the field, he excelled as well, leading the league in fielding percentage three times, assists twice, and putouts and double plays once each.

- Joe Cronin entered the major leagues in 1926 at the age of 19, and stayed for twenty years, starring at shortstop both at the plate and in the field. He fashioned a fancy .301 career batting average over that period, with 37 doubles, nine triples, 12 home runs, and 103 RBIs for every 550 at-bats. He led the American League in doubles twice, with 45 in 1933 and with 51 in 1938. He also led the league in triples in 1932 with 18. The stocky six-footer was no slouch in the field either, leading the league in fielding percentage twice, and putouts, assists, and double plays three times each. He batted over .300 ten times, with a high of .346 in 1930, the notorious "year of the hitter." Cronin was famous, not only for his play on the field, but also for his managerial career that began in 1933 when the 26-year-old shortstop assumed the reins of the Washington Senators and immediately led them to the American League pennant. Cronin's managerial career lasted 15 years, during which time his teams won a total of 1,236 games against 1,055 losses for an excellent .540 winning percentage.

- Luke Appling, "Old Aches and Pains" as he was called for his constant complaints about his physical condition, was a career .310 hitter, the fourth-highest career batting average of the fifteen shortstops in this study. The 5'10", 183-pound right-handed hitter was primarily a singles hitter, with just 27 doubles, six triples, and three home runs for every 550 at-bats. He had a keen batting eye that rewarded him with 81 bases on balls against 33 strikeouts, giving him a .399 on-base percentage, second only to Arky Vaughan. His .398 slugging percentage, however, was no better than eleventh out of fifteen. Appling also suffered on defense.

His .948 career fielding average was actually four points below the league average, and his range factor was in the middle of the pack. He did excel in two defensive categories. He led the league in assists seven times and in double plays three times. He is number seven all-time in career putouts with 4,398, number five in assists with 7,218, and number four in double plays with 1,424.

- Lou Boudreau was recognized as the best shortstop in the American League almost from day one of his career. He joined the Cleveland Indians in 1939 as a 22-year-old shortstop, and one year later he captured the hearts of the Cleveland fans with his all-around play. He led the league in fielding and double plays, and also wielded a potent bat, hitting .295, with 46 doubles, 10 triples, nine home runs, and 105 RBIs. Two years later, the precocious infielder was named player-manager of the Cleveland team, becoming the youngest manager in major league history. He continued his outstanding all-around play throughout the 1940s, leading the American League in fielding percentage eight times in nine years, and hitting the ball with authority, even winning the batting championship in 1944 with a .327 average. In 1948, Boudreau put it all together, guiding the Indians to the world championship with a masterful display of managing, hitting, and fielding. First he led his team to the American League pennant by defeating the Boston Red Sox, 8–3, in a one-game playoff after the two teams had finished the season in a tie for first place. The boy manager not only made all the right strategic moves, he also put two home runs over Fenway Park's Green Monster and added a single to pace his team at the plate. Then, in the World Series against the Boston Braves, won by Cleveland four games to two, he hit .273 with four doubles and three RBIs. And Boudreau received one final honor to cap off his dream season. He won the American League's Most Valuable Player award after ripping the ball at a .355 clip during the regular season, with 18 home runs and 106 RBIs, in addition to leading the league in fielding average and double plays. During his career, Lou Boudreau compiled a career .973 fielding average, a full 19 points above the league average, by far the widest differential of any shortstop in this study.

- Luis Aparicio was a dazzling all-around shortstop for the Chicago White Sox from 1956 to 1962, and again from 1968 to 1970. During his 18-year career, the 5'9", 160-pound rabbit covered acres of ground, both offensively and defensively, leading the American League in stolen bases his first nine years in the league and setting the pace in fielding average eight consecutive years, from 1959 to 1966. Aparicio, as a member of the famous "Go-Go" Chicago White Sox that ran wild on the bases during the late 1950s by stealing more than 100 bases a year from 1957 through 1961 with a high of 113 stolen bases in 1959, led the way with 56 stolen bases in the pennant year of 1959. The Sox's running game was stifled by the Los Angeles Dodgers in the World Series, as John Roseboro held them to just two stolen bases in six games, one of them by Aparicio, who hit .308 in a losing cause. Little Luis, in addition to leading the league in fielding average eight times, also led the league in putouts four times, assists seven times, and double plays twice. His twenty-one defensive awards are third highest of the fifteen shortstops, exceeded only by Cal Ripken and Ozzie Smith. The native of Maracaibo, Venezuela, is number one all-time in career games played at shortstop with 2,581, number six in career putouts with 4,548, number two in assists with 8,016, and number three in double plays with 1,553.

Lou Boudreau (right), shown here with Bucky Harris led the American League in fielding average a record eight times (courtesy Jay Sanford).

- Alan Trammell, one-half of the great double-play combination of Trammell and Whitaker that guarded the middle infield in Detroit for nineteen years, was a solid all-around shortstop who compiled a career fielding average of .977, ten points higher than the league average, and who stroked the ball at a .285 clip over his twenty-year career, with 2,365 base hits. Trammell averaged 27 doubles, four triples, and 12 home runs for every 550 at-bats, with 82 runs scored and 67 runs batted in. He batted over .300 seven times, with a high of .343 in 1987. That year he also slammed 34 doubles and 28 homers, and drove in 105 runners. He even stole 21 bases. In the field, Trammell was a sensational glove man during his career, as shown by his outstanding fielding average, the tenth-highest fielding average in baseball history. He is also number six in career double plays with 1,307. His Achilles heel was a lack of speed that limited his range considerably. He was actually last in range factor in the study, two points below the league average, the only shortstop with a negative range factor.

- Barry Larkin held down the shortstop position on the Cincinnati Reds for nineteen years, retiring in 2004 with a .295 career batting average, 379 stolen bases, and 2,340 base hits, including 715 for extra bases. The Cincinnati native, who averaged 14 home runs a year, slugged 33 round-trippers in 1996 and 20 in 1991. He batted over .300 nine times, with a high of .342 in 1989. In 1995, he batted .319 and stole 51 bases. Larkin played on two National League pennant winners and one world championship team. The 6', 196-pound right-handed hitter batted .353 in the 1990 World Series when the Reds swept the mighty Oakland A's of Canseco and McGwire four straight, outscoring them 22–8. Larkin was more than an offensive force; he was also one of the top defensive shortstops of his era, leading the league in putouts twice and assists and double plays once. His career fielding average of .974 was seven points higher than the league average, and his 4.34 range factor was 34 points above the league average.
- Joe Sewell was a 14-year major leaguer who compiled a .312 batting average and a .391 on-base percentage, the third-highest batting average and OBP of the fifteen shortstops in this study. The tiny, 5'6", 155-pound left-handed hitter was a bat-control specialist who struck out just nine times for every 550 at-bats while coaxing 65 bases on balls out of frustrated pitchers. He was not a power hitter, but he punched the ball to the gaps in the outfield well enough to average 34 doubles a year with 81 RBIs. Twice he drove in over 100 runs in a season. In 1923, he batted .353 with 41 doubles, 10 triples, and 109 RBIs. The following year, he hit .316 with a league-leading 45 doubles and 106 RBIs. And in 1925, he batted .336 with 37 doubles and 98 RBIs. Sewell was just as good on defense as he was on offense. He led the league in fielding average three times, putouts four times, assists five times, and double plays once. His .951 career fielding average was seven points above the league average, and his 5.37 range factor was fifty-three points above the league average, the fourth-highest RF differential in the study.

Active players

There are several active players who may replace some of the players on this list once their careers end. They include Alex "A-Rod" Rodriguez, Derek Jeter, Nomar Garciaparra, Miguel Tejada, and Omar Vizquel. Most of the active players, with the exception of Omar Vizquel, are basically offensive players. Vizquel is a defensive wizard in the mold of Ozzie Smith. A-Rod is arguably the greatest all-around player in the game today and, at the age of 33, the sky is still the limit for the slugging infielder. The 6'3", 190-pound right-handed hitter, now in his fifth year as a third baseman for the New York Yankees, was a shortstop during his first ten years in the major leagues. He is baseball's biggest offensive threat at the present time, averaging 39 homers and 112 RBIs a year to go along with a .306 batting average. He smashed his 500th career home run in 2007 and may well crack the 800 home run barrier if his health holds up. He is also solid on defense. Jeter is primarily an offensive player with a career .317 batting average, 102 runs scored, 14 home runs, and 69 RBIs for every 550 at-bats. Garciaparra is essentially a mirror image of Jeter, but he has been injury-prone over the past four years, and that has had an unfavorable effect on his statistics. Through 2007, Garciaparra had a career batting average of .315, with 93 runs scored, 23 home runs, and 93 RBIs. Tejada, a 31-year-old run-producer, has a .287 batting average, with 86 runs scored, 23 home runs, and 94 RBIs a season. Vizquel, who is nearing the end of a brilliant career, has a .274 batting average over 18 years, with 78 runs scored, four home runs, and 50 RBIs a year. In the field, the forty-one-year-old Venezuelan is a magician, still making defensive plays that tax the imagination. He has led the league in fielding average six times, putouts once, and double plays once. Only A-Rod among the other active players has led the league in fielding average, and he did it once. Vizquel's .984 career fielding average is the highest in baseball history.

Offensive Ratings

Normalized Adjusted On Base Percentage (NOBPA)

Arky Vaughan was the only shortstop with an on-base percentage greater than .400, at .406. Luke Appling had an OBP of .399, Joe Sewell and Honus Wagner were at .391, and Joe Cronin checked in with an even .390. When the statistics were adjusted for the era in which the player was active, Vaughan still retained his number one ranking with an OBPA of .399, edging Honus Wagner by .007. Appling finished with an OBPA of .387, the only other player with an OBPA above .373.

Normalized Adjusted Slugging Average (NXSLGA)

There were some notable sluggers patrolling the short field over the decades, led by Ernie Banks, whose 512 career home runs, an average of 30 home runs for every 550 at-bats, propelled him to a career slugging average of .500. Joe Cronin was next in line, but his .468 SLG left him far in arrears.

Honus Wagner had a slugging average of .466, and Arky Vaughan was at .453. These statistics were first adjusted for the player's home park peculiarities and then adjusted for the era in which the player was active. Banks fared well in the final adjusted slugging percentages (XSLGA) since his era adjustment was very small and his home run factor was a manageable 1.22. Honus Wagner, whose career was played primarily in the dead ball era, edged past Joe Cronin into second place thanks to a huge positive era adjustment of 68 points. Joe Cronin, who took a 14-point hit on the era adjustment, still managed to come in third, tying with Cal Ripken. Arky Vaughan had the only other XSLGA over .200, finishing at .214.

Normalized Stolen Bases (NSB)

There have been some rabbits holding down the shortstop job over the years, most notably Honus Wagner, who averaged 38 stolen bases a year; Ozzie Smith, who averaged 34 stolen bases a year; Luis Aparicio, who averaged 27 stolen bases a year; Barry Larkin, who averaged 26 stolen bases a year; and Alan Trammell, who averaged 22 stolen bases a year.

Normalized Sacrifice Hits (NSH)

The players who were active in the major leagues fifty or more years ago had a distinct advantage over the modern-day players when it came to evaluating them for their ability to lay down a sacrifice bunt. Bunting has almost become a lost art in the major leagues today, which is sad since many games are being lost because managers, most of whom disdain the sacrifice bunt, sit back and wait for the three-run homer that usually never comes. In the old days, even the big-name sluggers were well trained in the art of bunting. For example, in the 1955 World Series between the Brooklyn Dodgers and the New York Yankees, the big Dodger sluggers like Gil Hodges, Duke Snider, and Roy Campanella moved runners into scoring position with well-placed bunts. Joe Sewell, whose career spanned the years from 1920 to 1933, was one of the game's most skillful batsmen. He was a .312 career hitter who struck out just nine times and sacrificed 21 times for every 550 at-bats. Phil Rizzuto had 18 sacrifice bunts a year to his credit, and Lou Boudreau had 15 sacrifice bunts a year. Ozzie Smith laid down 13 sacrifice bunts a year, the only player in the past fifty years with more than nine.

Normalized Grounded Into Double Plays (NGIDP)

Shortstops, in general, had above-average speed, a characteristic that was essential for properly covering their position. As a result, they hit into fewer double plays than players at most other positions. Their GIDP totals ranged from six to 18, with only Arky Vaughan grounding into fewer than ten double plays a year. Honus Wagner and Ernie Banks were about average in that category, while Joe Cronin was one of the slower people at the position.

Final Offensive Ratings

The players who led the way in NOBPA and NXSLGA, from number one to number four, retained their positions in the final offensive ratings, but there was a slight adjustment in positions five through seven. Cal Ripken, who was in fifth place after the NOBPA and NXSLGA competitions, dropped to seventh place in the final offensive ratings as a result of his poor showings in the stolen base and sacrifice hit categories. Ripken had just two stolen bases and one sacrifice hit for every 550 at-bats, permitting both Lou Boudreau and Barry Larkin to pass him.

	NOBPA × 20	NXSLGA × 20	.05NSB × 20	.05NSH × 20	.05NGIDP × 20	Total Points	Final Offensive Rating
Cal Ripken	16.842	14.719	0.053	0.048	0.333	31.995	7
Honus Wagner	19.649	18.416	1.000	0.571	0.500	40.136	1
Ozzie Smith	16.892	5.809	0.895	0.619	0.600	24.815	15
Pee Wee Reese	17.995	9.901	0.421	0.524	0.500	29.341	10
Phil Rizzuto	17.193	7.789	0.368	0.857	0.600	26.807	13
Arky Vaughan	20.000	14.125	0.263	0.476	1.000	35.864	3
Robin Yount	17.293	12.475	0.368	0.238	0.545	30.919	8
Ernie Banks	16.692	20.000	0.079	0.143	0.462	37.376	2
Joe Cronin	18.697	14.719	0.158	0.571	0.375	34.520	4
Luke Appling	19.398	8.449	0.289	0.238	0.429	28.803	11
Lou Boudreau	18.697	12.607	0.132	0.714	0.429	32.579	5
Luis Aparicio	16.241	7.657	0.711	0.429	0.600	25.638	14
Alan Trammell	17.644	11.023	0.579	0.381	0.600	30.227	9
Barry Larkin	18.346	12.277	0.684	0.190	0.500	31.997	6
Joe Sewell	18.647	8.449	0.158	1.000	0.500	28.754	12

Defensive Ratings

Normalized Fielding Average Differential (NFAD)

Most of the shortstops in the study were outstanding defensive players who covered acres of ground and possessed powerful throwing arms and dependable gloves. Lou Boudreau, the defensive genius of the great Cleveland Indian teams of the late 1940s, compiled a brilliant .973 career fielding average, nineteen points above the league average. And he accomplished that in an era when a shortstop's glove was half the size of today's gloves and had a minimum of webbing between the thumb and forefinger. Honus Wagner, the clumsy-looking shortstop of the Pittsburgh Pirates during the first two decades of the twentieth century, had huge hands and long arms, and he dug balls out of the dirt as if he were wearing a shovel on his arms. Still, his .940 fielding average was a full thirteen points above the league average, the second-best fielding average differential of any of the top fifteen shortstops. Ozzie Smith, the "Wizard of Oz," had a twelve-point differential, while Alan Trammell and Cal Ripken were close behind with ten-point differentials. Ripken's .979 career fielding average and Smith's .978 average are numbers five and six all-time, respectively. Alan Trammell's .977 career fielding average was the tenth-best all-time. Luke Appling and Robin Yount were the only shortstops who did not have a fielding average above the league average. Yount finished exactly at the league average, while Appling's .948 career fielding average was four points below the league average.

Normalized Range Factor Differential (NRFD)

Most of the shortstops had outstanding range factors compared to the league average. The exception was Alan Trammell, whose range factor was two points below average. Ozzie Smith, not surprisingly, covered more ground than God, finishing 93 points above the league average with a range factor of 5.03. Robin Yount's 4.99 RF gave him an 83-point advantage, the only other shortstop with a range factor differential of more than plus 55. Ripken at plus 55 and Joe Sewell and Luis Aparicio at plus 53 points each followed Ripken and Yount. Honus Wagner, who covered more ground than any other shortstop of his time, had a 5.63 range factor, 45 points above the league average.

Final Defensive Ratings

Ozzie Smith, who finished third in Normalized Fielding Average Differential and first in Normalized Range Factor Differential, was crowned king of the defensive shortstops with a convincing lead over Lou Boudreau, who finished first in NFAD, but could do no better than ninth in NRFD. Honus Wagner finished third based on his second-place finish in NFAD and sixth-place finish in NRFD. Cal Ripken, in fourth place, finished in a tie for fourth place in NFAD and in third place in NRFD. Robin Yount, who finished second in NRFD, came in fifth overall as a result of his poor showing in the fielding average category.

	NFAD × 20	NRFD × 20	Total Points	Final Defensive Ratings
Cal Ripken	12.174	12.000	24.174	4
Honus Wagner	14.783	9.895	24.678	3
Ozzie Smith	13.913	20.000	33.913	1
Pee Wee Reese	6.957	5.895	12.852	12
Phil Rizzuto	11.304	4.000	15.304	10
Arky Vaughan	5.217	5.263	10.480	14
Robin Yount	3.478	17.895	21.373	6
Ernie Banks	9.565	9.684	19.249	8
Joe Cronin	7.826	7.158	14.984	11
Luke Appling	0.000	8.211	8.211	15
Lou Boudreau	20.000	7.579	27.579	2
Luis Aparicio	11.304	11.579	22.883	5
Alan Trammell	12.174	0.000	12.174	13
Barry Larkin	9.565	6.947	16.512	9
Joe Sewell	9.565	11.579	21.144	7

Final All-Around Ratings

The Final All-Around Ratings for shortstops were pretty much as expected, although it was a close race for the first five positions, with a spread of only 15 percent separating the first-place finisher from the fifth-place finisher. Honus Wagner, who finished first in offense and third in defense, won the title of baseball's greatest all-around shortstop. He was followed by Lou Boudreau, who finished fifth in offense and second in defense, and Ozzie Smith, who finished first in defense, but whose fifteenth-place finish in offense doomed his chances for the title. Ernie Banks, who finished second in offense and eighth in defense, came in fourth overall, and Cal Ripken, based on his sixth-place finish in offense and fourth-place finish in defense, won the number five spot.

	Offense Divided by 43	Defense Divided by 40	Total Points	Final All-Around Ratings	HOF
Cal Ripken	0.744	0.604	1.348	5	*
Honus Wagner	0.933	0.617	1.550	1	*
Ozzie Smith	0.577	0.848	1.425	3	*
Pee Wee Reese	0.682	0.321	1.003	14	*

	Offense Divided by 43	Defense Divided by 40	Total Points	Final All-Around Ratings	HOF
Phil Rizzuto	0.623	0.383	1.006	13	*
Arky Vaughan	0.834	0.262	1.096	11	*
Robin Yount	0.719	0.534	1.253	6	*
Ernie Banks	0.869	0.481	1.350	4	*
Joe Cronin	0.803	0.375	1.178	8	*
Luke Appling	0.670	0.205	0.875	15	*
Lou Boudreau	0.758	0.689	1.447	2	*
Luis Aparicio	0.596	0.572	1.168	9	*
Alan Trammell	0.703	0.304	1.007	12	
Barry Larkin	0.744	0.413	1.157	10	
Joe Sewell	0.669	0.529	1.198	7	*

The estimated rankings of the active players as of 2007 are shown below.

	Estimated Offensive Rating	Estimated Defensive Rating	Final Estimated All-Around Rating
Alex Rodriguez	2	12	6
Derek Jeter	10	17	17
Miguel Tejada	6	14	13
Nomar Garciaparra	3	15	15
Omar Vizquel	16	8	12

Jeter and Tejada are in the declining stages of their careers, and probably will drop below their present estimated ratings. Jeter's defensive problems revolve around his poor range factor differential that, at minus six, is the lowest range factor differential of any of the candidates, active or retired. Garciaparra has been playing first base since 2006, and may be a close call for the fifteenth position. Omar Vizquel's career is about over, so he may not see much more of a decline, making him a good prospect to finish in the top fifteen. A-Rod, who is about number six all-around, has been playing third base since 2004, so his high rating at shortstop may hold up. He could fall below number 12 on defense, but he shows no sign of slowing down on offense, which should help him retain his number six all-around rating.

CHAPTER 9

Baseball's Greatest Third Basemen

Fifteen players competed for the title of baseball's greatest all-time, all-around third baseman.

- Michael Jack Schmidt, a husky 6'2", 200-pound right-handed hitter, began playing minor league baseball in 1971 at the age of twenty-one. Within two years, the free-swinging youngster became a fixture at third base for the Philadelphia Phillies, a position he held for the next eighteen years. Initially, Schmidt had no idea of the strike zone, and although he led the National League in home runs with 38 in 1975, he also went down swinging 180 times. Over the years he became more disciplined at the plate, but he still averaged 124 strikeouts for every 550 at-bats. He compensated for that flaw by drawing 99 bases on balls, giving him a superior .376 on-base percentage. And when he did make contact with the ball, he made the pitcher pay, averaging 36 home runs and 105 RBIs a year. During his career, Schmidt led the league in home runs eight times, RBIs three times, bases on balls four times, on-base percentage three times, and slugging average five times.

    Schmidt was also one of the top defensive third basemen of his generation. He was a ten-time Gold Glove winner who led the league in assists seven times and in double plays six times. He was noted for his dependable glove and for his outstanding range in the field, reaching balls that the average third baseman would not even come close to. He won the first of his three Most Valuable Player awards in 1980, and he celebrated by pacing the Phillies to the world championship, ripping the ball at a .381 clip with two homers and seven RBIs in Philadelphia's six-game victory over the Kansas City Royals.

- Eddie Mathews was the big gun in the Milwaukee Braves' lineup during the 1950s, helping the Braves to two National League pennants and one world championship, a coveted World Series win over the New York Yankees in 1957. The stocky Texan averaged 33 homers and 94 RBIs over a 17-year career, giving him a total of 512 career homers, trailing only Mike Schmidt's 548 career homers for third basemen. Mathews led the National League in home runs twice, with 47 homers in 1953 and 46 homers in 1959. He had a fine .376 career on-base percentage and an excellent .509 slugging average, again second to Schmidt's .527 slugging average. His prowess with the bat was reported by *The Ballplayers*. "Mathews had a remarkable physique, and his powerful stroke and bat speed were marveled at by opponents, 'He swings the bat faster than anyone I ever saw,' commented Carl Erskine. 'You think you've got a called strike past him and he hits it out of the catcher's glove.' Even Ty Cobb, not known for his appreciation of the modern ballplayer, was impressed. 'I've only known three or four perfect swings in my time. This lad has one of them.'" But Mathews was more than a great slugger. He was a standout on defense as well, noted for his powerful throwing arm, his errorless play in the field, and his above-average range. He led the league in fielding average once, putouts twice, assists three times, and double plays once.

Eddie Mathews was a hard-hitting third baseman who also excelled with the glove (courtesy Jay Sanford).

- Al Rosen, a contemporary of Eddie Mathews, played major league baseball for only seven full years. His career totals would pale next to most of the other third basemen in this study, but he did not have to take a back seat to anyone when it came to playing the game. He was 26 years old when he played his first full season in Cleveland, and he was 32 when he retired. The tough former amateur boxer who had his nose broken eleven times led the American League in home runs as a rookie in 1950 with 37, and in 1953 with 43. He also led the league in RBIs twice and in slugging average once. Over his short career he averaged 28 home runs and 106 RBIs for every 550 at-bats, while striking out just 57 times and drawing 87 bases on balls. He had an excellent OBP and SLG. It was his defense that did him in. He overcame his early fielding problems to become a better-than-average defensive third baseman, but certainly not in the class of Brooks Robinson or Mike Schmidt. He retired after the 1956 season as a result of nagging injuries that reduced his skills considerably, particularly in the field.

- George Brett was one of the top hitters of his generation, with a .305 career batting average, and 35 doubles, seven triples, 17 home runs, and 85 RBIs for every 550 at-bats. In 1980, he had the baseball world in a tizzy as he challenged the sacred .400 mark for most of the summer before tapering off to .390. He also led the league that year in OBP with .454 and SLG with .664. The husky left-handed hitter, who stood six feet tall and weighed 200 pounds, led the league in batting two other years, with a .333 average in 1976 and a .329 average in 1990, and he led the league in slugging average two other years as well. Brett had excellent range at third base, his plus 40 range factor differential being the fourth widest differential in this study, but his work with the glove left something to be desired. His career fielding average of .951 was two points below the league average. Some experts point out that his excellent range factor allowed him to reach balls that other players could not get to and that that skill accounted for many of his errors. That may be true, but when measured against other world-class third basemen, the mediocre fielding average hurt him in the ratings. George Brett's career offensive statistics included 1,583 runs scored, 3,154 base hits, 665 doubles (number five all-time), 137 triples, 317 home runs, and 1,595 RBIs.

- Wade Boggs burst upon the major league scene like a runaway freight train, hitting a sensational .349 as a rookie, and following that up with five batting titles in the next six years. After the 1988 season, with seven years in the major leagues under his belt, Boggs owned a stratospheric .356 lifetime batting average, the fourth-highest career batting average in major league history, .0004 behind "Shoeless Joe" Jackson. He scored more than 100 runs and stroked over 200 hits in each of his first seven years. But the 30-year-old superstar could not maintain that pace as he tailed off dramatically over the final eleven years of his career, finally retiring in 1999 with a lifetime batting average of .328, number 29 all-time. The left-handed place hitter was not a power threat, averaging 35 doubles, four triples, and five home runs a year, but his base hits combined with 85 bases on balls a year gave him a sensational .415 on-base percentage. He led the league in OBP six times, with a high of .476 in 1988. Boggs, who was not a polished third baseman when he arrived in the major leagues, worked on his defense until he became one of the better third basemen in the league. He led the league in fielding average twice, putouts three times, assists once, and double plays four times.

- Frank "Home Run" Baker became an overnight sensation and earned his nickname after hitting home runs off New York Giant aces Rube Marquard and Christy Mathewson on consecutive days to pace the Philadelphia Athletics to a World Series victory in 1911. Baker led the American League in home runs four times, doubles once, and RBIs twice. He was also adept at other phases of the offensive game, averaging 22 stolen bases and 14 sacrifice bunts a year. On defense, he was a sure-handed fielder who led the league in fielding average three times, putouts seven times, assists twice, and double plays three times. He was a member of Connie Mack's famous $100,000 infield, joining Stuffy McInnis, Eddie Collins, and Jack Barry, who helped the A's capture four American League pennants and three world championships between 1910 and 1914.
- Bob Elliott was a hard-hitting third baseman for the Pittsburgh Pirates and Boston Braves in the 1940s. He led the Braves to the 1948 National League pennant by slamming 24 doubles and 23 home runs with 100 RBIs, plus a league-leading 131 bases on balls. He continued his cannonading in a losing effort against the Cleveland Indians in the World Series, leading the Braves with a .333 batting average while poling two home runs with five RBIs in six games. Elliott, who was often referred to as "Mr. Team," enjoyed a notable 15-year career that included a .289 career batting average, a fine .375 OBP, and a .440 slugging average. On defense, Elliott was better than average but probably not in the same category as the other candidates in this study, although he did lead the

Brooks Robinson became a legend during the 1970 World Series when he dazzled the fans with one spectacular play after another at third base (courtesy Jay Sanford).

league in fielding average once, putouts twice, assists three times, and double plays twice.
- Brooks Robinson, whose defensive magic had been well known in the small Baltimore market for sixteen years, became a legend in the 1970 World Series when he continually stymied Cincinnati Red rallies with spectacular defensive plays around third base, causing Reds manager Sparky Anderson to lament, "I'm beginning to see Brooks in my sleep. If I dropped this paper plate, he'd pick it up on one hop and throw me out at first base." Robinson's defensive brilliance rewarded him with 25 league-leading performances in the four major defensive categories over the years. He led the league in fielding average an unprecedented eleven times, compared to twenty times total by the other fourteen candidates. He led in assists a record eight times, and he led in putouts and double plays three times each. But Robinson was more than a defensive player; he also contributed on offense. He was a tough out, slamming an average of 25 doubles and 14 home runs a year, while driving in 70 runs. The 6'1", 190-pound right-handed hitter had a career year in 1964, earning American League Most Valuable Player honors after hitting .317 with 35 doubles, 28 homers, and a league-leading 118 RBIs. He also led the league in games played, innings played, fielding average, putouts, assists, and double plays. Robinson played on five American League pennant-winners in Baltimore between 1965 and 1974, and on two world championship teams. He hit a resounding .348 in eighteen American League Championship Series games and .263 in 21 World Series games. In the famous 1970 Series, won by the Orioles four games to one, in addition to his fielding gems, he also scorched the ball at a .429 clip with two homers and six RBIs. By the time he retired, Robinson had accumulated defensive statistics that still dominate the third-base position. He ranks first all-time in career games played with 2,870, career fielding average with .971, career putouts with 2,697, career assists with 6,205, and career double plays with 618.
- Harold "Pie" Traynor, the guardian of the hot corner for the Pittsburgh Pirates from 1920 to 1937, was arguably the greatest third baseman of the first half of the twentieth century. He was a career .320 hitter, the second-highest average of the fifteen candidates, and he averaged 86 runs scored and 93 RBIs during his career. He batted over .300 ten times, with a high of .366 in 1930, and he drove in more than 100 runs seven times. He played on two National League pennant-winners and one world championship team, batting .293 in the two Series, with a double, two triples, a homer, and four RBIs. He led the league in fielding average once, putouts seven times, assists three times, and double plays four times during his career. He had a strong throwing arm and was one of the best

at fielding bunts and gunning down the runner. He is number five all-time in career putouts with 2,289.

- Ron Santo is the Chicago Cubs' all-time greatest third baseman and one of the best of his generation. He played in the Windy City for fifteen years, leading the league in fielding average once, putouts seven times, assists seven times, and double plays six times, a record of defensive excellence exceeded only by Brooks Robinson. His .954 fielding average was six points above the league average, and his 3.07 range factor was 49 points above the league average, the second-widest range factor differential of the fifteen candidates in this study, trailing only Mike Schmidt. Santo was a defensive stalwart, but he was also an offensive threat, batting a hard .277 over his career with 25 doubles, 23 home runs, and 90 RBIs for every 550 at-bats. His best year was 1964 when he tattooed the ball at a .313 clip with 33 doubles, a league-leading 13 triples, 30 home runs, 114 RBIs, and a league-leading .398 on-base percentage. He also led the league in putouts, assists, and double plays. He is number five all-time in career assists with 4,581 and number eight all-time in career double plays with 395.

- Paul Molitor was one of the finest hitters of his generation, a career .308 hitter who averaged 31 doubles, six triples, 12 home runs, and 90 runs scored for every 550 at-bats. He had several outstanding seasons with the bat, notably 1987 when he hit .353 with 16 home runs and led the league with 114 runs scored and 41 doubles. Four years later, he batted .325 with 32 doubles and 17 homers while leading the league with 133 runs scored, 216 base hits, and 13 triples. He was not a big RBI man during his career, but in 1993, he drove in 111 runs and scored 121 on a league-leading 211 base hits while compiling a .332 batting average. After he turned 34 years old, he became a designated hitter for the final eight years of his career. His 3,319 base hits are the most ever recorded by a third baseman, although a high percentage of them were made as a DH. Molitor, who stood six feet tall and weighed 185 pounds, was an average third baseman with a slightly below average fielding average, but he had excellent range with a plus 43 range factor differential, the third-widest differential of the fifteen third basemen in the study.

- Stan Hack was another of the fine third basemen to hold down the hot corner in Wrigley Field. He handled the position for the Chicago Cubs from 1932 to 1947, helping the Cubs win four National League pennants. He batted a sizzling .348 in the four World Series, all losing efforts, with five doubles and a triple in 69 at-bats. The 6', 170-pound left-handed batter was a contact hitter who sprayed singles and doubles all around the outfield, but averaged only four home runs a year. He retired after 16 years with a .301 career batting average and a .394 on-base percentage,

Ron Santo gave the Cubs outstanding defense and a powerful bat for fifteen years (courtesy Jay Sanford).

the second-best OBP in the study. Hack added to his team's offense by stealing 12 bases a year, and he hit into the fewest double plays, six, of any third baseman in the study. Smiling Stan was also an excellent glove man who led the league in the four major defensive categories a total of 12 times, including five times in putouts, three times in double plays, and twice each in fielding average and assists. Hack's .957 career fielding average was eleven points above the league average, the second-widest differential among the third basemen in the study, trailing only the incomparable Brooks Robinson.

- Graig Nettles led the league in fielding average once, putouts twice, assists four times, and double plays three times. He is number two all-time in career assists with 5,279, and number two in double plays with 470. Nettles was not a force to be reckoned with on offense, however, compiling a mediocre .248 career batting average over twenty-two years. His best year with the bat was 1978, when he hit .276 with 27 homers and 93 RBIs. He also led the league with 32 homers in 1976 while driving in 93 runs with a .254 batting average, and he hit 37 homers with 107 RBIs and a .255 batting average in 1977. Over the course of his career, Nettles averaged 20 doubles, two triples, 24 home runs, and 67 bases on balls for every 550 at-bats, giving him a .329 on-base percentage, fourteenth out of fifteen players, and a .421 slugging average, good for eleventh. Defense was a different story for Nettles, however. He took a back seat to no one when he had a glove on his hand. He led the league in the four major defensive categories a total of 10 times, including once in fielding average, twice in putouts, four times in assists, and three times in double plays.

- Eddie Yost was known as "the Walking Man" because of his ability to draw numerous bases on balls during a season. He averaged 121 walks a year during his 18 years in the major leagues. The 5'10", 170-pound infielder led the league in walks six times with a high of 141 walks in 1950. He compiled a career batting average of just .254, but with his walks added to his base hits, he had a .394 on-base percentage, the second-highest career OBP of the candidates, trailing only Wade Boggs. He led the league in OBP twice, in runs scored once with 115, and in doubles once with 36. Yost was also an excellent defensive third baseman who led the league in the four major defensive categories 15 times, including a major league record eight times in putouts, three times in fielding average, and twice each in assists and double plays. He is number three all-time in career putouts with 2,356.

- Sal Bando, a member of the dysfunctional Oakland Athletics teams that won three consecutive world championships from 1972 to 1974, was a dangerous power hitter whose .254 career batting average belied his skill with a bat. The 6'2", 205-pound right-handed hitter averaged 23 doubles, three triples, 19 home runs, and 81 runs batted in for every 550 at-bats during his 16-year major league career. His best year was 1969, when he hit .281 with 25 doubles, 31 home runs, 106 runs scored, 111 bases on balls, 113 RBIs, and a .400 on-base percentage. He batted just .206 in three World Series with four RBIs, but in the sixth inning of the seventh game of the 1972 World Series against the Cincinnati Reds,

Bando doubled home the tying run and then scored the eventual Series-winning run on a double by Gene Tenace. Bando's .959 career fielding average was six points higher than the league average and his 2.83 range factor was thirteen points higher than the league average. He led the league in putouts twice and double plays once.

Active players

The two active players who stand ready to assume a place on the roster of the game's greatest players are Scott Rolen and Chipper Jones. Jones, a thirteen-year major league veteran who turned 35 in 2007, is nearing the end of a memorable career that, to date, has contributed to the Atlanta Braves' eleven consecutive division titles, three National League pennants, and one world championship. He owns a .307 career batting average with 31 home runs and 104 RBIs for every 550 at-bats. Rolen, an excellent all-around third baseman, has completed eleven years of major league service through 2007 with a .283 batting average, 26 homers and 101 RBIs a year. He is also in the upper echelon for fielding average and range factor.

Offensive Ratings

Normalized Adjusted On-Base Percentage (NOBPA)

Wade Boggs' .415 on-base percentage was the highest OBP of the third base candidates. Eddie Yost and Stan Hack were next with .394 each. Boggs and Yost maintained their lead after the era adjustments were made, but Stan Hack, who had a negative 19-point era adjustment, fell from third place to sixth. Sal Bando had a plus 11 era adjustment, while Brooks Robinson enjoyed a plus 13 adjustment. Pie Traynor had one of the larger negative era adjustments, a huge 18-point drop, while the active players, Scott Rolen and Chipper Jones, currently have a minus 11 era adjustment.

Normalized Adjusted Slugging Average (NXSLGA)

Mike Schmidt, with a .527 career slugging average, and Eddie Mathews, with a .509 slugging average, were the only players to have a career slugging average over 5.00. Al Rosen with .495 and George Brett with .487 were the nearest competitors. As usual, there were several era adjustments, both favorable and unfavorable. Home Run Baker had the biggest positive era adjustment, plus 43. Brooks Robinson was plus 15; Ron Santo was plus 13; Stan Hack was plus 14; Sal Bando was plus 17; Mike Schmidt was plus 13; and Bob Elliott was plus 12. On the flip side, Wade Boggs was penalized by a huge negative 23-point era adjustment, and Paul Molitor was minus 18. The individual park factors also played havoc with some of the candidates. Ron Santo, who averaged 23 home runs for every 550 at-bats during his career, had a highly unfavorable 1.71 home run factor (HRF) that significantly affected his overall park factor, reducing his average home runs to 18 per 550 at-bats. Al Rosen had a 1.19 HRF, and Graig Nettles had a 1.29 HRF. Curiously, only one player, George Brett, had a favorable home run factor, 0.79, that increased his average home runs per year from 17 to 19. When all the smoke cleared, the first four places were left unchanged, with Mike Schmidt still atop the heap, followed by Eddie Mathews, Al Rosen, and George Brett, in that order. One person who benefited from the era adjustment was Eddie Yost, whose .371 SLG was last out of fifteen players. But Yost, who had a slightly favorable era adjustment, finished ahead of Boggs, who had a huge negative era adjustment as noted above, and Hack, whose lack of power doomed him to fourteenth place, just ahead of Boggs.

Normalized Stolen Bases (NSB)

Very few third basemen were threats to steal bases on a regular basis. Only Paul Molitor, with an average of 26 stolen bases a year, and Home Run Baker, with 22, stole more than 12 bases a year. Mike Schmidt and Stan Hack had 12 stolen bases a year, and Pie Traynor had 12. Sal Bando was next with seven.

Normalized Sacrifice Hits (NSH)

Pie Traynor was the leader in sacrifice hits with 17 a year. Home Run Baker had 14, and Stan Hack had nine. It is quite obvious from the statistics that the sacrifice hit has become a lost art in recent years. Most modern-day players show only one or two sacrifice hits a year. The exceptions are Bando and Brooks Robinson with five, and Molitor with four.

Normalized Grounded Into Double Plays (NGIDP)

Third basemen were average when it came to grounding into double plays. The range of GIDP stretched from six to 20. Stan Hack grounded into only six double plays a year. Eddie Mathews grounded into eight double plays a year, and George Brett and Mike Schmidt grounded into nine. At the other end of the spectrum, Pie Traynor grounded into 20 double plays a year, and Al Rosen grounded into eighteen double plays a year.

Final Offensive Ratings

Mike Schmidt's early lead in NOBPA and NXSLGA combined held up throughout the remainder of the offensive competition, giving him a slight lead over Eddie Mathews and making him the top offensive third baseman in baseball history.

	NOBPA × 20	NXSLGA × 20	.05NSB × 20	.05NSH × 20	.05NGIDP × 20	Total Points	Final Offensive Ratings
Mike Schmidt	18.301	20.000	0.462	0.059	0.667	39.489	1
Eddie Mathews	18.252	18.781	0.115	0.118	0.889	38.155	2
Al Rosen	18.252	16.233	0.231	0.059	0.333	35.108	3
Home Run Baker	17.767	13.130	0.846	0.824	0.429	32.996	4
George Brett	18.010	13.629	0.192	0.118	0.667	32.616	5
Sal Bando	17.621	12.853	0.269	0.294	0.500	31.537	6
Bob Elliott	17.816	12.299	0.192	0.294	0.429	31.030	7
Ron Santo	18.816	12.299	0.077	0.059	0.316	30.567	8
Paul Molitor	17.864	9.917	1.000	0.235	0.600	29.616	9
Eddie Yost	18.932	8.864	0.192	0.059	0.600	28.647	10
Graig Nettles	16.214	11.745	0.115	0.000	0.462	28.536	11
Stan Hack	18.204	8.144	0.462	0.529	1.000	28.339	12
Brooks Robinson	16.262	10.693	0.077	0.294	0.353	27.679	13
Pie Traynor	16.699	8.753	0.423	1.000	0.300	27.175	14
Wade Boggs	20.000	6.427	0.077	0.118	0.429	27.051	15

Defensive Ratings

Normalized Fielding Average Differential (NFAD)

Brooks Robinson, to no one's surprise, had the highest fielding average in baseball history at .971 as well as the highest fielding average differential, a whopping eighteen points above the league average. Stan Hack had an eleven-point fielding average differential and, what might be a surprise to many people, Wade Boggs also checked in with an eleven-point differential, two points better than the New York Yankee vacuum cleaner, Graig Nettles. Paul Molitor and George Brett anchored the bottom of the list with a negative two point differential.

Normalized Range Factor Differential (NRFD)

Mike Schmidt, who was in the middle of the pack with regard to fielding average, captured first place in the range factor category, with a range factor of 3.00, giving him a plus 55-point range factor differential. George Brett was second with a plus 40 differential, and Brooks Robinson and Graig Nettles were close behind Brett with 36-point differentials each.

Final Defensive Ratings

The favorites justified everyone's confidence in them when the final returns were in to identify the game's greatest defensive third baseman. Brooks Robinson, who was first in fielding average differential and third in range factor differential, edged Mike Schmidt for first place in the final defensive ratings. Schmidt was number one in range factor differential, but could do no better than a tie for sixth in fielding average differential. Ron Santo, with a sixth-place tie for FAD and a second-place finish in RFD, came in third, just ahead of Graig Nettles, who finished third in FAD and tied for fifth in RFD.

Mike Schmidt did it all — hit 548 home runs, drove in 1,595 teammates, and won ten Gold Gloves — during his 18-year career.

	NFAD × 20	NRFD × 20	Total Points	Final Defensive Ratings
Mike Schmidt	8.000	20.000	28.000	2
Eddie Mathews	8.000	8.727	16.727	7
Al Rosen	9.000	0.727	9.727	14
George Brett	0.000	14.545	14.545	9
Wade Boggs	13.000	10.545	23.545	5
Home Run Baker	8.000	6.909	14.909	10
Bob Elliott	2.000	4.364	6.364	15
Brooks Robinson	20.000	13.090	33.090	1
Pie Traynor	2.000	10.909	12.909	11
Ron Santo	8.000	17.818	25.818	3
Paul Molitor	0.000	15.636	15.636	8
Stan Hack	13.000	4.000	17.000	6
Graig Nettles	11.000	13.090	24.090	4
Eddie Yost	5.000	5.091	10.091	13
Sal Bando	8.000	4.727	12.727	12

Final All-Around Ratings

The final all-around ratings for third basemen were based on the assumption that, although the position is regarded as a power position, it is also considered to be an important defensive position. It is not considered as important defensively as shortstop or catcher, but it ranks above most of the other positions, and it is considered to be on par with second base. Both positions require tenacious glove-work. The second baseman has to be adept at making the double play, but the third baseman has to have a powerful throwing arm in order to make the difficult plays around the hot corner. The final ratings for third basemen, therefore, rate the offense at twice the defense, the same ratio used for evaluating second basemen. Under those conditions, Mike Schmidt was able to sneak past Brooks Robinson to claim the title as the game's greatest all-around third baseman. Robinson's spectacular defense allowed him to hold off a challenge from Eddie Mathews, but Mathews' explosive offense was more than enough to overtake both Ron Santo and Graig Nettles for third place overall.

	Offense Divided by 43 × 2	Defense Divided by 40	Total Points	Final All-Around Ratings	HOF
Mike Schmidt	1.837	0.700	2.537	1	*
Brooks Robinson	1.287	0.827	2.114	2	*

	Offense Divided by 43 × 2	Defense Divided by 40	Total Points	Final All-Around Ratings	HOF
Eddie Mathews	1.684	0.418	2.102	3	*
Ron Santo	1.422	0.645	2.067	4	*
Graig Nettles	1.327	0.602	1.929	5	
George Brett	1.517	0.370	1.887	6	*
Al Rosen	1.633	0.243	1.876	7	
Wade Boggs	1.258	0.589	1.847	8	*
Home Run Baker	1.437	0.373	1.810	9	*
Sal Bando	1.467	0.318	1.785	10	
Paul Molitor	1.377	0.391	1.768	11	*
Stan Hack	1.225	0.425	1.650	12	
Bob Elliott	1.443	0.159	1.602	13	
Eddie Yost	1.332	0.252	1.584	14	
Pie Traynor	1.184	0.323	1.507	15	*

Scott Rolen and Chipper Jones have an excellent chance of competing for a place on the roster of the legendary all-star team. Based on his impressive .401 OBP and .538 SLG, and in spite of large negative era and park factor adjustments, Jones still has an outside chance of finishing in the top five offensively, but his average defensive statistics, which currently rank him about fourteenth, could drop him out of the top ten all-around, although he could still finish in the top fifteen. Rolen is in a better position to complete his career with a top ten finish, although his career has probably passed its peak as well. The eleven-year major league veteran turned 31 in 2007, so his statistics will probably begin to decline from this point on. He too will have a significant negative era adjustment, but he will probably retain his positive park factor, and that will serve him well in the final evaluation. At the present time, his statistics would give him about a number three finish in the offensive category, and his defensive numbers are even better. His career fielding average of .966 is thirteen points above the league average, while his plus 56 range factor differential is the best ever recorded. Those numbers, if they were to hold up throughout the remainder of his career, would give him a number one rating defensively and a number two rating overall, just 0.004 behind Mike Schmidt. But with perhaps another eight to ten years remaining in his career, his final rating is in danger of falling.

CHAPTER 10

Baseball's Greatest Right Fielders and Left Fielders

A total of twenty players competed for the title of baseball's greatest right and left fielder.

- Frank Robinson was the only man to win the Most Valuable Player trophy in both the National League and the American League. He walked off with the honor in the senior circuit in 1961 after leading the Cincinnati Reds to the World Series with a .323 batting average, 117 runs scored, 32 doubles, 37 home runs, and 124 RBIs. He duplicated the feat for the Baltimore Orioles five years later after winning the Triple Crown and leading the league in runs scored with 122, home runs with 49, RBIs with 122, and batting average with .316. Overall, Robinson helped his team win four league pennants and one world championship. The 6'1", 195-pound right-handed slugger exploded out of Columbia in the South Atlantic League in 1956 to capture the National League Rookie of the Year award after crushing 38 home runs, scoring a league-leading 122 runs, and batting .290 for the Cincinnati Reds. He went on to enjoy a 21-year career in which he batted over .300 nine times, with a high of .342 in 1962, en route to a career .294 batting average with 586 home runs. He led the league in doubles, home runs, RBIs, and batting once each, on-base percentage twice, and slugging average four times.
- Ted Williams was arguably the greatest hitter of the last eighty years. His .344 batting average is the highest batting average in the lively ball era that began in 1920. "The Kid," as he was called, always wanted to be known as baseball's greatest hitter, and he practiced his swing ad infinitum, to the exclusion of all other parts of the game. He may have

had the best hand-eye coordination the game has ever seen. He had more home runs than strikeouts four times. Williams did not completely ignore defense, but he played it with indifference. He compiled a sensational batting average as well as other offensive statistics over a 19-year career, but his numbers would have been even more impressive if he had not lost almost five years to military service in World War II and the Korean War. The gangly 6'3", 205-pound left-handed slugger was a true war hero, flying combat missions in Korea and escaping from a flaming jet after a crash-landing. In 1941 Williams had one of the greatest seasons in baseball history, batting a stratospheric .406, and leading the league with 37 homers, 135 runs scored, 147 bases on balls, a .553 on-base percentage, and a .735 slugging average. Williams had an even .400 average on the last day of the season, and his manager offered to let him sit out the final games to protect his magic number. Williams insisted on playing both games of the doubleheader and promptly went out and ripped six base hits in eight at-bats, to finish at .406. The next year, he won the Triple Crown, batting .356 with 36 homers and 137 RBIs. Over his remarkable career, Williams led the league in runs scored six times, doubles twice, home runs four times, RBIs four times, bases on balls eight times, batting average six times, on-base percentage twelve times, and slugging average eight times. If he had not lost five years to military service, it is likely he would have scored more than 2,400 runs, driven in more than 2,400 runs, and walked over 2,700 times. His home run total would have approached 700, and his batting average might have been even higher than .344.

- Carl Yastrzemski, Ted Williams' replacement, more than lived up to the Boston fans' expectations, holding down the left-field position in Beantown for 23 years, more than any other Red Sox outfielder. The handsome southpaw swinger helped Boston to two American League pennants, in 1967 and 1975. He batted over .300 six times in his career, with a high of .329 in 1970, and he won the Triple Crown in 1967 with 44 home runs, 121 runs batted in, and a .326 batting average. He then went on to bat .400 with three home runs and five RBIs in the club's seven-game losing effort to the St. Louis Cardinals in that year's Fall Classic. In the 1975 Series, a seven-game loss to the Cincinnati Reds, Yaz batted .310 with four RBIs. Over his career, the husky 5'11", 182-pound left-handed hitter exhibited outstanding bat control, striking out just 64 times a year while drawing 85 bases on balls. He was also an excellent defensive outfielder who led the league in fielding average once, putouts four times, assists nine times, and double plays three times. He is number two all-time in plate appearances with 13,991, number three in at-bats with 11,988, number seven in career base hits with 3,419, number seven in doubles with 646, number eleven in runs batted in with 1,844, and number six in bases on balls with 1,845.

- Goose Goslin was a pure hitter who spent every winter rubbing his bats and chomping at the bit to get to spring training and begin another baseball season. He lived to hit a baseball, and when he could no longer do it, he retired to the New Jersey shore and went fishing. The stocky left-handed hitter played major league baseball for 18 years, dividing his time with the Washington Senators, Detroit Tigers, and St. Louis Browns. He played on five pennant winners and two world championship teams. In 1924, he paced the Senators to the World Series title by hitting .344 with three homers and seven RBIs in seven games. Eleven years later he hit .273 with three RBIs in the Detroit Tigers' win over the Chicago Cubs, and he drove in the World Series-winning run with a two-out single in the bottom of the ninth inning of Game Seven. Goslin led the American League in triples twice, RBIs once, and batting once, with an average of .379 in 1928. He hit over .300 twelve times in eighteen years, scored more than 100 runs seven times, and drove in more than 100 runs twelve times, a record exceeded only by Foxx, Gehrig, and Ruth. He retired with a .316 batting average, 2,735 base hits, 500 doubles, 173 triples (number 22 all-time but number two in the lively ball era, behind Stan Musial), 248 home runs, and 1,609 RBIs.

- Al Simmons was a key member of the great Philadelphia Athletic teams that captured three consecutive American League pennants and two world championships between 1929 and 1931. Simmons batted a combined .378 during that span, winning batting titles in 1930 (.381) and 1931 (.390). He also led the league in RBIs in 1929 with 157, and runs scored (152) and fielding average (.990) in 1930. He continued his long-ball barrage in the Series, batting .333 in eighteen games with six home runs and 14 RBIs. He was a participant in the greatest comeback in World Series history. With the A's trailing the Chicago Cubs by an 8–0 score in the bottom of the seventh inning of Game Four of the 1929 Fall Classic, Simmons led off the inning with a home run onto the roof of the left-field stands at Shibe Park; later in the inning he singled and eventually scored what proved to be the winning run in the A's 10–8 victory. Over his storied 20-year career, the man they called "Bucketfoot Al," batted over .300 fourteen times, including his first eleven years in the major leagues, en route to a career average of .334, number twenty all-time. The rugged right-handed hitter ripped the ball at a .387 pace as a twenty-three-old second-year player in 1925, with 253 base hits (number five all-time), 122 runs scored, 43 doubles, 12 triples, 24 home runs, and 129 RBIs. He followed that performance with averages of .341, .392, .351, .365, .381, and .390, giving him a combined batting average of .363 after

Al Simmons batted .334 over a memorable 20-year career.

eight years in the big leagues. His career slowed slightly during his 30s, but he still maintained a .300 average with good power for another seven years.
- Rickey Henderson was the quintessential leadoff hitter, a 5'10", 180-pound right-handed batter with blazing speed and a powerful bat. He holds the all-time record for the most career home runs by a leadoff

batter, the most stolen bases in a season, and the most stolen bases in a career. His 81 career leadoff home runs broke the mark of 35 set by Bobby Bonds in 1981, his 130 stolen bases in 1982 broke the mark of 118 set by Lou Brock in 1974, and his 1,406 career stolen bases broke the mark of 897 set by Ty Cobb in 1928. The flamboyant outfielder, whose dash and cocky attitude fit right in with the garish gold and green uniform he wore as a member of the Oakland Athletics, played major league baseball for twenty-five years, usually with contending teams. He played on seven pennant winners and three world champions, batting .339 in fourteen World Series games with two homers and seven stolen bases. In 1982, Henderson set the all-time single-season stolen base record by swiping 130 bases in 172 attempts. He also stole 108 bases in 1983 and 100 bases in 1980. In 1985 he became the first man to steal fifty bases and hit twenty home runs in a season, a feat he duplicated the following year. During his career, he led the league in runs scored five times, bases on balls four times, on-base percentage once, and stolen bases a record twelve times. He is number one all-time in leadoff home runs, single-season stolen bases, and career stolen bases, as noted above. He is also number one in runs scored (2,294), number four in games played (3,081), number four in plate appearances (13,346), number ten in at-bats (10,961), number nineteen in base hits (3,055), number nine in doubles (510), number two in bases on balls (2,190), and number three in putouts (6,468).

- "Shoeless" Joe Jackson may have been the greatest natural hitter the game has ever produced. His smooth, compact swing was copied by no less a slugger than Babe Ruth, who carried it to the ultimate. The illiterate country boy from Pickens County, South Carolina, set a rookie record that will probably never be broken, hammering the ball to the tune of .408 in 1911. He led the American League in on-base percentage that year with .468, but lost the batting title to Ty Cobb, who hit .420, the fourth-highest single-season batting average of the twentieth century. Shoeless Joe's .408 mark was the sixth-highest single-season batting average of the twentieth century. The powerful 6'1", 200-pound left-handed hitter swung his favorite bat, "Black Betsy" with bad intentions, averaging 34 doubles, a major league record 19 triples, and six home runs with just 23 strikeouts for every 550 at-bats. He was barred from the game for life in 1920, at the peak of his career, after Commissioner Kenesaw Mountain Landis accused him of conspiring to throw the 1919 World Series, a charge that was flimsy at best. The fact is that Jackson led both teams at bat in the Series with a hefty .375 average, a Series-record twelve base hits, one home run, five runs scored, and six RBIs in eight games, and he played flawlessly in the field with sixteen putouts and one

Shoeless Joe Jackson may have been the greatest natural hitter in the history of the game.

assist. In his last year in the major leagues, Jackson batted a robust .382 with 42 doubles, a league-leading 20 triples, 12 homers, and 121 RBIs. His .356 career batting average is the third highest in baseball history, trailing only Ty Cobb (.366) and Rogers Hornsby (.358).

- Willie "Pops" Stargell was the heart and soul of the great Pittsburgh Pirate teams of the 1960s and 1970s. He led the Pirates to six division titles and two world championships. He batted .315 in fourteen World Series games with three home runs and eight RBIs. His two-run homer in the sixth inning of the seventh game of the 1979 Fall Classic provided the winning margin in a 4–1 Pirate triumph. Pops held down the left field spot in the Pittsburgh lineup for twenty-one years, but defense was not his strong suit. He was primarily a slugger who was paid to produce runs. And he did that with gusto, driving in an average of 107 runs a year. His best year was 1973 when he led the league in doubles with 43, home runs with 44, RBIs with 119, and slugging average with .646. He also led the league in home runs in 1971 with 48. Over his long career, Stargell batted .282 with 33 homers a year. And because he was not a strong defensive outfielder, opposing runners challenged his arm, often to their disappointment. He led the National League in assists four times and double plays three times.

- Pete Rose was one of the most competitive players ever to put on a uniform. The man they called "Charlie Hustle" gave 110 percent on every play, even if there was a wide discrepancy in the score. He always played hard and he always played to win. Rose did not have an abundance of talent, but he had desire and a dedicated work ethic that made him one of the top players in the game. His 24-year major league career produced seven division titles, six World Series appearances, and three world championships. In 1975, Rose pummeled Pittsburgh Pirate pitching to the tune of .357 in the NLCS, and he kept up the barrage against the Boston Red Sox in the World Series, hitting .370 as the Big Red Machine rolled to the world championship in seven games. Rose led the league in many offensive and defensive categories during his career. He led the league in runs scored four times, base hits seven times, doubles five times, batting average three times, on-base percentage twice, fielding average three times, putouts five times, and assists four times. His best year may have been 1969 when he led the league in batting (.348) and runs scored (120). Or it could have been 1976 when he led the league in runs scored (130), base hits (215), and doubles (42), while stroking the ball at a .323 clip. When he retired in 1986, he left a barrel of records behind. He broke Ty Cobb's record for the most base hits in a career in 1985, finishing with 4,256. He is also number one in games played (3,562) and at-bats (14,053), number six in runs scored (2,156), number two in doubles (746), number seven in total bases (5,752), and number five in career fielding average (.991).

- Joe Medwick, called "Ducky-Wucky" because of the way he walked, was one of the game's top sluggers during the 1930s. The rugged 5'10", 187-pound right-handed hitter was a notorious bad-ball hitter who hit balls off his shoe-tops or above his shoulders, driving them to all fields for extra bases. Over the course of his 17-year career, Medwick averaged 39 doubles, eight triples, 15 home runs, and 100 runs batted in for every 550 at-bats. He disdained the base on balls, as evidenced by his 31 walks a year, but he seldom struck out, fanning only 40 times a year. Medwick joined the St. Louis Cardinals as a 20-year-old outfielder in 1932 after literally destroying the pitching in the Texas League with a .354 batting average and 82 extra-base hits in 139 games. He batted .349 with St. Louis in 26 games at the end of that season, and went on to hit over .300 in each of the next eleven years. He won the National League's last Triple Crown in 1937, batting a sizzling .374 with 31 homers and 151 RBIs. He won the MVP that year while also leading the league in runs scored (111), base hits (237), doubles (56), slugging average (.641), and fielding average (.988). In all, Medwick led the league in base hits one more time, RBIs twice more, triples once, and doubles twice more, with a National League record 64 in 1936, second only to Earl Webb's 67 doubles in major league history. He retired in 1948 with a career batting average of .324.

- Harry Heilmann, a big 200-pound right-handed hitter, was strictly an offensive player. After playing a mediocre outfield in Detroit for four years, he was moved to first base, but when he led the league in errors for two years, he was returned to the outfield where he finished his career. He might not have been a standout with the glove, but he was a terror with the bat, winning four batting titles in seven years. In 1921, he beat Ty Cobb out of the batting title, hitting a blistering .394 to Cobb's .389. Two years later, Heilmann topped the magic .400 mark, taking his second batting title with a .403 average, ten points better than Babe Ruth's .393. He won his third crown in 1925 with a .393 average, four points better than Tris Speaker's .389, and in 1927 he ripped seven base hits in a season-ending doubleheader to come from behind to edge Al Simmons, .398 to .392. The man known as "Slug" arrived on the big league scene in 1914 as a 19-year-old phenom from the Northwest League, but it took him a few years to get his sea legs. He batted .320 in 1919, his fifth year in the American League, and followed that with a .309 season. Then, with the lively ball in full use in 1921, he went on a tear, averaging .380 over the next seven years. When arthritis in his wrists forced him to call it a day in 1930 at the age of 35, he could still hit, stinging the ball at a .333 clip in his last full season. His career batting average of .342 is number ten all-time and number three in the lively ball era, beginning in 1920.

- Stan Musial was a thorn in the side of all National League teams during his 22-year career, but he was particularly hard on the Brooklyn Dodgers' pitchers, raking them for a .356 batting average. During one visit to Ebbets Field, St. Louis swept a three-game series, with Musial's 11-for-15

10. Baseball's Greatest Right Fielders and Left Fielders

Stan Musial was a seven-time batting champion en route to a career .331 batting average.

performance at the plate leading the attack as usual. As he stepped to the plate for his last at-bat, one depressed Dodger rooter moaned, "Here comes that man again." The moniker stuck, and Musial was respectfully referred to as "Stan the Man" the rest of his career. The smooth-swinging left-handed hitter with the curious coiled batting stance had an excellent batting eye, striking out only 35 times a year while drawing 80 bases

Babe Ruth was baseball's all-time greatest home run hitter.

on balls. He also hit for average and hit with power, averaging .331 with 36 doubles, nine triples, 24 home runs, 98 runs scored, and 98 RBIs for every 550 at-bats. He is the greatest National League hitter-slugger of the last eighty years and second only to Rogers Hornsby in the lively ball era. Stan the Man led the National League in hitting seven times, with a high of .376 in 1948. He also led the league in runs scored four times, base hits six times, doubles eight times, triples five times, RBIs twice, on-base percentage six times, slugging average six times, and fielding average three times. He is number six in games played with 3,026, number eight in plate appearances with 12,712, number nine in at-bats with 10,972, number eight in runs scored with 1,949, number four in base hits with 3,630, number three in doubles with 725, number 19 in triples with 177 (number one in the lively ball era), number two in extra-base hits with 1,377, number two in total bases with 6,134, number five in RBIs with 1,951, number eleven in bases on balls with 1,599, number 20 in on base percentage with .417, and number 22 in slugging average with .559.

- Babe Ruth. The name conjures up visions of a Bunyan-type character standing astride the baseball world like a colossus. And in Ruth's case, truth is stranger than fiction. He almost single-handedly saved baseball after the infamous Black Sox scandal. The Baltimore native was the American League's top southpaw pitcher for several years, a two-time twenty-game winner prior to being converted to the outfield in 1918. The man known as "the Bambino" and "the Sultan of Swat" suddenly exploded with the bat when he became a full-time outfielder, hitting monstrous home runs from New York to St. Louis. In 1919 his 29 home runs broke the single-season record of 27 home runs set by Ned Williamson in 1884. He went on to break his own record three times, culminating in his sensational 60-home run season in 1927. Twice he hit more home runs than every other team in the American League — not man, but TEAM — in 1920 and again in 1927. Ruth set the career home run record with 139 in 1921, breaking the twenty-five-year-old mark set by Roger Connor. Every home run he hit after that just increased his own record. When he retired in 1935 with 714 home runs, his nearest rivals, Lou Gehrig and Jimmie Foxx, had just 378 homers and 302 homers, respectively. Gehrig retired with 493 homers, and Foxx retired with 534 homers, leaving him 180 home runs shy of Ruth's record. No other player of Ruth's era hit more than 301 home runs in his career; that is how good the Bambino was! He led the American League in home runs twelve times. Hank Aaron led the league four times, Barry Bonds twice, Mark McGwire four times, and Roger Maris once. In the most important offensive categories — batting average, runs scored, doubles, triples, home runs, RBIs, bases on balls, OBP, and SLG — Ruth led the league a total of 49 times. Ty Cobb was second with 42 times, and no other player in baseball history has led the league in those categories more than 31 times.
- Mel Ott was the greatest slugger produced by the New York Giants until the arrival of Willie Mays, and he took advantage of the short right-field wall in the Polo Grounds like no one else. Ott crushed 511 home runs during his 22-year career, and he quickly became proficient at lofting

fly balls over the friendly 257-foot right-field wall at the Polo Grounds, hitting 323 homers at home against 188 homers on the road. "Master Melvin" compiled a career batting average of .304 with the Giants, leading the league in runs scored twice, home runs six times, RBIs once, bases on balls five times, on-base percentage four times, and slugging average once. He was a dangerous hitter who hit 30 or more homers eight times and knocked in over 100 runs ten times. But he was also a patient hitter who drew 99 bases on balls a year against just 52 strikeouts. And he was just as dangerous in the three World Series he played in. When the Giants won their only world championship with a four games-to-one win over the Washington Senators in 1933, Ott batted .389 with two homers and four RBIs. He is still number eleven in both runs scored with 1,859 and RBIs with 1,860, and number eight in bases on balls with 1,708.

- Al Kaline was an outstanding all-around outfielder and a true five-tool player who could hit for average, hit with power, run, field, and throw. The 6' 2", 180-pound right-handed hitter burst upon the major league scene in 1953 at the age of 18. In his first full year, in 1954, he batted .276, and the following year he tore the league apart, capturing the batting title with a .340 average. He also led the league in base hits with 200, scored 121 runs, drove in 102 runners, and collected 24 doubles, eight triples, and 27 home runs. He continued in the same vein for the next nineteen years, batting over .300 eight more times, and helping the Tigers win two American League pennants and one world championship. Detroit defeated the St. Louis Cardinals in the 1968 Fall Classic, four games to three, with Mickey Lolich tossing three complete-game victories. Kaline chipped in with a torrid .379 batting average with two doubles, two home runs, and eight runs batted in. Over his career, Kaline only led the league once in base hits and once in doubles, but he was extremely consistent from year to year offensively, and he led the league in defensive categories ten times, including fielding average five times. When he retired in 1974, he left behind a .297 batting average and a total of 3,007 base hits, one of just 25 players with 3,000 or more hits. He is number six all-time in career games played in the outfield with 2,488, and number ten in career putouts with 5,035.

- Roberto Clemente along with Honus Wagner, is one of the Pittsburgh Pirates' greatest players. The flamboyant native of San Juan, Puerto Rico, was snatched out of the Brooklyn Dodger farm system in 1954 where the Dodgers were trying to hide him. The next year, the twenty-year-old outfielder played 124 games for the Pirates, batting .255, and in 1956 he upped his average to .311. He hit his stride in 1960, batting .314 with 16 homers and 94 RBIs. He batted over .300 in 13 of his last 14 years in a

Pittsburgh uniform, winning four batting championships — .351 in 1961, .339 in 1964, .329 the next year, and .357 in 1967. He also led the league in eleven defensive categories, including six times in assists. He is still number nine in games played in the outfield with 2,370. Clemente played on three National League pennant winners and in two World Series, winning the world championship both times. In 1960, the year Bill Mazeroski hit his dramatic ninth-inning home run off Bill Terry to bury the New York Yankees in Game Seven, Clemente batted .310. Eleven years later, when the Bucs edged the Baltimore Orioles in seven games, Clemente led both teams at bat with two doubles, one triple, two home runs, four RBIs and a .414 batting average. His fourth-inning home run in Game Seven proved to be the winning margin in the Pirates' 2–1 victory, and gave him the Series MVP trophy. His career ended prematurely on New Years Eve, 1972, when the plane he was on, carrying relief supplies to Managua, Nicaragua, crashed into the Atlantic Ocean. There were no survivors.

- Dwight "Dewey" Evans was one of the best right fielders in Boston Red Sox history. He arrived on the scene in 1972 at the age of twenty with a reputation as a strong-armed outfielder, and he was that, but he was also a threat with the bat. He played major league baseball for twenty years, all but one in Boston. He batted a tough .272, with 30 doubles, four triples, 24 home runs, 90 runs scored, and 85 RBIs for every 550 at-bats. He also drew 85 bases on balls a year, giving him a fancy .370 on-base percentage. Evans' best year was 1987 when he batted .305 with 37 doubles, 34 homers, 109 runs scored, and 123 RBIs. He led the league in runs scored once during his career, home runs once, walks three times, and OBP once. Even though he was a dangerous offensive player, he was best known as one of the game's best defensive outfielders with probably the strongest throwing arm in the major leagues during his career. The eight-time Gold Glove winner led the American League in fielding average three times, putouts and assists four times each, and double plays three times. He might have led the league in assists several more years but very few base runners challenged his arm. Evans played in two World Series, but was on the losing side both times. In 1975, when the Sox lost to the Cincinnati Reds in seven games, Evans batted .292 with a home run and five RBIs. In Game Six, eventually won by Boston on Carlton Fisk's dramatic twelfth-inning home run, Evans saved the game in the eleventh inning when he robbed Joe Morgan of a home run and started an inning-ending double play. In the 1986 Series, known for Bill Buckner's error in the ninth inning of Game Six that opened the door for an eventual Met victory in seven games, Evans crushed the ball at a .308 clip with two doubles, two homers, and nine RBIs.

- Bob Johnson, known as "Indian Bob," played in the American League for thirteen years, primarily with the Philadelphia Athletics. He was a hard-hitting outfielder who averaged .296 during his career, with 31 doubles, eight triples, 23 home runs, 98 runs scored, and 102 RBIs for every 550 at-bats. His 85 bases on balls a year combined with his good batting average gave him an excellent .393 on-base percentage. Indian Bob hit 20 or more home runs his first nine years in the major leagues, and he drove in more than 100 runs seven consecutive years. He did not have a best season; he was consistently good many years, with a good balance of runs scored, home runs, RBIs, and batting average. He did have several memorable days, however. On August 29, 1937, he set a major league record by hitting a grand slam homer and a two-run double in the same inning, good for six RBIs. In another game, he went six-for-six with two doubles and two homers. The seven-time All-Star retired from the game in 1945 at the age of 39, hitting a solid .280 in his final season.
- Reggie Smith may have been the greatest right fielder in Boston Red Sox history, although fans of Dewey Evans and Harry Hooper might object to the statement. Smith, who was a fixture in Fenway Park's right-field pasture for seven years, had a strong throwing arm and good range, but he was noted more for his big bat than his reliable glove. He batted over .300 six times in his 17-year major league career, with a high of .322 with the Los Angeles Dodgers in 1980. His best year was probably 1977, when he helped the Dodgers take the National League pennant. The 6', 190-pound switch-hitter caressed the ball to the tune of .307 that year, with 104 runs scored, 32 homers, and a league-leading .427 on-base percentage. He, Steve Garvey, Dusty Baker, and Ron Cey became the first quartet to hit 30 or more home runs each in the same season. Smith batted .287 over his career, averaging 28 doubles, 25 home runs, 88 runs scored, and 85 runs batted in for every 550 at-bats. He led the league in doubles twice, putouts twice, and assists and double plays once each.
- Paul Waner, known as "Big Poison," was one of the greatest hitters in Pittsburgh Pirate history, stroking the ball to the tune of .333 over a 20-year career. The 5' 8", 153-pound left-handed hitter was never a power hitter, but he could hit the ball in the gaps as well as anyone, averaging 35 doubles, 11 triples, and seven home runs a year. He and his brother Lloyd, a .316 hitter known as "Little Poison," patrolled the Forbes Field outfield from 1927 to 1941, giving Pirate fans some of the most exciting baseball ever seen in the Steel City. Paul Waner joined the San Francisco Seals in 1923 at the age of twenty, and after putting together averages of .369, .356, and .401 in the Pacific Coast League, his contract was purchased by Pittsburgh. In his rookie season, he batted .336 with a league-leading 22 triples. He went on to hit over .300 the

next twelve years, winning three batting championships along the way, with averages of .380, .362, and .373. He also led the league in runs scored twice, base hits twice, doubles twice, triples twice, and RBIs once. He scored over 100 runs nine times and posted eight seasons with more than 200 base hits. One of the keys to Waner's success was his keen batting eye. He struck out an average of just 22 times a year while walking 63 times, giving him an outstanding .404 on-base percentage, the tenth-highest OBP of the twenty players in the study.

Active Players

There are several active players who might deserve a place on this list once they retire, including Gary Sheffield, Vladimir Guerrero, Ichiro Suzuki, and Manny Ramirez. Gary Sheffield has been one the game's most dangerous hitters for 19 years. He has averaged .296 over that span with 99 runs scored, 31 home runs, and 102 runs batted in a year. He won the batting championship in 1992 with a .330 average. He is a decent defensive outfielder, although not outstanding. Vladimir Guerrero, who is in the middle of a potential Hall of Fame career, is primarily an offensive player. He sported a .325 career batting average through the 2007 season, with 33 homers and 107 RBIs for every 550 at-bats. Ichiro Suzuki, who played for ten years in Japan with a .355 batting average, was hitting .333 after seven years in the major leagues. He is a talented all-around player who has blazing speed on the bases and in the outfield. He averages 90 runs scored and 31 stolen bases a year. He also is among the leaders in outfield defense, with excellent range and a powerful throwing arm. Manny Ramirez is another pure hitter who is less than interested in playing defense. The 34-year-old right-handed hitter has a .313 batting average for 15 years in the big leagues, with an average of 105 runs scored, 38 home runs, and 125 RBIs a year. He had 490 career home runs through 2007 and broke the 500 career home run barrier in 2008.

Offensive Ratings

Normalized Adjusted On-Base Percentage (NOBPA)

Ted Williams had the highest published on-base percentage of any player in the study as well as the highest on-base percentage of any major league player in the history of the game. His .482 OBP is eight points higher than the next man, Babe Ruth. His 121-point favorable OBP differential from the league average was also the best of any player and again gave him the edge

Vladimir Guerrero, a .325 hitter who is averaging 34 home runs a year, is in the middle of a potential Hall of Fame career.

over Ruth, and he maintained that advantage after the era adjustment was made. Babe Ruth finished second to Williams in NOBPA, followed by Joe Jackson and Stan Musial. Ott, Heilmann, and Henderson, who had published OBPs over .400, rounded out the top five, but Paul Waner, who had a .404 OBP, had a negative era adjustment, allowing Al Kaline to pass him in the ratings.

Normalized Adjusted Slugging Average (NXSLGA)

Once again, Babe Ruth and Ted Williams stood head and shoulders above the competition in the slugging category. This time, Babe Ruth was number one with a .690 published slugging average, and Ted Williams was close behind at .634. Neither man had a significant advantage in either era adjustment or park factor, enabling Ruth to protect his first-place lead to the end. Stan Musial (.559), Frank Robinson (.537), Al Simmons (.535), Mel Ott (.533), Willie Stargell (.529), Harry Heilmann (.520), Joe Jackson (.517), Bob Johnson (.506), Ducky Medwick (.505), and Goose Goslin (.500), had published slugging averages over .500, and all of them except Goslin had a favorable differential to the league average of more than 100 points. Willie Stargell, thanks to favorable era and park factor adjustments, leapfrogged Musial, Robinson, Simmons, and Ott to finish in third place in NXSLGA. Al Simmons' negative era and park factor adjustments dropped him from fifth place to ninth place in the category. Musial held down fourth place, but Mel Ott, thanks to his higher batting average, was fifth, ahead of Frank Robinson.

Normalized Stolen Bases (NSB)

Ricky Henderson had no competition in the stolen-base category with his 72 stolen bases a year average. Joe Jackson, with 22 stolen bases, ranked second, while Frank Robinson with 12, Goose Goslin with 11, and Reggie

Ted Williams was the greatest hitter of the lively ball era, after 1920.

Smith with 10 were the only other candidates to have ten or more stolen bases a year.

Normalized Sacrifice Hits (NSH)

The corner gardeners were not big on sacrifice hits. Their job was to drive the ball for extra bases, not bunt. Harry Heilmann, although a slugger of note, laid down an average of 20 sacrifice bunts a year. Joe Jackson, another slugger, had 14, and Paul Waner had 10. No other candidate had more than seven.

Normalized Grounded Into Double Plays (NGIDP)

The big men in this category hit into more double plays than the average player. Al Simmons topped the list with 21 GIDPs. He was followed by Goose Goslin with 17 and Frank Robinson and Roberto Clemente with 16 each. Only Ricky Henderson and Willie Stargell with nine GIDPs each and Mel Ott with seven were below 10 GIDPs.

Final Offensive Ratings

There were some minor shifts, up and down, due to a player's skills in the stolen base, sacrifice hits, and grounded into double plays categories, but for the most part the players who led the way after the OBP and SLG competitions also led the way in the final offensive ratings. Babe Ruth and Ted Williams finished one-two, but Joe Jackson, thanks to his huge advantage over Stan Musial in stolen bases and sacrifice hits, passed "Stan the Man," for a third-place finish in the offensive ratings. The biggest change in the ratings was Rickey Henderson's jump from 18th place in the combined OBP and SLG categories to 14th place in the final overall ratings, thanks to his excellent showings in stolen bases and grounding into double plays. Passed by Mel Ott, Stan Musial dropped from third to fifth place because of his poor showing in the stolen base and sacrifice hit categories.

	NOBPA × 20	NXSLGA × 20	.05NSB × 20	.05NSH × 20	.05NGIDP × 20	Total Points	Final Offensive Rating
Frank Robinson	16.674	12.351	0.167	0.050	0.438	29.680	6
Ted Williams	20.000	16.716	0.028	0.000	0.528	37.244	2
Carl Yastrzemski	16.421	8.582	0.111	0.000	0.467	25.581	17
Goose Goslin	15.453	10.187	0.153	0.500	0.412	26.705	13

	NOBPA × 20	NXSLGA × 20	.05NSB × 20	.05NSH × 20	.05NGIDP × 20	Total Points	Final Offensive Rating
Al Simmons	15.200	10.746	0.083	0.350	0.333	26.712	12
Ricky Henderson	16.758	7.687	1.000	0.050	0.778	26.273	14
Joe Jackson	17.895	11.716	0.306	0.700	0.583	31.200	3
Willie Stargell	15.326	13.172	0.014	0.000	0.889	29.401	7
Pete Rose	15.958	5.896	0.097	0.100	0.700	22.751	20
Joe Medwick	14.947	10.336	0.042	0.150	0.467	25.942	15
Harry Heilmann	16.884	9.627	0.111	1.000	0.467	28.089	8
Stan Musial	17.305	12.649	0.056	0.100	0.583	30.693	5
Babe Ruth	19.326	20.000	0.111	0.350	0.583	40.370	1
Mel Ott	16,968	12.575	0.069	0.300	1.000	30.912	4
Al Kaline	16.716	9.552	0.111	0.100	0.467	26.946	11
Roberto Clemente	15.284	9.142	0.083	0.100	0.438	24.847	19
Dwight Evans	15.747	8.918	0.069	0.100	0.538	25.372	18
Bob Johnson	16.042	10.597	0.111	0.100	0.467	27.317	9
Reggie Smith	15.705	10.858	0.139	0.050	0.538	27.290	10
Paul Waner	16.547	8.097	0.083	0.500	0.538	25.765	16

Defensive Ratings

Normalized Fielding Average Differential (NFAD)

In general, the outer gardeners, in right field and left field, are not particularly good defensive players. However, in the case of the world-class cornermen in this study, many of them were better than average defenders. Al Simmons, for instance, had a fielding average of .982 compared to a league average of .968, a 14-point favorable differential. In fact, of the 2,142 games Al Simmons played in the outfield, 771 of them occurred in center field. Pete Rose was another outer gardener who stood out defensively in this competition. He also boasted a plus 14 fielding average differential. They were by far the best fielding outfielders in the group, but there were others who displayed significant defensive capabilities, such as Frank Robinson, Stan Musial, Al Kaline, and Dwight Evans, all of whom had a six-point positive differential. Players who were carried primarily for their slugging skills included Willie Stargell, who had a minus fifteen-point differential, Goose Goslin, who was at minus seven, and Harry Heilmann and Bob Johnson, who were at minus four. Reggie Smith was also at minus four, but in his case he covered acres of ground, and he reached balls that most of the other outfielders in this group could not reach.

Normalized Range Factor Differential (NRFD)

Reggie Smith, who showed a negative fielding average differential, was the leading outer gardener when it came to range factor, as noted above. Smith had a 2.28 range factor, a full 37 points above the league average. He was followed closely by Rickey Henderson, who had a plus 34-point differential, Roberto Clemente, who had a plus 22-point differential, and Al Kaline, who had a plus 16-point differential. Range factor is the area where the fielding deficiencies of the outer gardeners usually appear. Many of them can catch balls hit at or near them, but those same players do not have the quick reflexes or the foot speed that allows them to run down balls in the alleys or in foul territory.

Final Defensive Ratings

Al Simmons, who was number one in fielding average differential, finished in a tie for fourth place in the range factor differential category, assuring him the title of the best defensive player in either right or left field. Pete Rose, who tied Simmons for first place in the fielding average category, finished sixth in the range factor category, good enough for second place overall. Al Kaline and Frank Robinson, who tied for third place in fielding average differential, accumulated enough points in the range factor category to finish third and fifth overall, respectively. Rickey Henderson, who could do no better than thirteenth place in the fielding average differential category, finished a close second to Reggie Smith in the range factor category to edge ahead of Frank Robinson for third place overall.

	NFAD × 20	NRFD × 20	Total Points	Final Defensive Ratings
Frank Robinson	14.483	8.571	23.054	5
Ted Williams	8.276	2.857	11.133	18
Carl Yastrzemski	11.034	8.776	19.810	11
Goose Goslin	5.517	8.163	13.680	17
Al Simmons	20.000	10.408	30.408	1
Rickey Henderson	9.655	14.082	23.737	4
Joe Jackson	13.103	5.918	19.021	12
Willie Stargell	0.000	2.653	2.653	20
Pete Rose	20.000	10.000	30.000	2

	NFAD × 20	NRFD × 20	Total Points	Final Defensive Ratings
Joe Medwick	13.103	7.143	20.246	8
Harry Heilmann	7.586	0.000	7.586	19
Stan Musial	14.483	5.714	20.197	9
Babe Ruth	11.724	4.082	15.806	16
Mel Ott	13.793	3.061	16.854	14
Al Kaline	14.483	10.408	24.891	3
Roberto Clemente	8.276	11.633	19.909	10
Dwight Evans	14.483	6.939	21.422	7
Bob Johnson	7.586	8.980	16.566	15
Reggie Smith	7.586	14.694	22.280	6
Paul Waner	11.724	6.122	17.846	13

Two of the top finishers on the all-defensive team may surprise some people, namely Rickey Henderson and Pete Rose. Many in the baseball establishment considered Henderson and Rose to be average to mediocre defensive outfielders, but that was not the case as shown by this study. In Henderson's case, his dazzling speed gave him a favorable range factor that was 34 points above the average, putting him in the upper echelon in that category. His fielding percentage was just average, but as a left or right fielder, he outperformed the other players at that position. Most of the best fielding outfielders were, naturally, center fielders. Pete Rose was another matter. He was actually a very good left or right fielder who was above average in range factor and who led the league in fielding average three times, his career fielding average of .991 being a full 14 points above the league average.

Final All-Around Ratings

The offense, which was weighted at four-to-one over the defense, was a major factor in determining the best overall outer gardeners. It was no surprise, therefore, that Babe Ruth, who was the top offensive player in the group, was also number one in the final all-around ratings in spite of a 16th-place finish in defense. Likewise, Ted Williams, who finished second in the offensive ratings but no better than 18th in defense, claimed the number two spot in the final all-around ratings. Williams was a perfectionist whose goal was to be recognized as the greatest hitter in baseball history. In this study he finished at number two behind Babe Ruth, but with his power of concentration and his tremendous focus, if he had spent as much time and effort on

Ichiro Suzuki, Japan's all-time greatest hitter with a career average of .353, posted a .331 batting average after six years in the major leagues (courtesy James R. Madden, Jr.).

his defensive play as he did on his offensive play, it is very possible that he could have become a very solid outfielder, joining the same class as Al Simmons and Pete Rose. Under those circumstances, he might have passed Babe Ruth in combined offense-defense and been rated as the greatest all-around outfielder in major league baseball history. And, as noted above, Williams was probably penalized in the range factor category by the geometry of Fenway Park's tiny left-field area that greatly reduces a fielder's opportunities for putouts and assists.

	Offense Divided by 43 × 4	Defense Divided by 40 × 1	Total Points	Final All-Around Ratings	HOF
Frank Robinson	2.761	0.576	3.337	5	*
Ted Williams	3.465	0.278	3.743	2	*
Carl Yastrzemski	2.380	0.495	2.875	14	*
Goose Goslin	2.484	0.342	2.826	17	*
Al Simmons	2.485	0.760	3.471	7	*
Rickey Henderson	2.444	0.593	3.037	10	
Joe Jackson	2.902	0.476	3.378	3	
Willie Stargell	2.735	0.066	2.801	20	*
Pete Rose	2.116	0.750	2.866	15	
Joe Medwick	2.413	0.506	2.919	12	*
Harry Heilmann	2.613	0.189	2.802	19	*
Stan Musial	2.855	0.505	3.360	4	*
Babe Ruth	3.755	0.395	4.150	1	*
Mel Ott	2.876	0.421	3.297	6	*
Al Kaline	2.540	0.622	3.162	8	*
Roberto Clemente	2.311	0.498	2.809	18	*
Dwight Evans	2.360	0.536	2.896	13	
Bob Johnson	2.541	0.414	2.955	11	
Reggie Smith	2.539	0.567	3.106	9	
Paul Waner	2.397	0.446	2.843	16	*

Barry Bonds and Sammy Sosa are in limbo at the present time. If at some future date they qualify for the study, Bonds has an excellent chance to finish in the top three all-around, while Sosa might crack the top twenty.

Gary Sheffield's offensive contributions give him a fighting chance of crashing this list, perhaps in the top ten, if he can maintain his current level of production for the rest of his career; like other active players, he is hampered by negative era adjustments. His defense is above average for right and left fielders, and that should help him in the final overall ratings. Vladimir

Guerrero has an excellent chance of finishing in the top ten offensively when he retires, but his defense may derail his chances at crashing the final all-around top twenty. At the present time his fielding average differential is worse than any player in the study, retired or active, although his range factor differential is exceptional for the group. Ichiro Suzuki is one of baseball's greatest hitters, sporting a .333 batting average through 2007. He is also one of the game's outstanding defensive right fielders with exceptional reflexes, blazing speed, and a cannon for a throwing arm, but his lack of power will hurt him in his quest for a top ten finish. He averages only 20 doubles, seven triples, and eight home runs for every 550 at-bats. Manny Ramirez's statistics support the contention that he is primarily an offensive player. His published OBP of .409 would give him about a sixth-place finish in that category, and his .593 slugging average would probably put him in the top three for NXSLGA. If he were to retire today, he might finish in the top five offensively in spite of a huge negative era adjustment. His defense, however, is another matter. His fielding average differential is a negative ten points, and his range factor differential is also a negative ten points, relegating him to a very low finish in defense and probably dooming him to a near-bottom finish in the overall rating. In fairness to Manny, he, like Ted Williams and Carl Yastrzemski, may be the victim of Fenway Park's short left-field wall that punishes Red Sox left fielders in the range factor category.

CHAPTER 11

Baseball's Greatest Center Fielders

There were ten players competing for the title of baseball's greatest all-around center fielder.

- Willie Mays, a graduate of the Negro leagues, was a flashy bundle of talent and energy who was called "the Say Hey Kid" because of his way of addressing people. The 5'11", 180-pound right-handed hitter has been called the greatest player of the twentieth century by many baseball experts, or at least the greatest player of the last half of the century, sharing the honor with Joe DiMaggio. Mays was the prototypical five-tool player. He could hit for average, hit with power, run, field, and throw. He played for the Giants in both New York and San Francisco for 22 years, retiring in 1973 with a career average of .302, 3,283 base hits, 660 home runs, and 2,062 runs scored. He is number seven all-time in career runs scored, number ten in base hits, number four in home runs, and number nine in RBIs. Mays was Mister Giant during his career, leading the team to four World Series match-ups and one world championship, with the New York Giants in 1954. His back-to-the-plate catch of a drive off the bat of Vic Wertz in the eighth inning of Game One of that Series with two men on base protected a 2–2 tie, and the Giants eventually won the game in the bottom of the tenth inning on a three-run homer by Dusty Rhodes. Mays' catch has become legendary over the years, and has been called the greatest catch in World Series history. Mays did make a sensational catch off Wertz, but in many situations he demonstrated his flair for the dramatic by making the routine look extraordinary. For instance, he reportedly wore a hat one size too big so when he ran after a fly ball, his hat would fly off, giving the impression of much greater speed on his part. And he would often time his pursuit of a fly ball in order to

Willie Mays, shown here in a Minneapolis Millers uniform from 1951, may have been baseball's greatest all-around player during the second half of the twentieth century.

catch the ball on the run, giving the impression that he had made a sensational catch when in fact he had choreographed the entire scenario. Some outfielders, like Hank Aaron and Tris Speaker, would instinctively run to the spot where they had projected the ball to land, then turn and make the routine catch. Not so with Willie Mays. Nothing he did was routine. Still, in spite of his showmanship, he was one of the greatest players of his time. During his career, he led the league in batting one time, with a .345 batting average in 1954. He led the league in runs scored twice, base hits once, triples three times, home runs four times, on-base percentage three times, slugging average five times, stolen bases four times, putouts once, assists twice, and double plays five times. He scored over 100 runs for twelve consecutive years, drove in more than 100 runs ten times, and hit more than 30 home runs eleven times, with highs of 52 home runs in 1965 and 51 in 1955. He is number one all-time in career putouts by an outfielder with 7,095. In 1957, he put together a season unmatched in baseball history, hitting 26 doubles, a league-leading 20 triples, 35 home runs, and a league-leading 38 stolen bases, becoming the first and only player to equal or exceed 20 in all four categories.

- Mickey Mantle, "the Commerce Comet," might have been the greatest player to ever step on a baseball field if he could have exorcised his demons, but the demons got the best of him and slowly eroded his enormous skills. Several of Mantle's male ancestors, including his father, had died young, victims of Hodgkins disease. Mantle believed he would die young as well, and tried to enjoy life to the fullest while he lived. The result was a decade of debauchery and all-night partying in the nightspots around the American League, a practice that made him a shadow of his former self by the time he was 32. In addition to his wanton lifestyle, he also suffered from various knee injuries as well as from osteomyelitis, a severe bone disease that severely limited his range in the outfield and his base running capabilities. Still, the handsome, colorful 5'11", 198-pounder became one of the game's legends and the greatest switch-hitter the game has ever known. The Oklahoma strongman hit some of the longest home runs ever seen in a major league park, from both sides of the plate, including a 502-foot blast to right-center field in Yankee Stadium and a 565-foot homer over the left-field wall in Griffith Stadium. Mantle, who broke into the New York Yankee lineup in 1951 as a 19-year-old phenom, hit just .267 in 96 games in his rookie season. The following year, he upped his average to .311 with 23 home runs, and in 1955, entering the prime of his career, he batted .306 while leading the American League in triples with 11, home runs with 37, bases on balls with 113, on-base percentage with .431, and slugging average with .611. He went on to lead the league in runs scored six times, triples once, home runs four times, RBIs once, bases on balls five times, batting average once, on-base percentage three times, slugging average four times, fielding average once, assists once, and double plays twice. His greatest year was 1956, when he won the Triple Crown and led the American League in batting (.353), runs scored (132), home runs (52), RBIs (130), and slugging average (.705).

Mickey Mantle was the greatest switch-hitter in the history of the game.

The next year, he hit .365 and led the league in runs scored (121) and bases on balls (146). In 1961, the year he and Roger Maris both chased Babe Ruth's home run record before he was laid low with injuries, Mantle crushed 54 homers, batted .317, and led the league in runs scored (132), bases on balls (126), and slugging average (.617). Over the years, Mantle was one of the major contributors to the New York Yankees' twelve American League pennants and eight world championships. He batted a modest .257 in 65 Series clashes and 230 at-bats, but he established two World Series career records with 18 home runs and 45 RBIs. Mantle, who always swung as hard as he could on every pitch, struck out an average of 118 times a season over his 18-year career, but he also walked 116 times, and averaged 36 home runs, 114 runs scored, and 102 RBIs with a .421 on-base percentage, the third highest OBP of the ten candidates. Once while Detroit Tiger star Al Kaline was signing autographs, a young boy said to him, "You're not half as good as Mickey Mantle," to which Kaline replied, "Son, nobody is half as good as Mickey Mantle."

- Joe DiMaggio, "the Yankee Clipper," has been called the greatest all-around player of the twentieth century by many baseball experts, and his performance on the field for 13 years would seem to justify that title. Joltin' Joe arrived in New York in 1936 at the age of 21 after punishing Pacific Coast League pitching to the tune of .398, and he immediately took the big city by storm. He ripped into American League pitching with gusto, batting .323 with 44 doubles, a league-leading 15 triples, 29 home runs, 132 runs scored, and 125 RBIs. He continued his hard-hitting in the World Series with a .346 average as the Yankees took the measure of the New York Giants in six games. DiMaggio batted over .300 eleven times in his 13-year career, but lost three years in the prime of his life to military service during World War II. He led the American League in batting in both 1939 and 1940 with averages of .381 and .382, respectively, hit .357 in 1941, tailed off to .305 the next year, and then left to join the U.S. Army. The interruption robbed him of his best baseball years, but he did hit over .300 four more times after the war before retiring in 1951 at the age of 36. DiMaggio was a five-tool player and one of the game's greatest center fielders. He could do it all, and unlike some of his rivals, he did it with class, making everything look easy. He had quick reflexes, outstanding speed, and a powerful throwing arm, and he seemed to glide after fly balls. At the plate, his wide stance, short stride, and quick wrists gave him tremendous power, but unfortunately his power was neutralized by Yankee Stadium's enormous left-center field area, called "Death Valley," that extended 457 feet from home plate. Joe D. averaged just 24 home runs for every 550 at-bats in Yankee Stadium during his career, but he pounded 36 home runs away from the Bronx. He also had a great batting eye, striking out only 30 times a year while hitting 29 home runs. And he was an outstanding base runner, who ran the bases like a ballet dancer, gracefully and effortlessly. In 1941, DiMaggio set a major league record that has never been threatened. He hit in 56 consecutive games, from May 18 to July 17, when Jim Bagby of Cleveland finally shut him down in four at-bats with help from third baseman

Joe DiMaggio was arguably baseball's greatest all-around player during the first half of the twentieth century.

Ken Keltner, who made two sensational plays to rob the Yankee Clipper of base hits. DiMaggio was one of the main cogs in the great Yankee machine that won ten American League pennants and nine World Championships between 1936 and 1951. He won three Most Valuable Player trophies during his career, and retired with a career batting average of .325.

- Duke Snider, Brooklyn's answer to Mantle and Mays, out-hit hit his two rivals over the five-year period from 1953 through 1957, averaging 41 homers and 116 RBIs a year, compared to 39 and 100 for Mays and 37 and 112 for Mantle. Unfortunately for Snider, the Dodgers moved to Los Angeles in 1958, and Snider had to contend with the L.A. Coliseum's vast right-field territory that dramatically reduced his home run totals and took its toll on his aging legs. The man known as "the Silver Fox" was a Dodger fixture from 1948 until 1963, when he was traded to the fledgling New York Mets. During his 18-year career, Snider batted .295 with 27 doubles, 31 home runs, 97 runs scored, and 102 RBIs a year. He led the National League in runs scored three times, base hits, home runs, RBIs, bases on balls, and on-base percentage once each, and slugging average twice. Snider's greatest day in baseball may have been May 30, 1950, when he hit three home runs against the Philadelphia Phillies and missed a fourth one when the ball struck the right-field wall one foot from the top. Five years later, against Milwaukee, the big slugger hit three home runs and a double, driving in six runs in an 11–8 win over the Braves. "The Duke of Flatbush" played in six World Series, winning one World Championship. In 36 World Series games and 133 at-bats, he batted .286, with a National League record eleven home runs and 26 RBIs. Twice he hit four home runs in a Series, tying Babe Ruth's record for a single Series. He is the only man to ever hit four home runs in each of two World Series.

Duke Snider hit forty or more home runs in five consecutive seasons.

- Tris Speaker, "the Gray Eagle," was so-named because, like Duke Snider, his hair was prematurely gray. Speaker has long been considered the greatest defensive center fielder in baseball history. He was noted for playing an exceptionally shallow center field, with the quick reflexes and speed that was necessary to chase down and catch balls hit over his head. He was a great judge of how far and in what direction a batted ball would travel, and was able to turn his back on the ball when it was hit, run to the spot where the ball would land, turn and make a routine catch. The Gray Eagle was also an outstanding hitter and a dangerous base runner. The 6', 193-pound left-handed hitter played 22 years in the big leagues and hit over .300 eighteen times, including his first ten years as a full-time player, with a high of .389 in 1925. Six times he batted over .370, and in 1916 he led the league in batting with a .386 average. He also led the league twice in base hits, eight times in doubles, once in triples, four times in on-base percentage, once in slugging average, twice in fielding average, seven times in putouts, three times in assists, and six times in double plays. The Hubbard, Texas, native was not a power hitter but he drove the ball to the gaps in the outfield with regularity. His keen batting eye and his patience at the plate rewarded him with 75 bases on balls a year against just 15 strikeouts. The walks, combined with his .345 career batting average, gave him the best career on-base percentage .428, of any of the center field candidates. His 792 career doubles are the most in baseball history, and his 222 triples are number six all-time. He is number ten in runs scored (1,882) and extra-base hits (1,131), number nine in on-base percentage (.428), number five in batting average (.345), number two in putouts (6,788), and number one in assists (148) and double plays (139).
- Jimmy Wynn, "the Toy Cannon," so-named because of his explosive bat, played in the major leagues for fifteen years, most of it with the Houston Colt .45s, later the Astros. He was small by slugger standards, standing just 5'9" tall, but he weighed a husky 170 pounds, and he hit the ball with authority, averaging 24 doubles and 24 home runs for every 550 at-bats. The free-swinging Wynn struck out 118 times a year, but he also drew 101 bases on balls, scored 91 runs, and drove in 80. He led the league in walks twice, with 148 in 1969 and 127 in 1976. His best year was 1974 with the Los Angeles Dodgers when he hit .271 with 32 home runs, 104 runs scored, and 108 RBIs. He also had a big year in 1967 when, in spite of a mediocre .247 batting average, he slammed 37 homers, scored 102 runs, and drove in 107. Defensively, Wynn led the league in fielding average and putouts twice, assists three times, and double plays four times.

- Hank Aaron was the consummate baseball player. He could do it all — hit for average, hit for power, run, field, and throw. The man who broke Babe Ruth's career home run record was more than a slugger. In addition to leading the league in home runs three times, he also led the league in batting twice, runs scored three times, doubles four times, RBIs four times, and slugging average four times. He scored more than 100 runs in a season fifteen times in sixteen years, and drove in more than 100 runs eleven times. He hit 30 or more home runs fifteen times, with a high of 47 homers in 1971. He stole 240 bases during his 23-year career, and he batted over .300 fourteen times, finishing his career with a .305 batting average. One of his best years was 1963 when he batted .319, stole 31 bases, and led the league with 121 runs scored, 44 homers, 130 RBIs, and a .586 slugging average. His greatest day (or night) had to have been April 8, 1974, when he took an Al Downing slider downtown, depositing it into the Atlanta Braves' bullpen in left-center field for career home run number 715, breaking the record of Babe Ruth that had stood for 47 years. Hammerin' Hank was one of the game's most consistent players, and he was most dangerous and best in post-season play, where he hit a combined .362 with six home runs and 16 RBIs in 17 games. In 1957, after hitting the pennant-clinching home run for Atlanta, he went on to punish New York Yankee pitching in the World Series to the tune of a .393 batting average, with three home runs and seven RBIs, as the Braves spanked Casey Stengel's Bronx Bombers, four games to three. The next year, in a losing effort, Aaron batted .333 with two RBIs. And in 1969, in a losing National League Championship Series, he scorched the ball at a .357 clip with three home runs and seven RBIs in three games. Aaron was a humble man who did his job in a workman-like manner while serving as an excellent role model for the young children around the country. The man from Mobile, Alabama, quietly went about his business, maintaining a low profile while all the while establishing his legacy as a great all-around player. Offensively, he is number two in career home runs (755), number two in at-bats (12,364), number four in runs scored (2,174), number three in base hits (3,771), number nine in doubles (624), and number one in extra-base hits (1,477), total bases (6,856), and runs batted in (2,297). He was also one of the top defensive outfielders in the major leagues, leading the National League in putouts three times, assists once, and double plays four times, and he is number seven in career putouts with 5,539.
- Kirby Puckett, a squat 5'8", 210-pound right-handed hitter, was the heart and soul of the Minnesota Twins for twelve years until eye problems ended his career at the age of 34. The Chicago native raced through Minnesota's minor league farm system like a fiery comet, leading the

Appalachian League in batting with an average of .382 in 1982, and then hitting .314 for Visalia in the California League before moving up to AAA ball. Midway through the 1984 season, Puckett was promoted to the major league roster where he proceeded to punch out four base hits in his debut en route to winning American League Rookie of the Year honors. In 1986, the 25-year-old center fielder suddenly blossomed into a power hitter. After hitting just four home runs in his first two years, covering 1,248 at-bats, Puckett pounded 31 homers in 680 at-bats, to go along with a .328 batting average, 223 base hits, 119 runs scored, 37 doubles, 96 RBIs, and 20 stolen bases. The next year he produced similar numbers while leading the Twins to the American League pennant. He batted only .205 as the Twins dumped the Detroit Tigers in the ALCS four game to one, but he sizzled in the World Series, batting .357 to lead Tom Kelly's team to a seven-game triumph over Whitey Herzog's St. Louis Cardinals. In 1988, Kirby Puckett had one of his best years, batting a career-high .356 with 109 runs scored and a league-leading 234 base hits to go with 42 doubles, 24 homers, and 121 RBIs. The following year he won the batting title with a .339 average and once again led the league with 215 base hits. The Twins, with Puckett leading the way, beat the Chicago White Sox by eight games in the Western Division of the American League, and then took the measure of the Toronto Blue Jays in the ALCS, four games to one, with Puckett hitting a stratospheric .429 with two homers and six RBIs. In the Fall Classic, a four games-to-three victory over the Atlanta Braves, Puckett hit only .250, but he rose to the occasion in the last two games. With the Twins trailing the Braves three games to two, Puckett smashed an RBI triple off Steve Avery in the first inning of Game Six, and then carried the second run across himself. In the third inning, he quenched an Atlanta rally by making a sensational catch against the left-center field wall, robbing Ron Gant of an extra-base hit and the Braves of at least one run. Two innings later, he hit sacrifice fly to snap a 2–2 tie, after the Braves had scored in the top of the inning. And then he put the icing on the cake by driving a game-winning home run in the bottom of the eleventh inning, forcing Game Seven, an exciting pitching duel between Jack Morris and John Smoltz, won by the Twins, 1–0, in the bottom of the tenth inning on a bases-loaded single by Gene Larkin. Puckett's career ended four years later when glaucoma, a debilitating eye disease, forced him into premature retirement. During his career, he batted .318 and led the league in batting once, base hits four times, RBIs once, putouts three times, assists five times, and double plays four times.

- Ty Cobb compiled baseball's all-time highest batting average, stroking the ball at a .366 clip for twenty-four years. He may have been baseball's most hated player, but he played the game with a passion unmatched in baseball history by doing whatever it took to win a game. He was a fierce base runner who set the standard for stolen bases in the early part of the twentieth century. He was known to sharpen his spikes, sometimes in the dugout in full view of the opposing team, before a game so he could cause serious damage to an infielder when he slid into a base. Cobb, a sleek 6'1", 175-pound left-handed batter, had blazing speed that stood him in good stead both on the bases and in the field. It has been erroneously assumed that "the Georgia Peach" was strictly a singles hitter, but his .512 career slugging average belies that belief. Over his career, most of which was played in the dead-ball days, he averaged 35 doubles, 14 triples, six home runs, 108 runs scored, and 93 RBIs a year. He was a scientific hitter who held the bat with his hands several inches apart so he could shift them with the pitch and either pull a ball into right field or push a line drive to left. And his exceptional eyesight permitted him to wait until the last second to commit to a pitch. Cobb was one of the few players who did not adjust his approach to batting when the lively ball came into play in 1920. When many of his counterparts began holding the bat down at the end to generate more power, Cobb continued to choke up on the bat with his hands apart. He was always a sensational hitter who, after batting just .240 as an 18-year old rookie in 1905, ran off 23 consecutive years of hitting over .300, a major league record that will probably never be broken. He won twelve batting championships, including nine in a row, and had seven consecutive years over .367, with a high of .420 in 1911. He also led the league five times in runs scored, eight times in base hits, three times in doubles, four times in triples, four times in RBIs, six times in on-base percentage, and eight times in slugging average. In the field, he led the league in fielding average and putouts once each, assists twice, and double plays four times. Cobb's biggest disappointments were probably the three straight humiliations his teams suffered at the hands of National League clubs in the World Series and his sub-par performances. The toothless Bengals were defeated by the Chicago Cubs in the 1907 Fall Classic, four games to none with one tie. They fell to the Cubs again in 1908 in five games, and they were edged by the Pittsburgh Pirates the following year in seven games. Cobb batted a combined .262 in 17 games in the three Series after hitting a robust .350 during regular-season play.

- Tony Gwynn, the pride of San Diego, was the major league's leading batsmith during the 1980s and 1990s, placing the ball neatly to all fields depending on the pitch, the location of the pitch, and the game situation. The roly-poly left-handed hitter stroked the ball at a .338 clip during his 20-year career, the seventeenth-highest career batting average in baseball history, and the highest career batting average since Ted Williams retired in 1960. Over his career, Gwynn won eight batting titles, tying the National League record set by Honus Wagner in 1911. In 1994, he challenged the magic .400 mark most of summer but fell six points short, finishing with a .394 average when the baseball season was suddenly cut short by a players strike on August 11. In all, he batted over .367 four times and hit over .350 on three other occasions. He led the Padres into the postseason on three occasions and into the World Series twice, but his team never grabbed the gold ring, falling to the Detroit Tigers in five games in 1984 prior to being swept by the New York Yankees in 1998. In addition to winning eight batting championships, Gwynn led the league in runs scored once, base hits seven times, and on-base percentage once. He also had some outstanding seasons running the bases. He stole 319 bases during his career, including 56 stolen bases in 1987 and 40 stolen bases in 1989. Defensively, Gwynn became a good outfielder through hard work, and he combined his work ethic with exceptional speed to lead the league in fielding average, assists, and double plays once each and putouts three times.

Active Players

Ken Griffey, Jr., is the only active center fielder who appears ready to claim a place on this team when he retires. Cincinnati's sensational center fielder was on track to hit 800 career home runs until injuries derailed him in 2001. He suffered through six years of nagging injuries, hitting only 125 home runs over that stretch, but he was back on track in 2007. He can still top the 700 career home run mark if he plays another five years, but his dreams of hitting 800 home runs and perhaps being hailed as baseball's all-time greatest all-around player

Ken Griffey, Jr., cracked the 600 career home run barrier early in 2008, making him just the sixth player to reach that elevated level (courtesy James R. Madden, Jr.).

are a thing of the past. His offensive statistics through 2007 include a .290 career batting average, with 96 runs scored, 37 home runs, and 106 RBIs per 550 at-bats.

Offensive Ratings

Normalized Adjusted On-Base Percentage (NOBPA)

Ty Cobb (.431), Tris Speaker (.428), and Mickey Mantle (.421) were the only center fielders with published OBPs over .400. When the necessary era adjustments were made, the top three retained their positions, except that Mantle slipped past Speaker into second place. None of the other center fielders was able to challenge the top three. On the other hand, all the candidates had respectable numbers, with Jimmy Wynn, who was last in the group, still presenting a strong .371 OBPA.

Normalized Adjusted Slugging Average (NXSLGA)

Six of the center-field candidates had slugging averages over .500, with Joe DiMaggio (.579), Willie Mays (.557), Mickey Mantle (.557), and Hank Aaron (.555), not surprisingly, leading the way, with Duke Snider (.540) close behind. Snider, Puckett, and Gwynn were penalized by unfavorable era adjustments, while the other candidates benefited from favorable era adjustments, particularly Tris Speaker and Ty Cobb, who enjoyed 30-point and 21-point favorable adjustments, respectively. Joe DiMaggio, who had a 0.69 Home Run Factor, received the biggest boost from the park factor adjustment, and his .414 XSLGA was a full 38 points higher than the next man, Mickey Mantle. Ty Cobb had a 0.29 HRF, but his adjusted home run average of seven home runs for every 550 at-bats was too low to have a significant effect on his XSLGA. Duke Snider, hitting in friendly Ebbetts Field, had a 1.22 HRF, but the other big sluggers, Willie Mays (1.03 HRF), Hank Aaron (1.04 HRF), and Mickey Mantle (0.99 HRF), showed no advantage, either at home or on the road. That is somewhat surprising in Mantle's case. It might be assumed he would have had a significant home advantage from hitting left-handed in Yankee Stadium, especially when he hit 373 of his 536 home runs batting left-handed, but Mantle was more of a straightaway hitter than a pull hitter, and that neutralized his apparent home field advantage. DiMaggio, Mantle, Aaron, Mays, and Snider, in that order, easily outdistanced the other five candidates in the slugging average category.

Normalized Stolen Bases (NSB)

Ty Cobb, with his flaming afterburners, made a shambles of the stolen-base category, averaging 43 stolen bases a year compared to 24 stolen bases a year for Tris Speaker and 20 for Tony Gwynn. Joe DiMaggio, with only two stolen bases a year, finished in last place. Actually, Joe D. was an excellent base runner with good speed, but in a lineup that included such sluggers as Lou Gehrig, Bill Dickey, Charlie Keller, and Tommy Henrich, there was very little incentive for a Yankee base runner to try to steal a base. Duke Snider, who averaged eight steals a year, was in a similar situation with Roy Campanella, Gil Hodges, Jackie Robinson, and Carl Furillo waiting to drive him in.

Normalized Sacrifice Hits (NSH)

Sacrifice hits, like the corncob pipe, went out of style as the twentieth century progressed. Tri Speaker with 17 sacrifice hits and Ty Cobb with 14 topped the sacrifice-hit category, while Mays, Mantle, and DiMaggio, with one sacrifice hit each, tied for the bottom spot.

Normalized Grounded Into Double Plays (NGIDP)

Most of the candidates for the center-field position had above average speed, a necessary requirement for a position that was responsible for patrolling a vast expanse of territory beyond the infield grass, especially in those instances when the corner gardeners had lead feet, as often occurred. Mickey Mantle, who grounded into only eight double plays a year, set the pace in that category, with Jimmy Wynn close behind with nine GIDPs. Aaron and Gwynn with 16 GIDPs and Puckett with 15 brought up the rear.

Final Offensive Ratings

As might be expected, the final offensive center-field ratings were biased in favor of the big sluggers, especially ones with favorable era and park factor adjustments. Mickey Mantle, whose 116 bases on balls a year, compared to 74 bases on balls and 64 bases on balls for fellow sluggers Willie Mays and Joe DiMaggio, respectively, gave him a big lead in NOBPA, and his second-place finish, behind Joe D., in NXSLGA allowed him to maintain his lead throughout the remainder of the competition. DiMaggio finished second and Aaron came in third. Cobb and Speaker, who ran one and three in NOBPA, faltered in the slugging competition, finishing fifth and sixth overall. Willie Mays finished fourth in NOBPA, fourth in NXSLGA, and fourth overall.

	NOBPA × 20	NXSLGA × 20	.05NSB × 20	.05NSH × 20	.05GIDP × 20	Total Points	Final Offensive Ratings
Willie Mays	16.168	13.060	0.250	0.050	0.538	30.066	4
Mickey Mantle	17.979	14.030	0.139	0.050	0.875	33.073	1
Joe DiMaggio	16.126	15.448	0.028	0.050	0.700	32.352	2
Duke Snider	15.832	12.873	0.111	0.250	0.538	29.604	7
Tris Speaker	17.895	9.925	0.333	0.850	0.700	29.703	6
Jimmy Wynn	15.621	9.813	0.236	0.150	0.778	26.598	8
Hank Aaron	15.747	13.806	0.167	0.100	0.438	30.258	3
Kirby Puckett	15.158	7.015	0.125	0.100	0.467	22.865	10
Ty Cobb	18.274	9.664	0.597	0.700	0.700	29.935	5
Tony Gwynn	16.211	6.418	0.278	0.100	0.438	23.445	9

Defensive Ratings

Normalized Fielding Average Differential (NFAD)

All the center-field candidates were outstanding defensive players, and all of them had career fielding averages higher than the league average. Tris Speaker, who was noted for his shallow play, his quick reflexes, and his blazing speed, finished his career with a .970 fielding average, a full ten points higher than the league average. Kirby Puckett enjoyed a nine-point advantage, and Duke Snider had a seven-point advantage.

Normalized Range Factor Differential (NRFD)

Speaker's great speed gave him an excellent 2.68 range factor, 60 points above the league average, but that only gained him second place in the category. Willie Mays, who posted a 2.73 range factor, finished in first place as a result of his 63-point advantage over the league average. Kirby Puckett, with a plus 59-point advantage, pressed Speaker. Once again, all the candidates had positive range factors, justifying their place in the competition.

Final Defensive Ratings

The battle for number one in the defensive center-field category was a close race, particularly between Tris Speaker, Kirby Puckett, and Willie Mays. Speaker claimed the overall prize as a result of his first-place finish in the NFAD category and his second-place finish in the NRFD category. Kirby

Puckett nosed out Willie Mays for second place, with Joe DiMaggio and Jimmy Wynn finishing fourth and fifth, respectively.

	NFAD × 20	NRFD × 20	Total Points	Final Defensive Ratings
Willie Mays	13.103	20.000	33.103	3
Mickey Mantle	11.724	12.449	24.173	9
Joe DiMaggio	13.103	15.510	28.613	4
Duke Snider	15.172	10.000	25.172	6
Tris Speaker	17.241	19.388	36.629	1
Jimmy Wynn	13.793	14.694	28.487	5
Hank Aaron	13.103	11.224	24.327	8
Kirby Puckett	16.552	19.184	35.736	2
Ty Cobb	11.034	12.245	23.279	10
Tony Gwynn	14.483	10.204	24.687	7

Final All-Around Ratings

The final all-around ratings for center fielders favored the offense over the defense by a three-to-one ratio. Once again, the Gray Eagle, Tris Speaker, confounded the experts who predicted that either Joe DiMaggio or Willie Mays would grab the brass ring. Speaker parlayed his sixth-place finish in offensive ratings with a dominating first-place finish in the defensive ratings to narrowly defeat the Yankee Clipper for the overall title. DiMaggio enjoyed a big advantage over Speaker in the offensive ratings, but was severely outdistanced by Speaker in the defensive ratings. Mickey Mantle, who slugged his way to a convincing first-place rating in the offensive category, fell victim to his nagging leg injuries that greatly reduced his ability to cover large expanses of territory in the outfield, relegating him to a ninth-place finish in the defensive category and fourth place overall.

	Offense Divided by 43 × 3	Defense Divided by 40	Total Points	Final All-Around Ratings	HOF
Willie Mays	2.098	0.828	2.926	3	*
Mickey Mantle	2.307	0.604	2.911	4	*
Joe DiMaggio	2.257	0.715	2.972	2	*
Duke Snider	2.065	0.629	2.694	6	*
Tris Speaker	2.072	0.916	2.988	1	*

	Offense Divided by 43 × 3	Defense Divided by 40	Total Points	Final All-Around Ratings	HOF
Jimmy Wynn	1.856	0.712	2.568	8	
Hank Aaron	2.111	0.608	2.719	5	*
Kirby Puckett	1.595	0.893	2.488	9	*
Ty Cobb	2.088	0.582	2.670	7	*
Tony Gwynn	1.636	0.617	2.253	10	*

Ken Griffey Jr., one of the top sluggers of his era, could finish in the top ten offensively, but probably not in the top five because of his negative era and park factor adjustments. His 29-point negative era adjustment, in particular, cost him valuable points in the slugging average category. And on defense, he suffered from a negative fielding average differential. No center fielder in this study had a negative fielding average differential. He shows a decent range factor differential, but not great enough to overcome his low fielding average point total. The projected finish for Griffey at the present time is approximately an eighth-place finish in the offensive ratings, a tenth-place finish in the defensive ratings, and a tenth-place finish overall.

CHAPTER 12

Baseball's Legendary All-Stars

Baseball's Legendary All-Star Team, based on both the offensive and defensive skills of the candidates, is given below. The outfielders were rated on a 4-to-1 offense-to-defense ratio for this team. The team would have been slightly different if the center-field candidates were separated from the other outfield positions, and were rated with a 3-to-1 ratio, as they are in the four all-star teams that follow.

C	Roy Campanella	P	Dizzy Dean	OF	Ted Williams
	Gabby Hartnett		Ed Walsh		Joe DiMaggio
P	Walter Johnson	1B	Lou Gehrig		Mickey Mantle
	Grover Cleveland Alexander		Jimmie Foxx		Tris Speaker
	Cy Young	2B	Nap Lajoie		Willie Mays
	Lefty Grove		Bobby Grich		Al Simmons
	Tom Seaver	SS	Honus Wagner		Hank Aaron
	Christy Mathewson		Lou Boudreau		Duke Snider
	Sandy Koufax	3B	Mike Schmidt		Joe Jackson
	Whitey Ford		Brooks Robinson		
		OF	Babe Ruth		

Baseball's Legendary All-Star Teams

Top Four Teams

The following table identifies the top four all-time all-star teams as determined by this study. There are not many surprises on the teams. Even the younger fans will be happy to see such modern legends as Ozzie Smith, Mike

12. Baseball's Legendary All-Stars

Schmidt, Bobby Grich, and Gary Carter cavorting with the stars of yesteryear. And they should also agree with the estimated future ratings for active players like Pedro Martinez, Roger Clemens, Albert Pujols, Alex Rodriguez, and Vladimir Guerrero (see Appendix).

	Team 1	Team 2	Team 3	Team 4
Catcher	Campanella	Hartnett	Carter	Bench
Pitcher	W. Johnson	Alexander	Young	Grove
First Base	Gehrig	Foxx	Greenberg	Mize
Second Base	Lajoie	Grich	Collins	Doerr
Shortstop	Wagner	Boudreau	O. Smith	Banks
Third Base	Schmidt	B. Robinson	Mathews	Santo
Left Field	Williams	J. Jackson	F. Robinson	Simmons
Center Field	Speaker	DiMaggio	Mays	Mantle
Right Field	Ruth	Musial	Ott	Kaline

This study rated all the players, not only on their offensive contributions, but also on their defensive contributions. In the area of pitching, the candidates were evaluated on their combined pitching, batting, and fielding skills. In the past, all-time all-star teams were selected by vote (which is essentially nothing more than a popularity contest) or by rating the player's offensive skills only and, in the area of pitching, rating the candidates on their pitching skills only. The following table shows the weakness in those methods.

Position	Name	Offensive Rating	Defensive Rating	Final All-Around Rating
Catcher	Roy Campanella	4	1	1
First Base	Lou Gehrig	1	15	1
Second Base	Nap Lajoie	3	1	1
Shortstop	Honus Wagner	1	3	1
Third Base	Mike Schmidt	1	2	1
RF-LF	Babe Ruth	1	16	1
	Ted Williams	2	18	2
Center Field	Tris Speaker	6	1	1

PITCHERS

Name	Pitching Rating	Batting Rating	Fielding Rating	Final All-Around Rating
Walter Johnson	1	2	13	1

Roger Clemens, still active in 2007 at the age of 45, reached the 354 career victory total, moving him into eighth place on the all-time list (courtesy Boston Red Sox).

If the All-Time All-Star team had been selected on offense only, Gene Tenace would have been the catcher, with Mickey Cochrane a close second. Rogers Hornsby would have been the second baseman, and Mickey Mantle would have been the center fielder.

SECOND TEAM

Position	Name	Offensive Rating	Defensive Rating	Final All-Around Rating
Catcher	Gabby Hartnett	5	2	2
First Base	Jimmie Foxx	2	6	2
Second Base	Bobby Grich	8	4	2
Shortstop	Lou Boudreau	5	2	2
Third Base	Brooks Robinson	13	1	2
RF-LF	Joe Jackson	3	12	3
	Stan Musial	5	9	4
Center Field	Joe DiMaggio	2	4	2

PITCHERS

Name	Pitching Rating	Batting Rating	Fielding Rating	Final All-Around Rating
Grover Cleveland Alexander	3	10	5	2

Based on offense only, or pitching only in the case of the pitcher, the second team would have consisted of Cochrane, Foxx, Morgan, Banks, Mathews, Jackson, Musial, DiMaggio and Grove.

BASEBALL'S GREATEST OFFENSIVE TEAM—
AS DETERMINED BY THIS STUDY

C	Gene Tenace		3B	Mike Schmidt
	Mickey Cochrane			Eddie Mathews
P	Wes Ferrell		RF-LF	Babe Ruth
	Walter Johnson			Ted Williams
1B	Lou Gehrig			Joe Jackson
	Jimmie Foxx			Mel Ott
2B	Rogers Hornsby			Stan Musial
	Joe Morgan		CF	Mickey Mantle
SS	Honus Wagner			Joe DiMaggio
	Ernie Banks			

Baseball's Greatest Defensive Team—
As Determined by This Study

C	Roy Campanella	SS	Lou Boudreau
	Gabby Hartnett	3B	Brooks Robinson
P	Ed Walsh		Mike Schmidt
	Addie Joss	RF-LF	Al Simmons
1B	Vic Power		Pete Rose
	Keith Hernandez		Al Kaline
2B	Nap Lajoie		Rickey Henderson
	Bill Mazeroski	CF	Tris Speaker
SS	Ozzie Smith		Kirby Puckett

Baseball's Prospects

Potential Future Legendary All-Stars—
Active Players Plus Four Others

Catcher	Ivan Rodriguez	Shortstop	Alex Rodriguez
	Mike Piazza		Omar Vizquel
Pitcher	Pedro Martinez		Derek Jeter
	Roger Clemens		Nomar Garciaparra
	Greg Maddux		Miguel Tejada
	Randy Johnson	Third Base	Chipper Jones
First Base	Mark McGwire		Scott Rolen
	Albert Pujols	Outfield	Barry Bonds
	Todd Helton		Sammy Sosa
	Jim Thome		Ken Griffey, Jr.
	Paul Konerko		Ichiro Suzuki
	Frank Thomas		Gary Sheffield
	Rafael Palmeiro		Vladimir Guerrero
Second Base	Craig Biggio		Manny Ramirez
	Jeff Kent		

Comparison of the Legendary All-Star Team with MLB's All-Century Team

Position	MLB's All-Century Team Name	Legendary All-Stars Name
Catcher	Johnny Bench	Roy Campanella
	Yogi Berra	Gabby Hartnett

12. Baseball's Legendary All-Stars

Position	MLB's All-Century Team Name	Legendary All-Stars Name
Pitcher	Nolan Ryan	Walter Johnson
	Sandy Koufax	Grover Cleveland Alexander
	Cy Young	Cy Young
	Roger Clemens	Lefty Grove
	Bob Gibson	Tom Seaver
	Walter Johnson	Christy Mathewson
First Base	Lou Gehrig	Lou Gehrig
	Mark McGwire	Jimmie Foxx
Second Base	Jackie Robinson	Nap Lajoie
	Rogers Hornsby	Bobby Grich
Shortstop	Cal Ripken	Honus Wagner
	Ernie Banks	Lou Boudreau
Third Base	Mike Schmidt	Mike Schmidt
	Brooks Robinson	Brooks Robinson
Outfield	Babe Ruth	Babe Ruth
	Hank Aaron	Ted Williams
	Ted Williams	Joe DiMaggio
	Willie Mays	Mickey Mantle
	Joe DiMaggio	Tris Speaker
	Mickey Mantle	Willie Mays

Baseball's thirty greatest offensive players, as determined by the sum of their runs scored per total at-bats including bases on balls, and their runs batted in per official at-bats with walks excluded, were compared to the ratings of the OBP/SLG composite and the ratings from this study.

	Runs/ Tot. AB	RBIs/ Off. AB	Total Points	Rating	OBP/SLG Rating	This Study Rating
Babe Ruth	.208	.263	.471	1	1	1
Lou Gehrig	.199	.249	.448	2	3	3
Ted Williams	.185	.239	.424	3	2	2
Hank Greenberg	.174	.246	.420	4	5	7
Jimmie Foxx	.183	.236	.419	5	4	5
Joe DiMaggio	.183	.225	.408	6	8	6
Roy Campanella	.132	.244	.376	7		19
Rogers Hornsby	.171	.194	.365	8	6	8
Mel Ott	.167	.197	.364	9	11	9
Johnny Mize	.153	.208	.361	10	10	12
Mickey Mantle	.171	.186	.357	11	7	4

	Runs/ Tot. AB	RBIs/ Off. AB	Total Points	Rating	OBP/SLG Rating	This Study Rating
Harry Heilmann	.149	.198	.347	12	19	24
Ty Cobb	.177	.169	.346	13	13	11
Hank Aaron	.158	.186	.344	14	20	
Mike Schmidt	.153	.191	.344	14		14
Willie Mays	.167	.175	.342	16	15	16
Frank Robinson	.160	.181	.341	17	24	
Mickey Cochrane	.173	.161	.334	18	37	15
Stan Musial	.155	.178	.333	19	9	10
Yogi Berra	.142	.189	.331	20		
Eddie Mathews	.151	.170	.321	21	43	23
Duke Snider	.135	.186	.321	21	27	
Honus Wagner	.153	.166	.319	23		20
Willie McCovey	.129	.190	.319	24	39	22
Joe Jackson	.159	.158	.317	25	16	
Nap Lajoie	.149	.167	.316	26		27
Tris Speaker	.163	.150	.313	27	23	
Reggie Jackson	.138	.173	.311	28		
Johnny Bench	.128	.180	.308	29		17
Ernie Banks	.128	.174	.302	30		29

Note: Mark McGwire would be number seven in the Runs/RBI ratings, number eight in OBP/SLG, and number eight in this study. Barry Bonds would be number eight, number four, and number four, respectively. The Barry Bonds prior to 1999 would be number eleven in this study.

This study was not intended to be the end-all, greatest all-star team. It is simply the first all-time all-star team based on a complete evaluation of a player's skills, both offensively and defensively. My hope is that, in the near future, Pete Palmer will present his ultimate all-star team composed of the greatest players at each position. As the most talented and respected baseball statistician in the field today, Palmer has developed the most sophisticated formulas for evaluating the offensive and defensive contributions of major league baseball players, and he is well positioned to achieve the final result. From his existing Total Baseball Ranking (TBR) formulas, and from his correspondence, I believe he needs only to make a few minor modifications to his present formulas, such as including a caught-stealing percentage in his formula for catchers, and then replacing the generalized park factors with individual park factors and converting his formulas from a value system to a skill system. He can also eliminate the positional adjustment since each player will be evaluated against only players playing the same position.

Appendix:
The Steroid Problem

A study to identify the greatest players of the twentieth century would not be complete without a review of the steroid problem that has compromised the integrity of the game for the past twenty years. Barry Bonds, Mark McGwire, Sammy Sosa, and Rafael Palmeiro were ineligible for this study based on the suspicion that steroids may have contributed to their spectacular offensive statistics, particularly their home run totals. It is possible that all four of them will be persona non grata by the National Baseball Hall of Fame in Cooperstown, New York, when they become eligible for election into that elite body. That has already happened in the case of Mark McGwire. He was considered to be a shoo-in for election to the hallowed halls on the first ballot when he became eligible in 2007, but the voters shunned him, giving him just 23.5 percent of the vote, with 75 percent needed for election. A similar fate may await Palmeiro, Sosa, and Bonds. Two of the players, McGwire and Palmeiro, did not help their cause any when they testified before a congressional committee investigating steroid use in major

Mark McGwire thrilled the fans of the game when he chased Roger Maris' single-season home run record in 1998.

league baseball, on March 17, 2005. McGwire, who had previously admitted taking androstenedione, a muscle-building supplement that has since been added to the illegal steroid list, refused to answer questions about whether or not he took steroids, saying repeatedly that he did not want to discuss the past. Palmeiro emphatically denied taking steroids but, shockingly, was suspended by major league baseball less than five months later for testing positive for steroids. And this occurred just one month after he had joined Willie Mays, Hank Aaron, and Eddie Murray as the only major league players with 3,000 base hits and 500 home runs. He subsequently retired.

The evidence against the four players, most of which is circumstantial, ranges from flimsy to fairly strong. As far as I know, there is no credible evidence against Sammy Sosa except his Samsonian physique and his CHR curve that will be discussed shortly. The evidence against McGwire consists of his admission to taking andro, his CHR curve, his bulging physique, and the testimony of Jose Canseco that he had administered steroids to McGwire. The evidence against Palmeiro consists of his CHR curve, testimony of Jose Canseco, and a positive steroid test taken by MLB in 2005.

The strongest case seems to be the case against Barry Bonds. His enormous physique and puffy face have been interpreted as a sign that he was taking steroids. Reportedly, Bonds testified to the grand jury that he took "the Clear" and "the Cream," two steroids given to him by his trainer, Greg Anderson, but he denied that he knew the two substances were steroids that were undetectable by existing steroid testing procedures. He said he thought he was taking flaxseed oil and arthritis balm. Anderson, who spent three months in jail in 2003 for distributing steroids, went back to jail in August 2006 for refusing to testify against Barry Bonds in Bonds' perjury investigation prior to being released in late 2007. Many people feel that Anderson's refusal to testify is proof of Bonds' guilt. Bonds' alleged mistress, Kimberly Bell, who said she was Bonds' girlfriend for nine years, from 1994 to 2003, told Geraldo Rivera that Bonds said he was taking steroids as early as 1999.

In addition to testimony from former players and associates of Bonds, Sosa, McGwire and Palmeiro, statistical evidence is becoming more and more incriminating. Gabriel Costa, Michael Huber, and John Saccoman wrote an illuminating and informative treatise titled "Cumulative Home Run Frequency and the Recent Home Run Explosion," for SABR's *Baseball Research Journal* in 2005. In it, they graphed the cumulative home run ratios (CHR) for all players with more than 500 career home runs. Their findings were not unexpected. Most of the elite sluggers prior to the 1990s, including Babe Ruth, Hank Aaron, and Mike Schmidt, reached the peak of their CHRs by their mid-to-late twenties, with very little variability thereafter. A subsequent study by the author confirmed the findings of the first group. Today's active 500-career home runs sluggers — Jim Thome, Ken Griffey, Jr., Manny

Ramirez, Frank Thomas, and Alex Rodriguez — reached their peak CHRs by their late '20s or early '30s. And Gary Sheffield, who has periodically been implicated in the steroid scandal, has a fairly normal CHR curve that resembles the CHR curves of Mickey Mantle and Babe Ruth. Sheffield's CHR curve peaked in his late '20s. In the cases of Bonds, McGwire, Sosa, and Palmeiro, their CHRs continued to increase well into their '30s and, in the case of Bonds, his CHR was still on the rise as he approached the age of 40. When Bonds' year-by-year home run rates (HRR) were plotted graphically, they confirmed that his home run rate peaked initially when he was thirty years old and went into decline over the next four years, dropping from 52 homers for every 550 at-bats to 37 homers for every 550 at-bats. Then, in 1999, his home run rate suddenly exploded to 53 homers for every 550 at-bats and remained above that level for seven years.

BONDS' HOME RUN RATE PER 550 AT-BATS

Year	Age	Weight	Team	Home Run Rate Per 550 At-Bats	
1986	22	185	Pittsburgh	21	
1987	23	185	Pittsburgh	25	
1988	24	185	Pittsburgh	25	
1989	25	185	Pittsburgh	18	
1990	26	185	Pittsburgh	36	
1991	27	190	Pittsburgh	27	
1992	28	185	Pittsburgh	40	HRR 1986–92: 27
1993	29	185	San Francisco	47	
1994	30	185	San Francisco	52	
1995	31	185	San Francisco	36	
1996	32	190	San Francisco	45	
1997	33	206	San Francisco	41	
1998	34	206	San Francisco	37	HRR 1993–98: 43
					HRR 1986–98: 34
1999	35	210	San Francisco	53	
2000	36	210	San Francisco	56	
2001	37	228	San Francisco	84	
2002	38	228	San Francisco	63	
2003	39	228	San Francisco	63	
2004	40	228	San Francisco	66	
2005	41	228	San Francisco	65	
2006	42	228	San Francisco	39	HRR 1999–'06: 62
2007	43	236	San Francisco	49	

Based on the normal CHR for all career 500 home run hitters, with their CHR leveling off by the time they reach 30, and based on Bonds' own record, it was estimated that Barry Bonds should have hit between 570 and 618 home runs through 2006 under normal conditions. His actual home run total was 734, a discrepancy of at least 116 home runs.

In addition to the above studies, CHR curves of three players who had admitted using steroids — Jose Canseco, Ken Caminiti, and Jason Giambi — were plotted. The CHR curves of both Giambi and Caminiti followed the typical "steroid line," a sharp increase in CHR's well into their thirties. Caminiti's CHR showed a continuous sharp incline from the time he was 29 years old until his final major league season nine years later. Giambi's CHR curve was similar to Caminiti's, rising sharply from the time he was 27 years old until 2004, when at the age of 33 he admitted to the federal grand jury that he took steroids. He said he obtained "the Clear" and "the Cream" from Greg Anderson, Barry Bonds' personal trainer, in 2002. Surprisingly, Jose Canseco's CHR curve rose sharply from 1987 until 1991, when he was just 27 years old, and then flattened out. But it must be remembered that Canseco was injury prone and spent nine sessions on the disabled list, many of them for prolonged periods of time, between 1989 and 2000.

Another home run study that was discussed in my book *Ruth, Maris, McGwire, and Sosa* determined the number of home runs that might be attributed to the new Costa Rican rabbit baseball that was introduced in 1993 and the increased home run totals due to a player's increased weight. The effect of the rabbit ball, plus smaller ballparks and other factors, was estimated to be a 33 percent increase in the player's home run totals. It was also determined that the average player could be expected to hit one home run for every 3.3 pounds of weight added. Weight gains attributed to the four players by 1998 were 30 pounds for Barry Bonds (from 180 to 210), 25 pounds for Mark McGwire (225 to 250), 55 pounds for Sammy Sosa (165 to 220), and 34 pounds for Rafael Palmeiro (180 to 214). The following table of average home runs per 550 at-bats summarizes the results.

Name	Avg. HRs 1986–1992	HR due to rabbit ball	HR due to incr. weight	Predicted HRs 1993–1998	Actual HRs 1993–1998	Difference
Barry Bonds	27	9	9	45	43	−2
Mark McGwire	39	13	8	60	65	+5
Sammy Sosa	16	5	17	38	39	+1
Rafael Palmeiro	16	5	10	31	35	+4

The interesting thing about the above table is that there is no clear indication that any of the four players were experimenting with steroids during the 1993–1998 period. It supports the case that Barry Bonds' achievements through 1998 were strictly the result of his natural conditioning programs. The story, however, seems to be different after 1998. According to the year-by-year computation of Bonds' home run rates per 550 at-bats (HRR), he averaged 43 home runs for every 550 at-bats from 1993 through 1998, and then suddenly his rate skyrocketed to 55 homers for every 550 at-bats in 1999–2000, and to 84 homers for every 550 at-bats in 2001.

Barry Bonds' career statistics, presented here, tend to support the theory that a mystery supplement in addition to his normal conditioning program may have contributed to his success. One study has indicated that as many as 116 of Bonds' home runs and perhaps more can be attributed to that unknown supplement. Jose Canseco, in his book *Juiced* said that when Barry Bonds first saw him at the All-Star Game in 2000, he was amazed at Canseco's spectacular physique, and asked Canseco what his secret was. Over the next year, with Jose's secret in hand, Bonds added twenty pounds of muscle and proceeded to celebrate his new-found strength by crushing Mark McGwire's single-season home run record.

Years	Years	Age	AB	H	HR	Per 550 AB HR	RBI	BA
1986–1992	7	22–28	3584	984	176	27	85	.275
1993–1998	6	29–34	3037	933	235	43	120	.307
1999–2005	7	35–41	2519	825	297	65	139	.328

Another table, showing the home run averages of the four players between 2001 and 2004, highlights the problems that people have with Barry Bonds' achievements. The idea that a major league player could average 70 home runs a year between the ages of 37 and 40 is nothing short of miraculous. McGwire's numbers are inconclusive for the one year he played before he retired, and Palmeiro's numbers are also inconclusive. Sosa's numbers look suspicious.

Name	Predicted HRs 2001–2004	Actual HRs 2001–2004	Difference
Barry Bonds	51	70	+19
Mark McGwire	60	53 (one year)	−7
Sammy Sosa	38	49	+11
Rafael Palmeiro	31	37	+6

As I noted in a previous book, wine gets better with age. Baseball players, with the possible exception of Barry Bonds, do not. Remember the Team of the Century that was selected by a panel of writers and editors and the staff of Stats, Inc. in 1999? That survey, which chose the fifty greatest players of the twentieth century, did not identify Barry Bonds, a 13-year veteran, as one of them, although it did honor a number of active players, including Ken Griffey, Jr., Roger Clemens, Mike Piazza, and Mark McGwire. Seven years later, however, many baseball experts were calling Bonds not only a great player, but THE greatest player ever to play the game.

Bibliography

Carter, Craig, ed. *Daguerreotypes*, 8th edition. St. Louis: Sporting News, 1990.
Costa, Gabriel, Michael Huber, and John Saccoman. "Cumulative Home Run Frequency and the Recent Home Run Explosion." *Baseball Research Journal* 34 (2005): 37–41.
Couzens, Gerald Secor. *A Baseball Album ("...History & Trivia Never Before Published")*. New York: Lippincott & Crowell, 1980.
ESPN.com. MLB — All-Century Team Final Voting, 1–3. http://espn.go.com/mlb/news/1999/1023/129008.html.
Honig, Donald. *A Donald Honig Reader*. New York: Simon and Schuster, 1988.
Ivor-Campbell, Frederick, ed. *Baseball's First Stars*. Cleveland: Society for American Baseball Research, 1996.
James, Bill, and Rob Neyer. *The Neyer/James Guide to Pitchers*. New York: Simon and Schuster, 2004.
Kallay, Mike, ed. "Team of the Century," *Street & Smith's Baseball* (1999): 24–27.
Kavanagh, Gerard. "50 Years," *Street & Smith's Baseball* (1990): 54–59.
McConnell, Bob, and David Vincent, eds. *SABR Presents The Home Run Encyclopedia*. New York: Macmillan, 1996.
McNeil, William F. *Backstop*. Jefferson, N.C.: McFarland, 2005.
_____. *Baseball's Other All-Stars*. Jefferson, N.C.: McFarland, 2000.
_____. *Cool Papas and Double Duties*. Jefferson, N.C.: McFarland, 2001.
_____. *The Single Season Home Run Kings*. Jefferson, N.C.: McFarland, 2002.
Nemec, David. *The Beer and Whiskey League*. New York: Lyons & Burford, 1994.
Palmer, Pete, and Gary Gillette, eds. *The Baseball Encyclopedia*. New York: Barnes & Noble, 2004.
Reidenbaugh, Lowell. *Baseball's Hall of Fame: Cooperstown: Where Legends Live Forever*. New York: Arlington House, 1988.
Rickey, Branch, with Robert Riger. *The American Diamond*. New York: Simon and Schuster, 1965.
Santa Maria, Michael, and James Costello. *In the Shadows of the Diamond: Hard Times in the National Pastime*. Dubuque, Iowa: Elysian Fields Press, 1992.
Shatzkin, Mike, ed. *The Ballplayers*. New York: Arbor House, 1990.
Thorn, John, ed. *The National Pastime*. New York: Bell Publishing, 1987.

_____, Pete Palmer, Michael Gershman, and David Pietrusza, eds. *Total Baseball*. New York: Viking Penguin Books, 1997.

Tiemann, Robert L., and Mark Rucker. *Nineteenth Century Stars*. Kansas City: Society for American Baseball Research, 1989.

Index

Aaron, Henry "Hammerin' Hank" 8, 10, 11, 185, 200, 207, 211–216, 221, 222, 224
Adcock, Joe 132
Alexander, Grover Cleveland 6, 7, 10, 32, 85, 101–106, 108–111, 216, 217, 219, 221
Allen, Ethan 6
Allen & Ginter 5
Allison, Doug 4
Alomar, Roberto 136, 137, 142, 143, 145, 146
Anderson, Greg 224, 226
Anderson, Sparky 165
Anson, Cap 6, 45–47
Aparicio, Luis 8, 147, 148, 152, 153, 156–160
Appling, Luke 151, 152, 155, 157–160
Arroyo, Luis 95
Averill, Earl 90
Avery, Steve 208

Bagby, Jim 203
Bagwell, Jeff 121, 126–128, 130, 131, 138
Baker, Dusty 188
Baker, Frank "Home Run" 164, 169–171, 173, 174
Bando, Sal 168–171, 173, 174
Banks, Ernie 8, 10, 11, 147, 150, 151, 155–157, 159, 160, 217, 219, 221, 222
Barry, Jack 164
Battey, Earl 71, 75, 77, 81, 82
Beckley, Jake 45–47
Bell, Kimberly 224
Bench, Johnny 8, 10, 11, 63, 66, 75, 77, 79, 80–82, 217, 220, 222
Bennett, Charlie 6
Berra, Yogi 8, 10, 11, 13, 66, 67, 70, 75, 77, 79, 80–82, 220, 222
Biggio, Craig 121, 138, 143, 145, 146, 220
Blomberg, Ron 28
Blyleven, Bert 14
Boggs, Wade 163, 169–171, 173, 174

Bonds, Barry 9, 10, 35, 132, 185, 197, 220, 223–228
Bonds, Bobby 179
Boudreau, Lou 148, 152, 153, 156–160, 216, 217, 219–221
Brainard, Asa 4
Brett, George 11, 163, 169–174
Brock, Lou 8, 179
Brodie, Steve 60, 61
Brouthers, Dan 45–47
Brown, Mordecai "Three Finger" 96, 97, 100, 101, 104, 107, 109–111
Browning, Pete 57–59
Buckner, Bill 132
Burkett, Jesse "The Crab" 57–59
Burns, Thomas "Oyster" 57, 59

Caminiti, Ken 226
Campanella, Roy 7, 16, 18–28, 64, 73, 75, 77–82, 121, 156, 212, 216, 217, 220, 221
Canseco, Jose 154, 224, 226, 227
Carew, Rod 136, 140–146
Carlton, Steve 10, 11, 93, 94, 102–104, 106, 109–111
Carter, Craig 229
Carter, Gary 66–68, 77–82, 217
Caruthers, Bob 6, 41–44
Casey, Hugh 101, 102
Cash, Norm 71, 118, 119, 124–127, 129–131
Cepeda, Orlando 120, 123, 126–128, 130
Cepeda, Perucho 120
Cey, Ron 188
Chance, Frank 96
Chapman, John 4
Charlston, Oscar 9
Chesbro, Jack 95
Clark, Jack 121, 127, 130
Clark, Will "The Thrill" 119, 127–130
Clarkson, John 6, 41–44

Clemens, Roger 9–11, 84, 97, 99, 100, 105, 106, 108, 112, 217, 218, 220, 221, 228
Clemente, Roberto 8, 10, 11, 186, 187, 192–195, 197
Clements, Jack 38–40
Cobb, Ty 6–8, 10, 11, 84, 96, 162, 179, 180, 182, 185, 208, 209, 211–215, 222
Cochrane, Mickey 6, 7, 15, 62, 66, 74–76, 79, 80–83, 113, 115, 219, 222
Cody, Wild Bill 5
Collins, Eddie 6–8, 17, 135, 140–146, 164, 217
Combs, Earl 6
Comiskey, Charles 6
Connor, Roger 45, 47, 185
Cordeiro, Julie 107
Costa, Gabriel 224
Costello, James 229
Couzens, Gerald Secor 7, 229
Crandall, Otis "Doc" 100
Creighton, Jimmy 3
Cronin, Joe 6, 8, 99, 151, 155–157, 159, 160
Cross, Lave 54–56

Dahlen, William "Bad Bill" 50–53
Daly, Thomas "Tido" 48–50
Danning, Harry 69, 70, 77, 78, 81, 82
Davis, George 51–53
Dean, Dizzy 7, 90, 104, 106, 108–111, 216
Delahanty, Ed 56, 58, 59
Dickey, Bill 6, 13, 63, 64, 66, 67, 75, 77, 80–82, 212
Dihigo, Martin 9
DiMaggio, Joe 7, 8, 10, 11, 13, 63, 199, 203, 204, 211–214, 216, 217, 219, 221
Doerr, Bobby 8, 139, 141–146, 217
Downing, Al 207
Duffy, Hugh 56, 58, 59
Dugan, Joe 6
Dunlap, Fred "Sure Shot" 48–50

Eckersley, Dennis 10
Elliott, Bob 164, 165, 170, 171, 173, 174
Erskine, Carl 162
Evans, Dwight "Dewey" 187, 188, 193, 195, 197
Evers, Johnny 96
Ewing, Buck 37–40

Feller, Bob 7, 8, 10, 88, 98, 104, 106, 109–111
Ferguson, Bob 4, 5
Ferrell, Rick 99
Ferrell, Wes 29, 30, 32, 99, 103–110, 112, 219
Fingers, Rollie 8
Fisk, Carlton 11, 15, 66, 71, 75, 77, 79, 81, 82

Ford, Whitey 8, 10, 41, 93–95, 102–106, 109–111, 216
Foutz, Dave 41, 94
Fox, Nellie 139, 140, 142–146
Foxx, Jimmie 10, 11, 34, 99, 113, 115, 123, 127–131, 177, 185, 216, 217, 219, 221
Freehan, Bill 15, 66, 70, 71, 77, 81, 82
Frisch, Frankie 7, 137, 138, 142–146
Furillo, Carl 212

Gant, Ron 208
Garciaparra, Nomar 154, 155, 160, 220
Garvey, Steve 132, 188
Gehrig, Lou 6–11, 33, 34, 63, 99, 113–115, 123, 127–132, 147, 177, 185, 212, 216, 217, 219, 221
Gehringer, Charlie 8, 135, 136, 141–146
Gershman, Michael 230
Giambi, Jason 226
Gibson, Bob 8, 10, 11, 84, 90, 91, 104–106, 109–111, 119, 221
Gibson, Josh 9, 10
Gibson, Kirk 71
Gillette, Gary 42, 229
Glasscock, Jack 6, 51, 52
Glavine, Tom 99, 100, 112
Gordon, Joe "Flash" 139, 142–146
Gore, George 59–61
Goslin, Goose 177, 191–194, 197
Gould, Charley 4, 5
Greenberg, Hank 114, 115, 123, 127–131, 217, 221
Grich, Bobby 139, 142, 144–146, 216, 217, 219, 221
Griffey, Ken, Jr. 9–11, 210, 211, 215, 220, 224, 228
Griffin, Mike 59–61
Griffith, Clark 41–44
Grove, Lefty 8, 10, 11, 32, 87, 103, 106, 109–111, 216, 217, 219, 221
Guerrero, Vladimir 189, 190, 197, 198, 217, 220
Gwynn, Tony 9, 10, 209–215

Hack, Stan 166–171, 173, 174
Hall, George 4, 5
Hamilton, Billy 57–59
Harris, Bucky 153
Hartnett, Gabby 15, 16, 27, 28, 63–65, 67, 75, 76, 78, 80–82, 90, 216, 217, 219, 220
Hauser, Joe 115
Heilmann, Harry 182, 190–193, 195, 197, 222
Helton, Todd 20, 122, 127, 128, 132, 220
Henderson, Rickey 8, 178, 179, 190–195, 197, 220
Henrich, Tommy 212

Index

Hernandez, Keith 34, 117, 118, 127–131, 220
Herzog, Whitey 69, 208
Hines, Paul 59–61
Hodges, Gil 121, 122, 127–132, 156, 212
Hoiles, Chris 15, 70, 77–79, 81, 82
Honig, Donald 229
Hooper, Harry 188
Hornsby, Rogers "Rajah" 6–8, 10, 11, 134, 140–146, 180, 184, 219, 221
Horton, Willie 71
Howard, Elston 13
Hubbell, Carl 7, 8, 99, 104, 106, 107, 109, 110, 112
Huber, Michael 224
Huggins, Miller 85

Ivor-Campbell, Frederick 229

Jackson, Reggie 222
Jackson, "Shoeless Joe" 7, 163, 179, 180, 190–194, 197, 216, 217, 219, 222
James, Bill 13, 14, 229
James, Bill (pitcher) 94
Jennings, Hughie "Ee-Yah" 50–52
Jeter, Derek 154, 155, 160, 220
Johnson, Bob 188, 191, 193, 195, 197
Johnson, Randy 98–100, 105, 106, 112, 220
Johnson, Walter 6, 7, 9–11, 29–32, 84, 101–106, 109–112, 216, 217, 219, 221
Jones, Chipper 169, 174, 220
Joss, Addie 7, 95, 103, 104, 106, 108–111, 220

Kaline, Al 186, 190, 193–195, 197, 203, 217, 220
Kallay, Mike 8, 229
Kavanagh, Gerard 229
Keefe, Tim 6, 40, 42–44
Keeler, "Wee Willie" 57–59
Keller, Charlie "King Kong" 212
Kelly, Michael J. "King" 6, 37–40
Kelly, Tom 208
Keltner, Ken 204
Kent, Jeff 140, 146, 220
Killebrew, Harmon 8, 115, 116, 127, 129, 130
Kluszewski, Ted 132
Konerko, Paul 122, 127, 132, 220
Koufax, Sandy 8–11, 14, 87, 88, 90, 91, 93, 98, 103–106, 108–111, 216, 221

Lajoie, Nap 11, 134, 135, 140, 141, 216, 217, 220–222
Landis, Kenesaw Mountain 179
Larkin, Barry 154, 156, 157, 159, 160
Larkin, Gene 208
Latham, Arlie 54–56
Lazzeri, Tony 85, 113

Lemon, Bob 95
Leonard, Andy 4
Lloyd, John Henry 148
Lolich, Mickey 119, 186
Lombardi, Ernie 66, 78–80
Long, Herman "Germany" 51–53
Lopes, Davey 17
Lyons, Denny 54, 55

Mack, Connie 62, 86, 94, 113, 164
Mackey, Biz 64
Madden, James R. Jr. 9, 98, 196, 210
Maddux, Greg 9–11, 99, 100, 105, 106, 108, 112, 220
Mantle, Mickey 8, 10, 11, 151, 201–203, 205, 211–214, 216, 217, 219, 221, 225
Marberry, Firpo 101
Marichal, Juan 10, 93, 104–106, 109–111
Maris, Roger 132, 185, 226
Marquard, Rube 164
Martinez, Pedro 99, 100, 105–107, 112, 217, 220
Mathews, Eddie 10, 161, 162, 169–171, 173, 174, 217, 219, 222
Mathewson, Christie 6, 7, 10, 11, 29, 30, 32, 85–87, 94, 96, 104–106, 108–111, 164, 216, 221
Mattingly, Don 8, 34, 121, 127, 128, 130
Mays, Willie 7, 8, 10, 11, 34, 151, 185, 199–201, 205, 211–214, 216, 217, 221, 222, 224
Mazeroski, Bill 140, 142–146, 187, 220
McConnell, Bob 229
McCovey, Willie 8, 11, 117, 118, 127, 129, 130, 222
McDonald, Dan 4
McGraw, John 53–55, 100
McGriff, Fred 122, 127, 128, 130, 131
McGuire, James "Deacon" 37–40
McGwire, Mark 9–11, 35, 132, 154, 185, 220, 221, 223–228
McInnis, Stuffy 164
McNeil, William F. 229
McPhee, John "Bid" 47–50
McVey, Cal 4, 5
Medwick, Joe 181, 182, 191, 193, 195, 197
Merkle, Fred 96
Mize, Johnny 116, 117, 126–131, 217, 221
Molitor, Paul 166, 170, 171, 173, 174
Moore, Wilcy 101
Morgan, Joe 8, 10, 11, 17, 134, 142, 143, 145, 146, 219
Morris, Jack 208
Mueller, Ray 15, 70, 75–78, 82
Mulvey, Joe 6
Murphy, Johnny 101
Murray, Eddie 117, 118, 127, 129–131, 224

Musial, Stan 7, 8, 10, 11, 177, 182–185, 190–193, 195, 197, 217, 219, 222

Nash, Billy 53, 55, 56
Nemec, David 229
Nettles, Graig 168, 170–174
Newcombe, Don 29
Neyer, Rob 229
Nichols, Charles "Kid" 7, 40–44
Niedenfuer, Tom 148

Oakley, Annie 5
O'Rourke, James "Orator Jim" 57–59
Orr, Dave 45–47
Ott, Mel 185, 186, 190–193, 195, 197, 219, 221

Page, Joe 101, 102
Paige, Satchel 9–11, 90
Palmeiro, Rafael 35, 132, 220, 223–227
Palmer, Jim 10, 91–93, 103, 104, 106, 108, 109–111
Palmer, Pete 13, 14, 32, 33, 42, 111, 129, 222, 229, 230
Parrish, Lance 69, 75, 77–80, 82
Pearce, Dickey 4, 5
Pena, Tony 69, 75–77, 80, 82
Perez, Tony 132
Perranoski, Ron 101
Pfeffer, Fred 48–50
Phelps, Babe 66
Piazza, Mike 9, 10, 15, 72, 74, 76, 82, 83, 220, 228
Pietrusza, David 230
Pike, Lipman 4, 5
Plank, Eddie 94, 104, 106, 108, 109–111
Porter, Darrell 64–66, 74–78, 80, 82
Powell, Boog 120, 127, 130
Power, Vic 34, 119, 120, 123, 127–130, 220
Puckett, Kirby 34, 207, 208, 211–215, 220
Pujols, Albert 122, 123, 127, 128, 132, 217, 220

Radburne, Charles "Old Hoss" 41–44
Ramirez, Manny 189, 198, 220, 224, 225
Reese, Pee Wee 67, 121, 148, 149, 157, 159
Reidenbaugh, Lowell 229
Reitz, Ken 64
Rhodes, Dusty 199
Richardson, Bobby 117
Richardson, Hardy 48–50
Rickey, Branch 7, 229
Riger, Robert 229
Ripken, Cal, Jr. 9–11, 113, 147, 153, 156–159, 221
Rivera, Geraldo 224
Rizzuto, Phil "Scooter" 149, 156, 157, 159, 160

Roberts, Robin 95
Robinson, Brooks 8, 10, 11, 163–166, 168–174, 216, 217, 219–221
Robinson, Frank 8, 175, 191–194, 197, 217, 222
Robinson, Jackie 7, 8, 10, 11, 17, 67, 121, 133, 141–146, 212, 221
Rodriguez, Alex "A-Rod" 154, 155, 160, 217, 220, 225
Rodriguez, Ivan "Pudge" 15, 72–74, 76, 78, 83, 220
Rolen, Scott 169, 174, 220
Rose, Pete 8, 10, 11, 34, 181, 193–195, 197, 220
Rosen, Al 162, 163, 169–171, 173, 174
Rucker, Mark 230
Rusie, Amos 41–44
Ruth, Babe 6–11, 63, 99, 105, 113, 115, 132, 177, 182, 184, 185, 189, 190, 192, 193, 195, 197, 207, 216, 217, 219, 221, 224–226
Ryan, Nolan 10, 11, 84, 97–99, 102–105, 107–110, 112, 119, 221

Saccoman, John 224
Sandberg, Ryne 136, 142–146
Sanford, Jay 153, 162, 164, 167
Santa Maria, Michael 229
Santo, Ron 166, 167, 170–174, 217
Sax, Steve 17
Schmidt, Mike 8–11, 161–163, 166, 169, 170–174, 216, 217, 219–222, 224
Seaver, Tom 10, 91, 92, 104, 106, 108–111, 216, 221
Seitz, Peter 101
Sewell, Joe 154–160
Shatzkin, Mike 229
Sheffield, Gary 189, 197, 220, 225
Shindle, Billy 54–56
Simmons, Al 6, 34, 99, 177, 178, 182, 191–194, 197, 216, 217, 220
Simmons, Ted 64
Sisler, George 6–8, 117, 123, 124, 126–130
Smith, Charles 4
Smith, George "Germany" 51–53
Smith, Ozzie 8, 10, 11, 147–149, 153, 154, 156–159, 216, 217, 220
Smith, Reggie 188, 191–195, 197
Smoltz, John 208
Snider, Duke 121, 156, 205, 206, 211, 213, 214, 216, 222
Sosa, Sammy 35, 197, 220, 223–227
Spahn, Warren 7, 10, 11, 88–90, 93, 95, 102, 104, 106, 109–111
Speaker, Tris 6–8, 10, 34, 182, 200, 206, 211–214, 216, 217, 220–222
Stargell, Willie "Pops" 180, 181, 191–194, 197

Start, Joe 4, 5
Stengel, Casey 66, 67, 94, 116, 207
Stivetts, Jack 41, 43, 44, 104
Stovey, Harry 56, 59
Sullivan, John L. 5
Sundberg, Jim 15, 66–68, 70, 75–78, 80–82
Sutter, Bruce 8
Sutton, Don 99
Suzuki, Ichiro 117, 189, 196, 198, 220
Sweasy, Charlie 4

Tejeda, Miguel 154, 155, 160, 220
Tenace, Gene 62, 64, 74–76, 80–83, 169, 219
Terry, Bill 99, 119, 126–130
Terry, Ralph 117, 187
Thomas, Frank "The Big Hurt" 122, 127, 128, 132, 220, 225
Thome, Jim 122, 127, 127, 132, 220, 224
Thompson, Samuel "Big Sam" 56, 58, 59
Thorn, John 229
Tiant, Luis 29
Tiemann, Robert L. 230
Tiernan, Mike 57, 59
Tinker, Joe 96
Torre, Joe 64, 66, 75, 77, 80–82
Trammell, Alan 138, 153, 154, 156–160
Traynor, Pie 6–8, 165, 166, 169–171, 173, 174

Van Haltren George 60, 61
Vaughan, Arky 149, 151, 155–157, 159, 160
Vincent, David 229
Vizquel, Omar 154, 155, 160, 220

Waddell, Rube 7
Wagner, Honus 6–8, 10, 11, 147, 148, 155–159, 186, 210, 216, 217, 219, 221, 222
Walsh, Ed 7, 95, 96, 101, 103, 104, 106, 108–111, 216, 220
Waner, Lloyd 188
Waner, Paul 6, 188–190, 192, 193, 195, 197
Ward, John Montgomery 6, 50, 52, 53
Waterman, Fred 4
Weaver, Earl 92
Webb, Earl 182
Welch, Michael Francis "Smiling Mickey" 40, 42–44
Wertz, Vic 199
Westrum, Wes 15
Whitaker, Lou 138, 143, 145, 146, 153
Wilhelm Hoyt 10, 93, 99
Williams, "Smokey Joe" 9
Williams, Ted 7, 8, 10, 11, 175, 176, 189–192, 194, 195, 197, 198, 216, 217, 219, 221
Williamson, Ned 185
Wood, Smoky Joe 104, 105
Wright, George 3, 4
Wright, Harry 3, 4
Wynn, Jimmy 206, 211–215

Yastrzemski, Carl 8, 176, 177, 192, 194, 197, 198
Yost, Eddie 168–171, 173, 174
Young, Cy 6, 7, 10, 11, 84, 91, 93, 97, 100, 104, 107, 109, 110, 112, 216, 217, 221
Yount, Robin 149, 150, 157–160

Zettlein, George 4, 5
Zimmer, Charles "Chief" 37–40

www.ingramcontent.com/pod-product-compliance
Lightning Source LLC
Chambersburg PA
CBHW051219300426
44116CB00006B/637